PHOENIX RISING

From the Ashes of Desert One to the Rebirth of
U.S. Special Operations

COL KEITH M. NIGHTINGALE (RET)

CASEMATE
Philadelphia & Oxford

Published in the United States of America and Great Britain in 2020 by
CASEMATE PUBLISHERS
1950 Lawrence Road, Havertown, PA 19083, USA
and
The Old Music Hall, 106–108 Cowley Road, Oxford OX4 1JE, UK

Copyright 2020 © Col Keith M. Nightingale (Ret)

Hardback Edition: ISBN 978-1-61200-877-6
Digital Edition: ISBN 978-1-61200-878-3

A CIP record for this book is available from the British Library

Printed and bound in the United States of America by Sheridan

For a complete list of Casemate titles, please contact:

CASEMATE PUBLISHERS (US)
Telephone (610) 853-9131
Fax (610) 853-9146
Email: casemate@casematepublishers.com
www.casematepublishers.com

CASEMATE PUBLISHERS (UK)
Telephone (01865) 241249
Email: casemate-uk@casematepublishers.co.uk
www.casematepublishers.co.uk

Contents

The single lone exception was Army Chief of Staff Shy Myer, who saw terrorism and asymmetrical warfare as the emerging threat to U.S. interests and worked to build a missing capability. He did this as a lone wolf, in that much of the Army leadership as well as the other services looked upon SOF as a high-risk loose cannon on their stable conventional deck.

I am certain that had Desert One/*Eagle Claw* succeeded, the services and the JCS, less Army, would have congratulated themselves and disbanded the capability and relegated their historical SOF-like forces to their traditional service backwaters. Events prevented that for which we can be eternally thankful. What we see today and revere was essentially institutional anathema then. This is a description of the birth of SOF through the prism of the Iran Hostage Rescue attempt by a direct observer.

I have chosen only to write about what I saw, did, or heard directly. The operational details are available in other literature.

The Bottom Line

The RH-53 helicopter is a very complex bird. Its internal organs are a maze of wires, pipes, bolts, and buttons. It usually performs very well but operates on a thin mechanical margin. To help the pilot stay ahead of the margin, there is a bank of rectangles, plastic and black. They are arrayed in front of the pilot, each connected to the complex and inter-related systems that monitors performance. The visual cues provided advise the pilot as to the status of performance and indicate specific actions to be taken to adjust a discrete portion of the system to maintain essential synchronization. At approximately 2207 on the night of 24 April 1980, one of them turned red on a remote part of the central Iranian desert. This machine without a soul told the pilot that it had quit. Accordingly, the United States of America terminated its attempt to rescue the 52 hostages in our embassy in Tehran.

In the Beginning

And God saw the light, that it was good: and God divided the light from the darkness.
And God called the light Day, and the darkness he called Night.

—Chapter One, Genesis

Everything we take for granted today in the Special Operations Forces (SOF) world began with the Iran rescue attempt in 1980/1981 of 52 American hostages being held in Tehran by the Iranian government. Before this issue became a national priority to resolve, "Special Operations" was reserved for some small elements within each service that performed discrete unique tasks outside of the conventional mainspring. They rarely, if ever, worked together in common cause. The hostage crisis changed all that as we came to grips with the operational realities and necessities of the world.

In the beginning, with the requirement to rescue the hostages in Iran, the SOF shelf was essentially bare. We had to invent capabilities that heretofore had never existed. In light of what we enjoy today, these initial efforts were quaint at the least and shocking at the worst. Regardless, all that we enjoy today began at this event.

When the U.S. Embassy in Tehran was stormed and its U.S. citizens taken as prisoners, the Joint Chiefs of Staff examined its inventory of capabilities and concluded it had in reality no capabilities other than nuclear weapons or mass conventional forces, neither of which were rational tools to respond to this event. Any capability tailored for this form of conflict would have to be built from scratch. In a quintessentially American way, we began from nothing and progressed to something unique and competent.

In the Tank session with the Joint Chiefs, after it was clear no viable options could be provided, General Meyer, Army Chief of Staff, said, "We need a specialized force for a reasonable chance to free our hostages. I will provide the commander and we will start from there."

That commander was Major General James Vaught, the head of the Army Department of the Army Management Office-Operational Directorate (DAMO-OD). He would have as his base staff, the members of the Joint Special Operations Directorate (JCS-SOD) located in Pentagon Room 2C840. The rest of a staff he would have to create from whole cloth.

I was a member of General Vaught's DAMO staff, responsible for the Africa-Middle East desk. He asked, without explaining, that I go to 2C840 and see a Colonel Jerry King, the Director of JCS-SOD. I was met by Colonel King, signed a form and the journey began.

The Office

In that the rescue attempt was to be a Joint Chiefs of Staff operation, the location chosen for the Task Force was the existing spaces occupied by JCS Special Operations Directorate. It would remain so for the entire program.

JCS-SOD (Joint Chiefs of Staff, Special Operations Directorate) is located in the Pentagon as Room 2C840. It is an adjunct to the "Chairman's Corridor"; the walls of the corridor are lined with large pictures of each previous chairman, his heroic deeds, and contributions to the nation. Also included are several explanations of how the joint system works. This has not been explained to the members of the joint staff. In all, the corridor is a monument to the Graphic Arts Division.

The door to SOD is controlled by a cipher lock. Knowledge of this cipher, which is routinely changed, opens the cover to the book on the Iran rescue. The door opens into an anteroom from which several smaller offices access. On the left side are three offices with windows. A window here is a status symbol. However for us it is a pain; it means we can't post any material in those offices and we can't speak of any classified issue. The corridor itself is jammed with security safes.

To the right of the entranceway is the director's office. It has a frosted glass window; such as you would see in a bathroom. It is guarded by a secretary, blonde, indeterminate age, predictable makeup and surly disposition. She is not at all happy to see us descend on her and her previously quiet life. She did make a positive comment about the coffee cup so she has a spark of life.

The heart of the SOD is Room 2C840B. It has a separate cipher lock and a door that looks like a Mosler safe. That is where the "plan" is.

Inside, it looks like a storage locker in a submarine. Every inch of usable space, about 400 square feet, is jammed with desks, safes, maps, people, and pipes. In the Pentagon, everything was designed for easy access. The wiring and plumbing hang from the ceiling where it is easy to access, but the workspace is not. On average, 15 people work in here full time with another

15 constantly moving in and out, holding meetings and coordinating. There is no air conditioning, we had it turned off and sealed for security. We are going to get very familiar with each other.

Next to the secretary, there is a TV. It is cabled to a tape machine. The Pentagon tapes all relevant news and provides us with the tapes. Twice a day we gather around the tube and watch the three network reports from Tehran. These twice-daily events provide us with our greatest sense of frustration, but also our greatest sense of purpose. What we do behind these doors has a direct impact on the lives of the hostages and their captors. It is a rare event in the military where the soldier can simultaneously see the object of his planning efforts in a graphically real sense and translate this into a specific plan directed toward those same human beings.

Staff Selection

General Vaught's first problem, after deciphering the mission, was to select a staff to put together a plan. The Unconventional Warfare branch of the Special Operations Division of JCS became the foundation for growth. The Intelligence Officer, the Operations Officer and the Chief of Staff were frocked from their previous JCS-SOD assignment. This meant, as an extra benefit, they wouldn't have to move out of the cipher-secured area that became the rescue force planning spaces.

The position of personnel officer was filled by no one and everyone. Each staff member became his own recruiter for known talent and the unusual skills needed to assist. This followed the traditional "old boy" network and resulted in a constant stream of unique personalities and capabilities appearing in front of the secure door. While no formal personnel officer was assigned, the Chief of Staff, as a shrewd judge of character and with knowledge of the organizational needs and the tolerance levels of the joint system, began to assign personnel to key roles. In less than 10 days a total headquarters of 32 highly qualified people including the commander had been created.

The staff was small enough to get things done efficiently and keep everybody informed, and over-worked enough to avoid the creation of unnecessary work or needlessly expend effort. The chief was able to physically monitor about 25 of these people at all times. Like a Roman galley captain, he verbally beat the drum or flogged the laggard who seemed to be drifting from the mainstream of requirements.

The support personnel, a tiny but crucial part of the 32, came with the local furniture. The administrative chief was a Navy yeoman. Extraordinarily efficient and capable of dealing with any problem including manipulating divergent officer personalities, he came with a major additional benefit—a wife who unselfishly prepared dinner for the 32 JTF internees and the Chairman of the JCS on numerous occasions out of the goodness of her heart. The yeoman's catering service became an essential part of the morale support system. This devotion to duty and comrades is not mentioned in any service manual.

The secretaries were the standard Pentagon issue—hard-boiled, efficient, and totally unsympathetic. Requests were met with a clear internal computation of the requestors' congeniality factor before the request, position in the local power structure, and the potential result of noncompliance.

The New General

A new personality showed up today in SOD wearing civilian clothes. Air Force Lieutenant General Philip Gast. He recently returned from Iran where he was the Chief of the Military Assistance Group. He is en route to a new assignment and will spend some time with us. His knowledge of the city and the Iranian military could be of value. The group of cynics believes he is a spy for the Chairman. It is believed the Chairman feels uncomfortable with General Vaught, now code-named Hammer. He talks very straight and in precise terms. He even says "shit" occasionally and uses precise names when discussing uncooperative people or agencies. That's refreshing.

Lieutenant General Gast is serving as special advisor on "Iranian" affairs and will be helping out General Vaught. Seems like a good man. He answers questions quietly without pontificating and even knows how to say "Sorry, I don't know anything about that." That's refreshing too. Maybe he can be helpful.

About a week after his arrival, he comes to work wearing a uniform, blue in color, with wings and several stars. His permanent change of station orders to Langley Air Force Base, Virginia, have been deferred. It appears we have a "de facto" Lieutenant General air deputy. The general has served in Korea and Vietnam and been shot at several times. Hammer accepts him. Good enough credentials for the rest of us. It is odd to have a three-star ostensibly subordinate to a two-star but it's not a problem for us; the entire organization is odd.

Charlie Charges

Within a few days of the creation of the Task Force, Colonel Charlie Beckwith, the Delta Commander, came to our spaces in 2C840. I saw him routinely through the program and after.

Army Colonel Charlie Beckwith "invaded" our spaces today. He is a big man with big gestures and pre-emptive statements. He does not display a great deal of sensitivity. which makes life around the Chairman and some of his joint seniors difficult. The Joint Director of Operations, Vice Admiral Thor Hansen, is particularly off-put by Beckwith. Apparently the Navy is not used to direct discussions in mono-syllabic words.

Charlie has a very clear understanding of what he wants and how he wants it and is very clear in all aspects. What he doesn't seem to appreciate is that few people responsible for the program other than General Vaught either know or understand the specific nature of what Delta Force is being asked to do. Delta is an elite unit established in the 70s to combat terrorism and take direct action as required. Charlie wants 100 percent of everything he desires and he wants it immediately. Delay or caveat draws immediate ire.

General Meyer has a soothing effect on him and General Vaught clearly communicates in his own language when required. Others around him are hesitant to speak as he immediately displays in body language and gestures his evaluation of the comment and the speaker.

Being a member of his organization must have issues of balance. Clearly he is a man who can fight. It remains to be seen if he can successfully fight his way through the labyrinth of personalities and issues that we all face before Charlie can get to the embassy.

most of the United States government, including the majority of the Department of Defense.

- There will be no funding line, nor money directly provided for the program, nor normal administrative orders cut.
- Most service staffs, organizations, agencies, or commands or units cannot be approached except through specific points-of-contact.
- Execution of the entire operation must take place in darkness under good weather conditions.

This particular planning/organizational session takes only 20 minutes. Everyone involved feels in a better sense of humor when the meeting terminates except the man who compiled the list. He knew it to be true and the next briefing that would focus on possible solutions was only two hours away.

Key Questions

The JTF Chief of Staff, Colonel Jerry King, presides over his normal post-briefing meeting. He is becoming increasingly impatient. The staff has been unable to develop a cogent plan that made sense and his received guidance from above was becoming increasingly imprecise.

The chief did not like this situation. He was personally a very hard worker and routinely became very involved with his people's efforts. He liked people to solve each problem as it arose and then to move on to the next. In such a manner, most problems could be reduced to manageable proportions. However, this case was different. There were so many imponderables, so many unknowns, that it was very difficult to even define all the problems to be resolved. By and large, there were no precedents for many of the situations they were asked to resolve. The chief felt that the most practical solution was simply to list the questions, with their possible resolution becoming second priority. In this manner, at least everyone would have an appreciation of the problem. A very nagging fact was that each question and its answer both drove the next question and answer and developed more. Nothing could be done independently and each step required a known resolution of the preceding case. The Junior Operations Officer (me) began to list the questions on his butcher pad with a blue felt tip pen. There was no particular order.

How do we get the assault force into Iran? Helicopter or fixed wing?
How many people can we take on the assault force and how many people do we actually need?
How do we get the force into the city and out again?
How do we refuel the helicopters?
How do we enter the Embassy and Foreign Ministry?
How do we ensure the helicopters and fixed wing rendezvous at the same place?
What flight routes will avoid detection?

Colonel King briefed the Chairman and Service Chiefs on this in the evening brief. The Chief of Naval Operations approved the selection and said he would message the appropriate folks still in port at Norfolk. The helicopter force crews would have to stay behind for the long-distance flight profile training and night operations, which we knew were required.

If we don't have a plan yet, at least we know most of the players. This was a big day.

Entebbe

Throughout the planning process, we were constantly told about Entebbe operation and how we should follow the Israeli example. This came from very highly placed personnel who were acutely ignorant of the facts but mesmerized by the outcome. Accordingly, Lieutenant Colonel Lenahan and Colonel King created an Entebbe briefing to be shown whenever we were asked to follow that model.

Our intelligence officer (Air Force Lieutenant Colonel Rod Lenahan) has been receiving callers all day. In the custom of the commander, anyone with an idea, regardless of how sophisticated it might be, is granted an audience with someone on the planning staff. This is in hopes that a germ of an idea might bring forth the key to a difficult puzzle. Several people had mentioned to the intelligence officer that the Entebbe raid by the Israelis might be a good model. Shortly before, he had heard on TV a news editorial criticizing the ability of the U.S. to mount such a raid to rescue its own hostages. He was becoming increasingly disgusted with the Entebbe analogy, particularly after he spoke with several first-person sources. He began to complete a list on the subject, which he neatly placed in a manila folder entitled Entebbe, and placed it on the shelf next to his desk. The paper was hand-written and done with some anger. It outlined the following points:

- The Israelis had built the airport and had plans on hand.
- The hostages were in a single hangar that was part of the airfield immediately adjacent to the aircraft-parking ramp.
- The Israelis had a man on the telephone who was able to view both the hostages and the guards.
- The government of Kenya granted landing rights to the Israelis prior to mission execution.
- It's a lot closer from Israel to Entebbe than from the United States to Tehran.
- Israel has a history of acting with single-minded determination when the requirements are obvious.

The intelligence officer has become emotionally involved with his job.

Who Are We Fighting Here?

In the early stages of the JTF, we had liaison with the Department of State. Within two weeks of this bridge, it was clear that State was increasingly uncooperative for whatever reason and would become a potential OPSEC disaster.

I thought we were on the same team. I am clearly wrong. Since the beginning of the planning, we have had discussions with knowledgeable folks from State. It is their employees who are hostages, and we (the military) are working to bring them back, so this is perfectly natural. For whatever reason, this has significantly changed.

Lieutenant Colonel Lenahan just returned from Foggy Bottom and had a long discussion with Colonel King and General Vaught. Apparently the State folks have suddenly become quite hostile and uncooperative. We have no idea why. King tells us to cease any communications with State unless authorized by either him or General Vaught.

At the evening briefing, General Vaught had a sidebar discussion with the Chairman on the subject. Today, the Chairman visited State. He returned and informed us that henceforth we would have no further communications.

The good news is that we got the architectural drawings for the embassy compound, primarily from the CIA, which "owns" an internal complex.

I thought we were one country with one fight. Obviously naive.

Myth and Reality

At one time, the organization's ability to gather and decipher intelligence and to conduct selected operations was unmatched in the world. This capability was largely due to human beings.

Then science began to take hold.

Machines were invented that could do wonderful things. They did these things from locations far removed from the objects of their targeted attention. They were low risk and what they did was very good. But it wasn't a complete picture. Only a person could make a complete picture and truly judge what was being observed or reported.

But people also entailed risk. Risk that the person may not be totally reliable. Risk that he may be caught. And the greatest risk of all, that he also might be difficult to control. In a management-oriented society, risks are reduced to the barest minimum. Man went, and the Machine replaced him.

The general presents a problem that a machine cannot solve. The exterior of the building is well developed and clear. The interior of that building is totally invisible. The humans are inside. With luck, the rescue force will get inside also. But where and how and what will they find? This is a "people" question that cannot be programmed into a machine.

The intelligence "community" has several problems. An asset if inserted may be found. There may be no person capable of doing the job, most have been fired or retired, and his existence may be compromised for a project of dubious worth and his long-term value to the "community" destroyed.

These problems are noted by the general. He has several questions that he must answer. Where are the hostages? How are they guarded? Who guards them?

Machines can't answer these questions. Like the Luck of Roaring Camp, man is the weakest and yet the strongest link.

All Ideas Welcome

There were always many more questions than answers and General Vaught had to have them resolved in very short order. Accordingly, he encouraged ideas and eliminated most staff processes along the way. In my entire career, I never met a Flag Officer more open to random ideas and options than he. Yet he was also able to immediately judge the worth of the proposal in the operational timeframe. Even if your idea was rejected, you did not feel bad about the process.

Any thoughts considered. All ideas will be tested. That is one of the general's best traits. He is open to anything and has the sense not to prejudge its worth. His interest is the mission, not the trappings or protocol. People who wouldn't normally come near a general are providing ideas that could eventually be briefed to the President.

This week is devoted to the Ground Transport Option. What busses, trains, and planes transit Iran? Where do they start and where do they end? Who gets on board and where? Who checks the passengers and the cargo? How are they checked? What are the schedules? How do travelers eat, drink, dress? And of course, how can we take advantage of this information to transit 75 American-looking males into Iran and out again with another 60+ American civilians when the nearest international border is 300 miles away? At least the answers might be useful if we want to infiltrate someone with reliable eyes and ears beforehand.

Various categories of people that have been there before are asked their knowledge. It is impossible to ask State for help. State does not like anything that even suggests the possibility of a military option. State does not accept the fact that a mellifluous voice backed by an expensive education and an impressive vocabulary usually can't overcome something that isn't willing to be overcome.

Information continues to flow in. Daily stimulus is provided by a steady stream of strange people who occupied the outer lobby waiting to talk to a staff principal regarding a single piece of archaic knowledge that only such a visitor would know or deliver a unique set of data or equipment. The pieces of the puzzle were coming slowly together with the aid of many people, most of whom did not know and could not be told the purpose of the request or the utility of the information they provided. Train schedule for Bangladesh. Food shipments in Turkey. Customs procedures in Dogubazet. Sh'ia holy days. Commercial flight routes. Bus stops in the desert. (See Appendix F.)

The Truck Option

Trucks look pretty good. Concept: We buy some local-looking trucks, put our people in them and drive to town. Where do we start? The options are the Soviet Union, Turkey, Iraq, Pakistan, or Afghanistan. Such a deal. Maybe we can get mileage points from Hertz.

Some minor problems are showing up. No country is apparently willing to overtly support us. Trucks take a long time to cover 300–500 miles in Iran. No one is quite sure how long the trucks will have to sit at the border check points before beginning the in-country trek or how exactly 30–40 people get fed, kept warm and undetected in a truck that is supposed to be carrying things that do not require food, heat, or rest stops.

An old aide of the general's is brought in who served with him in Turkey. I spent several months in the same area—the Iran–Turkey border. We got our roadmap, compared notes, and came up with a fairly good test plan on paper. We brief it to General Vaught and 30 minutes later he delivers a synopsis to the Chairman. This was not an easy feeling. We could visualize a scene where the President, in the heat of the moment gives the go-ahead to a plan put together by two majors who devoted a whole four hours of study to it. Fate of Nation hangs in the balance. Nonetheless, it's nice to know your work gets a hearing. Rather than being mesmerized by new-found visibility, I am frightened by my potential responsibility.

Chairman in 30.

TIR in Tears

One of the first options to bring in the force to Tehran was by truck. Accordingly, we began to seriously examine the details of such an option. This ranged from developing suitable trucks to understanding the details regarding an actual crossing. This is a description of the reconnaissance of the crossing point most likely to be used. It was assumed the Turkish government would permit a clandestine infiltration. The acronym TIR is the European customs transit description used by all cross-border freight trucks throughout the continent. It is painted on the side and rear of virtually all freight trucks. Usually, the customs at the government of origin will seal the doors with a lead seal. Others may be added as the truck passes several borders.

Dogubazet, Turkey, lies atop the Turkish corridor near Lake Van where it crosses into the Iranian border. It is the only crossing point in the area that permitted non-Turks or -Iranians to transit. The difficulties associated with a correct pronunciation of the formal name caused us to immediately label it Dog Biscuit. This became the code word used between ourselves and the CIA regarding working the site. Accordingly, a man was sent to investigate the specifics regarding the site. This is the story.

The truck, laden with frozen lamb, more properly, an amalgam of fat tailed sheep and goat carcasses, approached the exit lane at Dog Biscuit. It pulled slowly behind the last truck in line and halted. There were more than 20 trucks ahead, all waiting for processing. The driver and passenger both descended to the ground from their lofty perches and slowly walked up the road to the customs and security building. At an altitude in excess of 5,000 feet it was bitingly cold. And this was September. Both grabbed their dirty woolen jackets and pulled them tighter with their sleeve-encased arms. The passenger also stopped for a moment to re-pin a large brass laundry safety pin through his pants to the now-tightened jacket. He had a week's beard, well-weathered eyes and cheap Bulgarian shoes with the cardboard inners now exposed as white pulp next to his dark blue socks. This was our agent.

Along the line of parked trucks, people were sitting with their backs to the tires as wind relief. Some were smoking, others cooking on small charcoal braziers. Some trucks harbored families with wives and children wrapped in camouflaging quilts and blankets with only eyes showing. The fires all exuded odors of burning manure, fat from questionable sources, and a uniformly piercing blue haze. The smoke hung low over the ground and saturated all that passed, causing momentary stinging sensations as the pair traveled between belts of local smog. By the time they arrived at the process station, their eyes were heavily watering. While the driver wiped his eyes clear with a large blue bandanna, the passenger just wiped his sleeve across his eyes allowing the water to streak across his cheeks and further add to the image of dissoluteness.

Once inside the building and clear from the wind, the atmosphere was no better but markedly different. It stank from hundreds of unwashed drivers yelling and screaming at a dozen different process stations. The building was a large square with dilapidated windows lining the top. Neon lights hung on naked wires from the ceiling with more than half the bulbs dead in the fixtures. Off to one side were several cold water taps for Muslim ablutions and a line of a dozen open urinals projecting from the walls in various states of disrepair. That portion smelt decidedly worse than the rest but it was a matter of nuance rather than significant difference.

The rear third of the building was a loosely walled boundary delineating the formal work spaces from the applicants. The bottom portion was concrete cinderblock that had been painted at one time and was now worn by hands and feet to an undulating series of grime-marked crevices. At the top of the wall was a continuous steel-barred fence with openings for the officials to administer their stations. Above each opening was a rough block-printed sign in Turkish, Persian, and Arabic indicating the station. Many had an English addition undoubtedly hand-painted by a frustrated driver or tourist. Lines were behind each. Drivers shuffled and smoked incessantly with their hands filled with TIR forms, customs declarations and visa applications. No line was moving particularly fast. The ground by each station was littered with cigarette butts, spit, and the mud of the moment. It is doubtful that the area was ever cleaned in a normal sense. Rather like ancient cities, they just built on top of the older portions.

The overall effect was stink and noise. From the outside, it sounded like a constant screech and rumble of machinery and manpower. Inside, there was the unabated noise attendant with some 500 people constantly shouting, spitting, shuffling, and rustling papers. Inside, the deafening effect sublimated the senses and allowed the body to assimilate the roar to an acceptable level. Both driver and passenger engaged in some form of continuous low conversation with the others as they waited to progress in the line. While the talk was seemingly casual, it began to glean important data points.

At the station, papers would be processed. Currency would be pinned to the underside, out of sight, to be quickly removed by the attending official. Depending upon the size of the bribe, a transit could take several hours to three days. No bribe meant a three- to five-day wait. The amount drivers were allocated by their customer or owners depended upon the necessary speed. Dry goods took several days with minimal Baksheesh. Other cargoes cost a lot more and were processed more quickly. There also appeared to be a pecking order to the stations. Several to the extreme right processed paperwork quickly but at considerable expense, whatever the economy would bear.

Once the paperwork had been passed, each driver would receive a large cardboard number and be directed to a second building. Here, he would wait to be called by an inspector. The inspector would take the paperwork, go to the truck, and undertake his own inspection. In most cases, this would include a walk through the interior to check cargo. Whether or not the inspector had an issue would depend on the stipend offered to overlook. Once satisfied as to the cargo, a stamp would be affixed to the transit papers and the truck could proceed to the Iranian side for a significantly less onerous passage.

The passenger, now uncommitted, used the time to walk around the inspection lanes and observe.

He began to ascertain a specific pattern of inspection and clearance regardless of the inspector. Trucks with dry cargo were routinely opened at the rear and through the cab if such a portal existed. Trucks with liquid were probed by a long stick throughout their length and depth. Frozen food trucks were opened just sufficiently to see the cargo and feel the breath of ice air and quickly re-shut. In some of these, a large frozen package or carcass would be pulled through, dropped to the ground and left for later retrieval by the inspector. This would be an important observation.

Several other discussions resulted in some disquieting data points. Winter was exceedingly bitter as September presaged. Often, snows would block the single mountain road for days or weeks until plows from both sides cleared them, an act that was highly problematic. Several drivers indicated they had been stopped for more than a week. A Siberian winter began in mid-November and dragged on through early April. Any transit would have to be before or after.

Bribes had a clear place in the process but the amount would have to be carefully determined and the target window identified. If the bribe was offered too hastily, especially by an unfamiliar face, suspicions could be aroused, a risk that could not be taken.

The lead customs seals were rarely broken but the connecting wire would be cut and then re-wired as if no one cared as to the integrity. The inspectors did look at the seal and confirm its legitimacy with the paperwork. In a very erratic pattern, an inspector might affix his own seal within the confines of the older seal. This often resulted in a mass of lead illegible until separated. The passenger noted that our seals would have to be from a non-Western European country that had a common trade in whatever product would be utilized as cover.

After about 48 hours, the driver and passenger were permitted to cross. The bribe had been average for a dry cargo load. The second adventure would now begin: Iran.

Once beyond the Iranian crossing site, a simple painless process, the truck proceeded down a large but unpaved highway through the mountains into the high plains of Kurdistan. Several truck caravansaries dotted the road, offering fuel, food, bazooka music, and questionable bathrooms. Lights were predominately provided by Olympus-brand Coleman-type lanterns, with the blaring black-and-white TVs powered by a loud overbearing generator. Rarely were refrigerated drinks or food available. Most drivers hung hammocks inside their cab. Passengers slept on the cushions or inside the freight area accessed by the magic opening customs seals.

With the fall of night, the formal Iranian gendarmes departed in their Daihatsu jeeps. They were replaced within an hour by Kurdish Peshmerga, who would walk through the rest stops, knock on cab doors and inspect papers. The Dog Biscuit agents had cargo indicated for Kurdistan. Accordingly, they were allowed to proceed without a bribe. Cargoes bound for the interior of Iran were taxed.

In time, the truck and its passengers arrived at a large Kurdish town where they turned the truck over to a third party. Agent Dog Biscuit was then joined by a person with whom he was familiar and in record time arrived at 2C840 with a plan.

We could use trucks from Turkey ostensibly carrying frozen lamb carcasses, but not during the winter due to concerns about roads being closed. Total transit time from where Delta would mount the vehicles to dismount in Tehran would take between five and eight days. Charlie Beckwith is decidedly unhappy but we have an option. Maybe; it depends on the dates and we are closing on November.

Carcasses—Frozen and Otherwise

Now that we have settled on a frozen lamb carcass truck, we have to actually fabricate one so that we can pack the force inside in relative comfort for an extended cross-country drive of several hundred miles. We needed to imbed some form of covert communication means as well as associated "comfort" items, not the least of which are heat and air. In due time, the Agency produced a prototype for Charlie to try out with some of his force. Once designed, we would need a number of these trucks to move the entire force. This is representative of the steps taken for all our entry options that were examined and weighted throughout the planning period, a point for which General Vaught never received any credit.

Today, we went to a secret undisclosed location, one we have visited quite frequently lately. It is isolated enough to play with stuff in a small way and close enough that we can get back to the real world of the Pentagon. Travel there also has a way of relieving the make-believe we have to tolerate in the corridors of power. It is warm, breezy and near the water. If nothing else, a good respite and recharge.

Once we arrive, we are introduced to the "truck." This is a prototype of a possible design we could use to get the boys across the border. It looks very much like all the others we saw at Dog Biscuit, which was the point. But this one had some unique aspects not visible. The Agency guy took General Vaught, myself and a number of Charlie's boys around the chassis.

The fabricators had managed to acquire a real truck dashboard and bench seat from the region. The window was dripping small cotton balls dangling from the ceiling. The bench seat stank of tobacco, strong tea and a lifetime of spilled greasy goat-meat sandwiches and dirt. The floor mats were the rough-cut scrap carpet pieces utilized to keep some protection between the floor boards and the freezing outside. The instrumentation was an amalgam of scrap parts and a uniform appearance of poor homemade fabrications. Perfection.

The top of the ceiling was plastered with a variety of glued religious pictures. They covered the gamut from Hindu to Christian to Muslim. The Agency man demonstrated one unique feature.

By pressing Vishnu's head, a small crack was revealed that ran the width of the roof. By gently pulling at the crack, it dropped about six inches. A small set of ear phones and a very small voice microphone descended. Above them, between the interior and roof, a satellite antenna had been constructed. It was invisible from the outside because the top of the roof was, in fact, the antenna material. The instrumentation was a glowing face revealed when the earphones were extracted.

The troop entrance was equally clever. There was a small pin under the freight floor board hidden by the large transmission running the length of the truck. Once pulled (it worked from both in and out of the compartment), a door would drop resting on the top of the transmission. There was approximately 20 inches of space between the transmission top and the cargo floor. Sufficient for troops to move in and out and pass gear.

Inside, the compartment was lined with thin prison-type mattresses on the floor with a foam sound-dampening material lining the walls and ceiling. A compost toilet with a dump door was arranged in a corner. With a pull on a cable, the contents would drop on the pavement. Racks were arranged halfway up the sides like a ship's galley, holding water bottles and packaged food. There was plenty of room for gear and weapons. Small lights were arranged on the ceiling and sides that were powered by the truck battery. The mattresses and side foam provided significant insulation. A small vent joined the cab and the cargo area. Encased within the normal hydraulic lines connecting the cabin to the cargo area and brakes was a communications line and speaker that was imbedded into the rear of the driver's headrest.

The rear of the truck was a large insulated split door, standard for refrigerator trucks. Opened, as it would be for an inspection, frozen lamb carcasses were stacked to the ceiling. Sufficient overpressure had been built into the pumping system so that any opening would create a large continuing wall of fog. The guide showed where several carcasses were loose that could be easily pulled out of a minimal opening to satiate the inspector's needs. This frozen compartment was one carcass deep in depth. Adding to the illusion was a series of sheep's heads between the legs of the first row, facing out and affixed to the troop interior wall, providing an illusion of further cargo but well camouflaged by the emitting clouds of near-frozen moisture.

All looked good, but now the real test began. We all crawled into the interior, arranged ourselves in semi-darkness and began a four-hour cross-country transit. At first, the ride was simply bumpy as our senses adjusted to this all. Then the mind began to wander and wonder as we were constantly jolted, battered, and vibrated into both emotional and physical submission.

A particularly bad jolt would throw us together or bounce us against each other. Over time, the lack of vision, the vibrations and oddly disconcerting noises of the engine, the refrigeration unit, and the road became mentally troublesome.

After about four hours of representative roads ranging from dirt to smooth pavement, the truck halted, and we unloaded. We all agreed that while it was a doable means of transport, it was not ideal. If the trucks had to remain stationary at Dog Biscuit for more than four hours, which was highly likely, there would be issues with both heat and toilet use. An inadvertent dump in a parking lot could raise considerable suspicion.

By count, we would need about a dozen trucks to haul the force. Getting them all through Dog Biscuit simultaneously would be a miracle. Well, we at least had an option while searching for a better solution. Now, for the first time, I-95 was looking pretty good.

The Base Force

General Meyer has indicated that the newly created Delta Force, commanded by Colonel Charlie Beckwith at Fort Bragg, will be the primary assault force. We immediately begin working with his staff. The key issues remain: How do we get Delta there and how do we get them back?

Within a few days, we have developed a new base concept of methodology and force mix to resolve the problems. We examined *Jane's Fighting Planes* and identified the RH-53 as a likely lift helicopter. The Navy and Marines have a quantity of these.

The Navy version is used for mine-sweeping and anti-submarine work off of carriers. With tactical fighter wing tanks, these helicopters can fly a notional 1,100 miles just right.

The Air Force has a number of EC-130s. These are C-130 Hercules airlifters with mid-air refueling capability. The force could initially ride in these to a location and off load into the RH-53s and then get to the embassy and back. It's a start point. So are trucks, trains and buses … and everything else to be discovered.

Help Wanted!
Driver, Knows Tehran and Speaks Farsi

In a short time, we understood this would be a two-night operation with troops in position on Night One, and assault on Day Two. We had no idea what either Desert One or Desert Two looked like. A key issue was how to get the assault force from Desert Two to the embassy. Invariably, this became a truck movement. But we needed drivers that looked Iranian and spoke fluent Farsi. We could not risk a vehicle being stopped and searched. Lieutenant Colonel Lenahan and Major Richard Friedel then began locating and integrating Iranian expatriates of a trustworthy nature. This describes our beginning efforts.

Now that we have decided to infiltrate the force into the city and close with the embassy by vehicle, we need to make sure they get there and on schedule. Thanks to Colonel Lenahan and overhead imagery, the actual act of driving, even through the streets of Tehran, is doable. We can map out every foot of the way and identify every turn and landmark. We can even work out a respectably precise timetable given the time of night and where the force will be moving.

What we can't predict, or take for granted, is the unexpected road block thrown up by the Pasdaran (the Islamic Revolutionary Guard Corps), or the highway accident that occurred just before we reach that spot on the journey. We will need people that look like Iranians, speak Farsi, and can BS their way around, or out of the unexpected road adventure.

The Agency says it can provide the genuine article. We need seven drivers but decide to create our own reliability insurance. These come in two forms—a Delta shooter and an American military-type who speaks Farsi.

The search is on. The J2 guys working with Defense Intelligence Agency (DIA) contacts who then work with the service personnel staffs, crank up the computers looking for Farsi speakers. The initial run does not look good. We confirm you could be fluent in 16 languages, be on active duty for 10 years, and be invisible to the personnel system and its computers unless you have been formally tested for each of the languages, or attended a certified language training program, or hold a military occupation specialty that requires that language. The fluent speaker of a foreign language that learned to speak on the knee of his mother is not in the computer unless one of the other three circumstances occurred subsequently. So we push the button again. Anybody that served in Iran in the past four years?

Now the second list is bigger. There is a correlation between the first list and the second. Fortunately, our new Deputy Commander, Lieutenant General Gast (the former Military Assistance Advisory Group [MAAG] Chief), provided names of some candidates early on. We use these early candidates after they have passed our language vetting, driving skills, and volunteer status to sort out a few more known quantities from the computer lists.

Within 10 days we have our roster. It includes a Navy captain from Annapolis, two Army Special Forces/Ranger officers, one from Defense Intelligence Agency and other from the Army staff. Two sets of Air Force flight wings are also part of the equation plus what turned out to be a real prize.

By the time this search program is terminated, we will have examined almost every form of transport known to man. Yes Sir! Elephant option coming right up!

Inside an RH-53

We had settled on the RH-53 as the helicopter of choice. No other aircraft would provide the OPSEC profile. A CH-47 looks like an Army CH-47 on a carrier and is therefore a dead giveaway. We became quickly familiar with the eccentricities of this Naval/Marine airframe.

The aircraft itself looks rather impressive and somewhat foreboding from the outside. It has a distinctive shape, readily recognizable by those who have watched astronaut recovery shots on television. The main rotor blade shades almost the entire fuselage and the tail rotor is high and obvious at the top of a cylindrical boom that juts up sharply from the main body. Inside it is not so sleek-looking; industrial/functional may be more accurate.

The interior shell is rectangular and painted a light green. Red nylon seats attached to spun aluminum frames line the walls of the cargo bay. The seats will be taken out for the mission. Any riders will have to sit on the beaded aluminum floors interspersed with clasps for shackles and tie-down straps. The vibration of the engine turbines and blade wash are passed directly through the floor. The fuselage sides are pierced in several places by clear plastic bubble windows. Most are covered with a slight coating of grease or scratched so that the outside world appears to be somewhat impressionistic and unfocused to the inside observer.

A portion of the pilot crew compartment can be seen from the rear of the helicopter. The pilots are elevated from the deck floor as is their instrumentation. The result is that passengers can only catch occasional glimpses of the cockpit—a disembodied hand grasping the collective stick or the greenish glow of the instrument panel. This is the total world as it will be seen by the rescue force as they fly toward Tehran in utter darkness.

At this moment, the entire center portion of the helicopter's interior is filled with oblong fiberglass tanks. These are the just-invented long-range fuel tanks that will permit the helicopters to fly from an aircraft carrier somewhere in the Indian Ocean to Desert One without refueling. The tanks are about three-quarters full now and a careful viewer can see the thin, almost opaque line where the fuel is sloshing about in the interior. Each tank is connected with a small maze of pipes and hoses and control knobs that connect the auxiliary fuel system to the main fuel system. The overall impression is not factory showroom but garage functional.

If the helicopters work as planned, tested, and predicted, things will work out fine. If they don't, a lot of people will be tested beyond that which they anticipated.

A Typical Day

This is a decent description of my day when not deployed out west.

0600. We update the book and give it to the Chairman. We get an intelligence dump from Rod Lenahan and read the night's message traffic. We talk to the units in the field if something is critical and get a cup of extraordinarily strong coffee.

Chairman comes in about 0800 for an informal brief. Nothing is informal with the Chairman. Colonel Knight and Rod review the bidding. I sit at the rear and take notes. The Chairman provides some guidance that will create several centuries of work. We drink more coffee.

1000. I go downstairs to give the Army a heads-up on what's needed. I get 20 minutes of lecture on how we need to have a realistic view of the possible with a concurrent character assassination of a convenient scapegoat. Back upstairs.

1215. About lunchtime. Wait, the afternoon crisis is about to begin. Whatever it is, the minimum requirement will be three options accompanied by graphic charts, several phone calls, at least one out-of-the-building visit, two memos, a guidance session with General Vaught, and another page for the Book. Crisis resolves itself about 1600 concurrent with the Chairman's afternoon visit. Same scenario as 0800. "Lunch" is ossified potato patties accompanied by a Coke courtesy of the Pentagon cafe. Mmm, good!

1645. Chairman leaves. Colonel Knight provides guidance along with General Vaughn as to what the Chairman meant to say. We begin filing, researching, or collating as required. Europe is shutting down so we get our last list of phone calls from the mother countries.

Anytime between 1800 and 0600 is used to finish the work we each have been trying to do all day. After 2000 people start to depart. The advantage to this schedule is that there is no traffic on the Beltway coming or going. However, no buses are running either. Well, we rarely see our wives, we never see our children. We cannot car pool. There is no such thing as a weekend or holiday.

Graphics

As in any Pentagon program, a briefing was a key part of the decision process. For this event, I was the principal briefer twice a day taking input from a variety of sources and directives and then translating all that to a simple set of explanatory graphics. How to do this became a daily challenge.

I have found the key national strategic asset: the graphics department of the Joint Chiefs of Staff. You cannot have a plan without a briefing. You can't have a briefing without a chart or map. You can't have a map or chart without graphic aids. Without graphics, there is nothing. What's that worth to the Soviets?

My point of contact is a female Navy Lieutenant JG with a well-fitted uniform. About 5 foot 1 inch, she had short-cut brown hair and a nice smile. The overall effect is harmed by a dominant malocclusion. But, she does great work. Any name, place, or title within the hour. In this place, time is invaluable. I often worry about the security of the whole thing. Supposedly only about 50 people know what's going on but it won't take a genius to figure out the answer if he just reads what titles we asked for. I am most concerned about this aspect when Colonel Knight tells me that the Chairman is coming in 30 minutes and wants a once-over brief.

Graphic titles are black on a white background and come with wax backing. Easy to move and reset. They are made on photocopy paper and waxed. Very quick and neat. I'm becoming an expert on designing.

We have cornered every type of colored stripe tape made. We cover the whole color spectrum and further divide subsets with dashes, stripes, and alternating colors. Each colored stripe is a route or PERT chart event of the Myriad of Options under consideration. If someone makes an error, we will be briefing commercial flights from Saudi Arabia transiting truck stops in Pakistan. Fortunately, everyone is so busy now and has no time to provide "guidance" so it usually ends up correct.

I have a Letterset collection that must rival any architectural department. We have all the symbology of the world's known defense systems, most print fonts of the English language, and all the geometric forms Pythagoras knew. The quality of the products may be thin but the graphics are first-rate.

Pentagon truism; it's not what you read but how you brief that counts. If it looks good, it will probably sail.

Maps

It is virtually impossible for the military to run an operation without a map. Different elements need different maps—aviators, ground forces, intelligence collectors etc. We found that very few maps existed for Iran that were applicable. Accordingly, the J2, Lieutenant Colonel Lenahan, went to extra lengths with the key Department of Defense map purveyors.

One of the best assets we have is the Defense Mapping Agency. They can print anything on anything in addition to reducing photos, making maps, and finding maps.

Rod gave them several satellite photos and asked them to print up some maps. Within a week they had converted them to standard maps and included the actual photos on the back, blown up, for extra credit.

Every unit that needs a map or photo print has one. The Defense Mapping Agency made rescue maps for the pilots and troops on rubber sheet paper. One is an extended Iran tourist map and the other a large-scale Iran map.

It's amazing what this nation can produce when pressed or gets behind a program.

The Tank

On some occasions, we were required to brief issues in the famous "Tank."

The end of a Pentagon corridor, blocked off from normal access, is the Tank. The Tank is where the JCS meet to ponder the weighty issues of the day.

It is a small room, much smaller than what the uneducated would believe. It has cream and gold curtains and plush carpet. It is dominated by a large almost-square table. At one end of the room is a large world map, and at the other is a rear projection screen for briefings.

There is a small room to the side for the someone to take notes. Around the edge of the room on two sides are some chairs. Not many. They don't encourage much of an audience.

The deliberation table is wood. Next to each seat is an ashtray, paper and pencils. The centerpiece usually has fruit and candy. Each person has a nameplate. Protocol is very important.

The members sit around the table and debate the issues in tongues ranging from moderated to hushed to irritated, depending on the subject. While they are usually polite to each other, it is not a requirement. Here, the most august members of each service can and will speak their minds without the usual niceties.

The briefer is ushered in, introduced by his appropriate service representative and then is on his own. Questions follow. Briefing is terminated. Briefer leaves. Later, we find out the result.

Once you become a member of the Tank, the resident NCO learns your various likes: you get iced tea, Coke, Sprite, water, or coffee. You can munch on peanuts or small Hershey's Kisses or miniature Krackle bars.

The Tank is very nice and can be very terminal.

Clandestine Committees

The Chairman has a distinct management style. He rarely makes a decision in our presence, but reserves those for private moments with Major General Vaught after consideration. He also uses a myriad of people and ad hoc organizations to examine pieces of the program without reference to the whole. These pieces and parts would advise us as to arcane points that were then required to be integrated or rejected. Every day brought a new personality into the fold.

The Chairman, by his nature, is a reserved commander. He keeps his counsel to himself and demurs from taking strong positions. He is noted for his "clandestine" committee approach to doing things. Scattered throughout the building are groups of people or trusted individuals all working on projects or tasks he has passed out. Each element is directed to report only to him and reveal their intent to no one. Many seem to be working on the same thing.

I originally thought that this was rather improper and an impediment to the "system." But the more I observe the joint "system," the more convinced I am that he is right. If he makes these projects a traditional "Joint" action requiring consensus prior to execution, it will die of its own weight. Each service will adjust for its own self-interest, object to the other services' position, and in order to ensure comity, obfuscate and deliberate, generally killing any idea with kindness. Forward operational progress would be hopeless. It is apparent that one of the last things the Joint Chiefs want is a clear consensus that could lead to deliberate action and responsibility. They will cover this position with professional terms such as "consensus" and "prudent deliberation," but it all boils down to nothing happens of a positive nature. Score one for the Chairman.

The Navy is right, the only positive thing that can come out of a joint action is no harm.

Andrew Jackson was also right: one man with courage makes a majority.

Part of the Problem

One of the things that struck me about the very senior people on the Joint Chiefs Staff was how naïve and unfamiliar they were with real world combat or combat situations. They had spent their careers in rarified sanitary environments and suddenly we were forcing them into a world in which they were decidedly uncomfortable.

One of the many events today was a briefing by Charlie Beckwith on how the embassy would be "taken down." As usual, it took place in the back room around the conference table with the usual attendees; General Vaught and General Gast, our staff, Director Joint Staff (General Shutler), and a variety of lesser lights. Crowded and hot.

The basic plan is reviewed and various questions answered. We then come to the embassy plan. Charlie indicates the wall will be approached that parallels Roosevelt Avenue. "What about the guards?" says a naval person.

Charlie leans his formidable self across the table, looks at the questioner directly in the eye and replies that he will be "taken out." "You mean killed," asks the questioner. Clearly he did not expect that answer. Equally clearly, the thought is distasteful.

Charlie momentarily hesitates to gather his thoughts and looks back at his tormentor and replies;, "I'll shoot him right between the eyes and then do it again just to make sure."

End of questions.

There were several people in that room that thought the original question was quite logical.

Gas!

Prior to Tehran, as part of their initial standup, Delta personnel had meetings with French, German, and British counter-terrorist elements. Colonel Beckwith had trained early in his career with the British SAS and had been an observer with them in Malaya. During a liaison visit with the French CT unit commanded by Captain Pretou, Charlie received an extensive briefing on the French use of gas of various kinds in counter-terrorist operations. Soon after being tapped to lead the Iran rescue ground assault effort, he made a point of requesting the use of gas.

Charlie has asked to use gas as part of his assault at the embassy. He is rightfully concerned about the possibility of crowd control should the operation be compromised. He can also evacuate the hostages if need be by gassing the student guards rather than shooting them. This is a sensible request but it is fraught with all sorts of emotional and political connotations for the seniors.

The Chairman was taken aback at the briefing and clearly unsettled. Secretary Brown was stunned. Brown muttered that this would require a presidential decision.

We do some cursory research on the subject and discover that there is a fair array of various products on the shelf that will incapacitate but not kill. An issue is that even a cursory check of wind drift and acreage indicates that a lot more people than the embassy crowd will probably be exposed. However, the use of gas would greatly minimize the necessity for lethal gunfire. Delta will not aim to wound. A drawback is that Delta will have to carry each hostage more than 100 yards to the helicopter evacuation site.

A second discussion with Brown occurs describing the various gas options. Later, the Chairman informs us that we "may consider the employment of riot gas." Vaught asks for that in writing. Not yet forthcoming. (See Appendix F.)

Ground Planners

Grouped around the rectangular wooden table are three men. Spread on the table is a large colored map of the city of Tehran, several satellite photos, an 18-inch ruler, some clear plastic acetate and several colored marking pens. Surrounding them are a dozen people all intently working at their own desks or talking to each other. The walls are surrounded by heavy metal Mosler safe filing cabinets. Piled on top of the cabinets are maps, charts, and a variety of miscellaneous material ranging from coffee cups to encyclopedias. The room is very noisy, but the planners hear none of it. Like football players huddled in a crowded stadium, they are oblivious to the crowd and totally intent on their work.

One man is tall with very curly hair and a very English-looking face. Another is about 6 feet and heavily built. He has a receding hairline and excellent muscle definition. He and the curly-haired man are dressed in very casual, almost western-style clothes, almost as if they had stepped off the train in Boulder, Colorado.

The well-built man has a plastic coffee cup in his hand which he frequently uses to spit into. The third man is dressed in a standard Army green uniform with open collar. He is taller than the others but hides the fact by resting his head on his balled fist on the table as he listens to the other two talk. This group is working on the ground assault plan.

The tall man circles each intersection on the map that is contiguous to the Embassy. He then places an X over the soccer stadium adjacent to the embassy and several more smaller circles inside the Embassy compound. The other casual dresser places numbers by each circle and an X as he refers to the satellite photos that matched the map. The uniformed planner busies himself making a list of numbers. He totals the numbers represented by each circle and X and then refers to the numbers available to be lifted by helicopter. They don't match.

It will take more people to conduct the assault and secure the force than the present assault force has. That is what planners do. They bring reality to a concept and cause hard decisions to be made. The noise surrounding the planners continues. While the planners can shut out the interference, they can't avoid reality.

General Vaught will have to make another hard decision. He has been in three wars and absolutely understands that under each circle and X are human beings that he commits to fate. One of the problems in being an experienced general is that you know what you are doing and the likely cost.

Feed the Troops

Just down the corridor from 2C840 is the Pentagon cafeteria. This place sustains us at a survival level for the entirety of our participation. Most of us rarely make breakfast or dinner with our families. We are surreptitious visitors that sneak in and out of our houses trying not to wake occupants. Our hours and necessary appearances are such that a normal meal routine is unheard of.

General Vaught will take a briefing, be intrigued by the prospects and ask the Chairman to come and hear about it … and make a decision. I've got 20 minutes to spare.

I race down to the cafeteria and grab the quickest obtainable meal. This usually equates to a paper cone of Tater Tots and a large cup of lemonade.

In the morning, I substitute a large cup of very dark coffee and a Baby Ruth candy bar.

Everyone else seems to be on a similar diet with minor menu adjustments.

I have to remind myself to wash my hands as the first time I flipped the chart for the Chairman, I left a large greasy stain where my fingers held the paper. The Chairman looked at me and said, "Are you leaking?"

Eyes on the Target

The primary question always in our forefront was; where are the hostages? The corollary requirement was to develop quality operational intelligence regarding the known hostage sites: the embassy and the foreign ministry complex just to the north where chargé d'affaires, Bruce Laingen, and two companions were located. These were standing tasks for the CIA—tasks that they could not seem to fill.

If there is one thing next to the mission statement that is important, it is intelligence; either its availability or lack thereof, and its quality and timeliness. If we don't know where the hostages are in a very precise way, we can't launch a rescue with a high probability of success. Likewise, we must know the guard routine, the warning system, the door construction and reaction capability. This sort of thing can't be picked up from a satellite photo. There is no substitute for credible eyes on the ground. Right now we don't have any.

The general is fit to be tied. He has a pair of spooks in daily from the supposed font of all knowledge and is given a dry hole on virtually every question he asks. Stand Still Burner (Admiral Stansfield Turner) and his Clowns In Action (CIA) either won't or can't produce the information. Sometimes it's a combination of both. It's maddening. We thought we were doing what the President ordered, but we can't do squat until one of his other subordinates begins to help.

What seems to have happened is that the Great Saturday Night Massacre at Langley disemboweled the ranks of field soldiers in favor of sexy, high-tech systems. The systems are very attractive to the state-side bureaucrat—although expensive, they're prestigious, provide high-quality, and most importantly, low risk and brief well to the uneducated. However, they usually can't provide the ground level pulse of the intended operating area and their coverage cycle is largely fixed and predictable. We know all about the roof of the embassy and virtually nothing about what's inside. Without that inside information, we are almost wasting our time. The Agency is very reluctant to commit to a HUMINT (covert intelligence-gathering by people) operation. They aren't convinced the mission will really happen.

The J2 is working on developing an "in-house" solution to the problem. Most are betting that the Clowns will object to that once they get wind of it. They troop through here daily in their pinstripes and speak in hushed, cultured tones. What we need is a grubby gardener who knows the layout of the embassy compound inside and out and still has access to the kitchen. A secretary with ambivalent morals and in debt will also help.

Some predict that the mission will be launched in spite of the Clowns but only after we develop our own HUMINT capability and battle the bureaucrats to insert them.

Scouts Out

The cavalry of old used the term "scouts out," at least in the Hollywood version of *She Wore a Yellow Ribbon* and other big-scene westerns. I remember hearing it again from the lips of Lieutenant General Sam Wilson, U.S. Army, retired, and former Director of the Defense Intelligence Agency in one of his lectures at the Air Force Special Operations School in the mid-70s.

Two hundred years earlier, General George Washington gave the same order to a select handful of volunteers, including Nathan Hale. It made sense then, it makes sense now, and it will also make sense particularly when we are about to commit American lives to the unknown and the risk of death and possible defeat.

We needed scouts on 5 November. We had none. On the 7th we were told another government agency would provide them. In spite of the valiant efforts of three civilian contract hires (who did accomplish some very essential tasks), it was not enough. We needed to launch our own scouts. We needed individuals who could view the environment with the awareness of a soldier, and see and evaluate things that would remain unnoticed to the typical civilian.

Nearly a dozen volunteers came forward, most without being asked. They just knew of the need. We selected four. Remarkably, none of the four have the pedigree of the regulars of the other government organization. Our volunteers are more the American hybrid than the American blue blood. All four come from working-class families. All four have their roots in the enlisted corps. Three of the four could be categorized, by the politically and culturally correct, as Hyphenated-Americans.

Prize Package

The U.S. military harbors a wide variety of ethnicities within its structure. We reached out and got lucky. Fred Arooji became a huge indispensable asset.

About two weeks into the crisis, sometime in the third week in November, a young airman working on the F-4 flight line of Shaw AFB quietly asked his line chief for an appointment to see the unit commander. Accomplished within hours. The Commander contacted a friend and former SOW classmate in the Defense Intelligence Agency. The DIA contacted the JTF. The airman was on the JTF doorstep within 48 hours. When he first arrived neither the JTF nor the young married E-4 knew exactly how he would be used, but both know his natural Iranian looks, fluent Farsi and familiarity with Tehran would come in handy as well as his willingness to help his adopted country. The airman called his wife and explained that he would be on temporary duty for a while. The line chief and commander and their wives made sure she was not abandoned. This pledge held for the duration—which for him was longer than the rest of us. Welcome Fred.

Two Sergeants

The Iranian Foreign Ministry held the chargé d'affaires, Bruce Laingen, and two of his staff. They had been sequestered there by the same "students" that took over the embassy. We had to plan on rescuing them as well as the embassy location. Hard as it was to develop quality intelligence on the embassy, it was impossible to develop intelligence on the consulate. Finally in frustration, and at the suggestion of Colonel Beckwith with the approval of the Chairman and General Meyer, we recruited several NCOs from Special Forces Berlin to assume a cover and collect intelligence about the consulate.

Standstill Burner won't or can't help with some HUMINT so what we develop is an internal capability. Two sergeants. The mission is to find out what's happening in "town" and in particular, what's happening in Laingen's location.

They do a great job. They arrive, take on the tourist profile and wander as they please. They enticed a guard to pose for pictures in front of the residence for cigarettes and gauge the door entrance. They get a lot of good information a satellite won't show.

Each earned about $1,000 a month.

Like the Army says—you want to get a job done, ask a sergeant to do it.

Penetration, However Slight

The actual flight route for the helicopters and fixed wings was a crucial part of the puzzle. It drove intelligence, flight profiles and security as well as follow-on extraction tasks. There were many variables that drove selection. Chief among them were Iranian ground and air security, radar profiles (we previously installed the Iranian radars), isolated laager sites and just plain distance and flight times within the capacity of the various aircraft.

Rod has been trying to firm up the final flight route. Where can we coast in? What altitude can we fly out? What is the best route? Fortunately, the Air Force did a ground radar profile for the Shah just recently before he was deposed.

The map is of a standard JOGG (Joint Operation Ground Graphic) with the analyzed radar profile over-printed in pink. The pink outlines the actual ground profile of the radar. Unlike the standard school depiction of a radar range, this map is all spikes and angles indicating the effect of the terrain on the radar pulse.

There is a massive blank area in the extreme south near Chabahar and virtually no pink all the way north. Eureka, we found it!

If the map is right, the pilots have their coast-in point within reasonable range for the carrier and clear sailing through the Eastern Mountain area to the Dahst e'Kavir Desert, if they stay below commercial airline altitudes.

There is some concern over portable radar possibly being moved to block that corridor. But reports indicate that maintenance has been a problem and the border problems with Iraq should keep them occupied.

We have ways to find such things out!

The Shrink

The psychological state of the hostages was always a crucial issue for the recovery force. Would they move quickly without hesitation or would they be stricken with Stockholm Syndrome? The assault force was prepared for all contingencies ranging from slip cuffs to injectable drugs. Lieutenant Colonel Lenahan and Major Friedel created a dossier on each hostage and developed background data based on news video, letters, and associate interviews.

The intelligence officer is concerned about the effect of imprisonment on the hostages. He makes a phone call to an expert and arranges a meeting.

Walter Reed Army Hospital has a significant amount of resources devoted to understanding the human mind. The intelligence officer sits down at a small table with one of those resources. Arrayed on the table is a manila folder for each hostage, inside is a photo of the person and a single sheet of typewritten bond paper. On the paper is a basic description of the hostage, background, and personnel reports. Under the paper are a variety of documents that refer to the hostage's personality, work habits, and basic nature.

The psychologist examines each dossier and promises to provide a more detailed review to the intelligence officer.

Several days later, the psychologist calls. The intelligence officer makes three stacks of folders—those that might be a "problem," those that will not be a problem, and those that the psychologist is unsure of. This information is passed to the assault force.

The assault force begins to gather some additional material. Slip cuffs made of plastic, sand bags, and selected injections. Treating some of the hostages like terrorists will be necessary to ensure their release. Dependent personalities tend to grow very close to their captors and to resist liberation. This will be no place for misplaced affection.

Ego and Evolution

For the past several days, I have been trying to develop the weather patterns over the border-crossing site for the truck option. Concurrently I have been trying to get an idea of what the road really looks like; locations of roadblocks, checkpoints, gas stations, etc.

The Air Force daily brings me a captain with a weather map and local temps. This inspired me to timidly ask Rod if I might borrow a satellite pass to examine key spots on the road. Sure! I am now introduced to the big-time high-tech world. Who am I competing with? Just every other high-priority target in the whole free world. We end up with the majority of daily draft choices—and all NFL quarterbacks and big money rankings. At first, I got a big ego thrill out of actually snagging such a critical national asset—then I got to thinking that it was only fair. We have a real mission with real people's lives involved. We should be given everything available. I'm sure I would get an argument from the National Targeting Center in Nebraska or the Nuclear Regulatory Commission.

Charlie and the Rangers

Once serious planning against specific targets was initiated, the true manpower requirements became painfully obvious. This was noted fairly early into the planning, but Charlie Beckwith resisted any suggestion that "outsiders" be brought in. Finally General Vaught forced the issue in order to completely assemble an operational force.

Charlie Beckwith and General Vaught are having a minor struggle. It is clear that there is a greater requirement for people in the compound area than Charlie has at his disposal. Not only will we have to clear the 27 acres, room by room, but we will also have to secure the embassy grounds and the extraction site. This problem is further complicated by the very limited lift going into the country.

General Vaught wants Charlie to take in some Rangers to do the basic security and infantry work so that Delta can concentrate their high-priced talent in the embassy. Charlie doesn't like it because he doesn't know them like he knows his own people and, I believe, there may be a touch of parochial jealousy. Eventually, Charlie will have to give in because the mathematics alone can drive one to that conclusion. Having Delta guard a street corner is like having Da Vinci paint barns.

Rangers Lead the Way and Sometimes Follow

The Rangers were not initially included in the forces. The ground operation was to be solely done by Delta. After the program planning matured, it became obvious that Delta was over-stretched. General Vaught had seen the Rangers when he commanded Fort Stewart and thought them an ideal augmentation. Colonel Beckwith was adamant that no personnel other than Delta would participate on ground ops. I was charged, based on previous membership, with conducting the liaison between the Rangers and the JTF. This was not a comfortable fit—at least initially.

General Vaught called me into his office and asked me to again recount the simple ground security requirements for each stage of the raid. I used flip charts for each location and annotated the minimum forces needed. This included Desert One (the desert or Nain), Desert Two, the airfield seizure, and extraction at our exfiltration location. The general quizzed me closely as to numbers. Previously, I had met with Captain Dave Grange and gave him notional scenarios accompanied by approximate distances and physical descriptions. The Grange numbers would be the numbers.

The general believes the Rangers are ideal for the task. They are superb light infantry and are not required for the more sensitive and sophisticated tasks. Charlie can devote 100 percent of his men to appropriate tasks—the largest challenge being clearing 27 acres of embassy grounds including three distinct compounds and extract within 30 minutes or less.

General Meyer and the Chairman agree to their inclusion for planning, but Meyer warns that the Army community will not be entirely happy. The spooky stuff is exactly what the Rangers were enjoined not to be part of on their formation. Not a big deal now as few will know until after the fact. Beckwith is another story.

Vaught asks that we call Delta and ask for Beckwith to join us tomorrow. Stay tuned.

Getting There Is Half the Fun

The inclusion of the Rangers was a very painful process for several days. It pitted egos against realities.

It is becoming painfully clear that a significant force will be required to perform all the tasks. This was fine with Charlie Beckwith, but a source of concern for General Vaught who sees the unit as becoming seriously over-stretched, if not beyond the ability to perform.

Our gradually evolving scenario eats large bites out of the posited force. Security forces would be needed at the following sites:

- Desert One (the refuel/helicopter-fixed wing meeting site) and TBD.
- Plan B. An airfield seizure at a small remote field identified as an alternate to Desert One.
- Desert Two. The site for the lift birds after dropping the assault force on Night One prior to the assault on Night Two.
- The soccer stadium across from the embassy that was the extraction point.
- The street access to the embassy grounds (27 acres).
- Seizure of the unoccupied extraction airfield and destroying the helicopters prior to fixed-wing takeoff.

As we begin to game actions at each location, we assign the minimum forces for security, tasks that Delta would have to do in addition to its focused rescue attempt. In Vaught's mind, these tasks, if done by Delta, would be a distraction from the key task and probably beyond Delta's capability in totality. After mulling this over with Colonel King, the Chief, and myself one afternoon, the general decided to address the issue with Charlie.

I use paper flip charts and magic marker outlines of each objective and assign the best guess number for each station. These numbers had been previously agreed to by Charlie. The totality exceeded 100—more than half of Delta's available force. This is presented in the late afternoon with the basic question: How are you going to do this with available forces? Might we not be well-served to bring in the Rangers to do this?

Charlie was heatedly adamant. No new forces. No Rangers. No rubber-neckers. The discussion became somewhat heated to the point where Beckwith said he would not continue if Rangers were involved. Vaught adjourns the meeting to his office with himself, Colonel King, and Beckwith. After less than 30 minutes, Charlie storms out and returns to Fort Bragg, unmoved in his position.

Hammer directs that we provide this briefing to General Meyer in Vaught's office the following afternoon. General Vaught lays out the manning issue and Beckwith's objection. Meyer asks that Beckwith return to the Pentagon the following morning for a further discussion. He asks that Vaught attend, and I brief the charts.

We set up ahead of time in the Chief of Staff of the Army briefing room and Beckwith comes in. I repeat my discussion, showing the numbers by location. Meyer asks Beckwith if he agreed to the figures. Yes. At the conclusion, he then asks Charlie how he intended to perform the dual tasks of security rescue. Charlie says he would figure it out. Meyer then asks Vaught what he thought was the right answer. Vaught says the Rangers. Meyer pauses and then said he agrees and that the Rangers would be added to the force, size to be determined.

He turns to Beckwith, now clutching his briefcase and looking down at the floor, and asks if he, Beckwith, would support this and if he, Beckwith, recognized that Vaught was in command and needed his 100 percent loyalty: Could you do that? Absolutely. Not an issue. General Meyer quietly said, "Meeting is over. Issue resolved."

Plan B—For Desert One

There still is no final decision on exactly where Desert One will be. Dick Friedel, the assistant J2, and myself have been tasked with finding an alternative to the location now suggested. The selection parameters were fairly straightforward:

- Within range of the helicopters with crew only.
- Within reasonable range of Desert Two.
- Ramp space suitable for the C-130 package and the helicopters together.
- Isolated from general or chance observation.
- Minimal on-site elements to control.

We pulled out the JOG Map (Joint Operational Ground) and stretched a string from the notional launch site at sea to its range end in country for the RH-53s. An arc was drawn. Everything south of that line was fair game.

Iran is dotted with landing strips throughout its territory. These were built by the U.S. and used as pilot training sites throughout our engagement in country. Some of these were abandoned and some were occupied as part of the existing Iranian security system. We go to Lenahan with several targets that show promise. We will need to get overhead to validate each site as to fitness and manning. Lenahan also sends a note to our NSA rep to determine if any have live communications.

Within two days, we are intimately familiar with each of our candidates. Unfortunately, none of the deserted strips can hold the force. By process of elimination, we both agree that a small post named Nain is the right answer.

Nain has a small airfield control group and a security force that doesn't seem to exceed 20 people. It has excellent runways and a lot of surplus space to play with. We are informed the base has a single landline and a radio plugged into the National Gendarmerie net. This will have to be taken out very quickly. Daily volleyball games appear to be the activity of choice. I wonder what they would think if they knew how far up the priority pole for overhead their daily games were? We will monitor on a daily basis until this place is rejected. We soon have every playing personality reasonably identified by body type and dress as well as his play schedule.

Now that we have a place, what do we do with it? Answer: Rangers Lead The Way! I am tasked with making a diagram of the place with accurate dimensions while Friedel builds the potential Iranian force structure and locations to be neutralized. I take this package to Savannah to brief Company C, 1st Ranger Battalion. The company commander, Dave Grange, reviews the situation and begins to assign teams. It will take the entire company dropped by EC-130s for the job.

We are also looking at an EC-130 air assault with Rangers going out the back of air-landed birds.

The options are briefed to the Chairman and Secretary of Defense at the afternoon brief. Vertical head nods.

Selecting Desert One

We used a variety of resources to select an appropriate Desert One and Desert Two. This is an example.

He's not a very impressive-looking individual. He is beyond middle age with a rough beard. His belly hangs somewhat loosely over a dirty striped shirt and an old pair of gabardine slacks. The pants are pinned with a large brass safety pin and a black button that hangs precariously through its eye. His shoes are of a very cheap Eastern European manufacture with well-worn heels. Holding everything up is a pair of dark, worn leather suspenders arrayed with greasy tassels and brass decorations. A common adornment for his people. Behind one decoration was a well camouflaged hole which concealed a small lens of a very unique camera. He covers his chest with a well-worn Turkish movie magazine, to be removed as needed. His lack of presence and ordinariness hides his task, which is to make a physical examination of what may be Desert One. He is a spy.

He examines the bus schedule and knows from experience that the table is largely invalid. He learns much more with the results gleaned from idle conversation with drivers and people hanging around the bus stop and tea shops. He sits outside a cafe next to the bus stop, making mental notes of the departures and arrivals and was happy to conclude that his opinion coincided with his boss's desires. It was time to confirm things.

He mounts the bus. It is a well-worn Blue Bird bus of mid-sixties vintage. It has been painted with numerous clashing colors. The large driver's mirror is lined with yarn balls that hang around the frame and sway rhythmically with the bus's movement. The walls and ceilings around the driver are plastered with religious pictures and movie magazine cut outs.

About twice as many people as the original manufacturer recommended enter the bus, all laden with cardboard boxes, bags, dirty children, and greasy packages of curiously smelling food and drink bottles. Very quickly, the bus fills with a conglomerate odor that can neither be described or ignored. Our man, ensuring he was first to board, placed himself directly behind the driver.

eye piece. The other man does so and sits back. They both conclude the same thing. They have caught the entire garrison of Nain Airfield playing volleyball.

The airfield provides a solution to a vexing problem. With an existing runway, the aircraft can land on a reliable surface, refuel the helicopters and then depart. Without the asphalt strip, the aircraft will have to land on the surface of the desert floor of the Dash e'Kevir, a salt desert wasteland of unproven reliability. Nain also fits easily into the flight profile required to move the helicopters from the carrier to a refuel point.

Twelve people in the desert do not appear to be a problem. The lieutenant begins to sweep the acetate slide again. He notes the wires for power and telephones. He marks the vehicles, notes the buildings with foot tracks, trash piles and the nature of the ground outside the airfield. The second officer makes notes and then confirms with his own eyes what he has been told.

Vaught absorbs this information. He recognizes that this presents a solution but also a problem. How does he get a force into Nain ahead of the heliborne and fixed-wing assets to secure the airfield without sounding the alarm? How does he ensure that surprise is not lost on an enemy airfield with 24 hours still to go before the assault on the embassy? The photo interpreter turns off the light switch illuminating the table. His job is completed.

Developing Plan B

The enemy always gets to vote and a wise commander plans for potential outcomes to his actions.

We spent the best part of the day addressing the possible Iranian reactions to a rescue. We tried to determine what the Iranian capabilities were to react, how long it would take them to be generated and how we could deal with them. Most of the answers came from Lieutenant Colonel Lenahan after his due diligence. These were major issues in finalizing our assault and extraction plans.

At this level, certain options that might appeal to the military would be non-starters for the civilian bosses. Killing people, potentially a lot of them, causes a great deal of angst and often results in desired options coming off the table.

What If?

What can we expect the Revolutionary Guards and Iranian government to do if they learn of a rescue attempt? Most importantly, what can they do if we are still in the compound? We drill this from a variety of sources.

The Iranians hold daily media demonstrations to coincide with our East Coast news cycle. They put 100,000 folks in the street around the embassy for specific periods, but all in daylight. It's clear that any rescue has to be well after dark.

The mullahs have a fairly sophisticated alert system consisting of loudspeakers on rooftops to call out their folks. We guesstimate that it would take about 30 minutes for a sizeable crowd to gather at night. This means we have to be in and out in less than 30 minutes. Good luck, Charlie.

We have excellent conduits inside the Iranian Gendarmerie system. This police force is pretty efficient and formidable. They also seem to be the best intelligence source everywhere in country; hence, we need to keep our ears on their system as the best chance for early warning of knowledge regarding our intrusion.

The Chairman is particularly concerned about the Iranian F-4 jet fighters. While the Shah was in power, we gave them top-of-the-line aircraft and systems and General Gast says they have some excellent pilots. Chairman asks Colonel Kyle to figure out how to neutralize the threat other than with a U.S. combat air patrol. Kyle is examining the option of using the AC-130 gunship over the Iranian air base. We know where the F-4s are housed, but need to examine how best to engage them. Hopefully when they are still on the ground.

In sum, this is a clear requirement for the AC-130 gunships to be in the mix on the night we do this. That means tankers in country. Nothing is simple.

Panic City

We were very sensitive to the ability of the local leadership to mass demonstrations. We had observed the daily staged media of street actions and had excellent intelligence as to how these were managed. Our greatest fear was that during the extraction, this system would be activated and we would be faced with defending our forces from thousands of Iranians. The Chairman charged us with developing "management" capabilities ranging from non-lethal to highly lethal as options.

It is estimated that the Iranians can probably mass about 400,000 people outside the embassy within an hour of alert. The thought of half a million people screaming is hard to handle. What do we do if the troops are inside the embassy and the locals begin to pour into the streets?

We have to rescue our own people and the hostages, so we can't very well abandon them to the mob. Do we begin to massively hose the hordes as they press toward the wall with an AC-130?

No problem with the backroom vote!

How many rioters can an AC-130 kill before it runs out of ammo?

Freedom of the Skies

The Chairman, a devil for detail, raised concerns regarding the Iranian F-4 fighters located in Tehran. He, as well as our Air Force personnel with Iranian experience, is abundantly aware of the potential for their interfering with this rescue.

How do you get "assured destruction" of the Iranian F-4s sitting alert at Mehrebad Airfield? One of our greatest concerns is the reaction of the Iranian Air Force. They have equipment comparable and in some cases better than our own. But can they use it? And will it fly? We have to assume yes to both questions. Our answer: kill them on the ground before they can do any damage.

The alert birds are sitting in hardened hangars near the end of the runway. They must taxi to their launch point. The plan is to knock them out while they are exposed with a well-aimed and selective barrage of fire from an orbiting AC-130 Spectre gunship. The Chairman wants assurance that this can be done. Colonel Jim Kyle, the fixed-wing air mission commander is back in the "Air Force Room" with his cast working on the problem.

Jim has photographs of the airfield and detailed drawings of the hangar and the taxiway on the table. He has the AC-130 jocks around him and a protractor in hand. He is working on the angle of attack for the 105mm round, the opening of the hangar and the proximate location of the aircraft on the ground to determine the point of impact and the correct angle the AC-130 must make to assure the hit. He then repeats the process all along the alert taxiway the F-4s must transit. Interesting how important geometry can become after the 10th grade.

The Hide Site

We always planned for a two-stage infiltration. Stage One would be to carry the assault force and helicopter refuel loads on EC-130s into country at a location to be named Desert One. The RH-53s would proceed empty from the carrier to meet this force. From there, the force would board the refueled helicopters and proceed to Desert Two. Stage Two would see the force would move by ground from Desert Two to the embassy. The helicopter force would then meet the recovered hostages and assault force and move to the final exfiltration site.

After departing from Desert One, the force will have to laager overnight somewhere short of the city and conduct the final reconnaissance and planning. We are looking for a place to hide the helicopters and to drop off Delta where they can be in a good position to launch the operation. The location has to be close enough to Tehran to allow easy access and far enough away to be isolated from casual observation. Also, it has to be at about that point where Iran turns into daylight after departing from Desert One. We can't be flying around when the sun comes up.

The major and the retired major are huddled over a large overhead photo of a uniformly barren portion of Iran. Next to them is an imagery interpretation technician and a qualified RH-53 pilot. They are intently looking at an extremely sparse portion of Iran to select a Desert Two, the location where Delta will land, be met by the average looking retired major, transported into Tehran and conduct the rescue. The helicopter force will laager close by and await extraction instructions the next day.

Close by is an abandoned mine and a reasonable dirt road, the desired drop-off point. Here, the retired major and his trucks can hide, load the assault force and quietly and undetected move into the city. We hope.

A map inspection narrows the possibilities down to a large mountain mass south of the city. It has an ancient caravansary corral in it, an abandoned mine complex, and a secondary access road to Tehran. The reconnaissance imagery indicated that the mining camp is abandoned and that there is a reasonable place to hide the helicopters some 10 miles away higher up in the rugged terrain. The plan is to drop the Delta force near the mine site and laager the helicopters in the mountains until assault time. It all seems so simple.

A key issue is the slope of the laager site and the irregular growth of pine trees. If the slope angle is too steep, the helicopters cannot hold on the ground. There is no flat ground. A spot will have to be selected for each bird that has an acceptable slope angle and is surrounded by pine trees that will enhance each bird's camouflage screen netting. The imagery tech and the pilot select and reject a number of locations and eventually identify specific spots for the requisite number of birds. A precise GPS coordinate is selected for each site, noted and will be passed to the helicopter crews. It will be their ultimate test to make them work. Nothing is simple.

In time, the group concludes their work. Later in the day, the major briefs the Chairman, Secretary of Defense, JCS Operations Deputy, Major General Vaught, Lieutenant General Gast, General Meyer, and Colonel Beckwith on the site. Lieutenant Colonel Lenahan discusses the light data and selection process. The helicopter expert addresses slope, and the average retired major summarizes the plan. It is approved.

The not-very-average retired Major Dick Meadows completes his notes and departs to manage the in-country support program.

Close to Desert Two. It was on a butte covered in sparse pine that hid a road to a mine.

An Important Event

The single most vexing and crucial question was: "Where are the hostages?" Despite constant requests for this, the CIA was consistently unable to answer it. In the absence of such knowledge, we had to plan for a worst case assault clearing 27 acres and three building complexes. This required a large force as well as the helicopter transport to move it. The issue reached a point to where General Vaught simply told the Chairman, without the data point, our risk was great and our probability of success low. He also stated a fact that we knew for months, the Agency either didn't believe the op would ever happen or it simply did not have the capability to answer the question. This note is based on General Vaught's description to me.

The Director of the Central Intelligence Agency is ushered into the Oval Office. He advances tentatively at first, then with greater confidence as he recognizes the President. He breaks out into a broad grin that causes his rather bushy eyebrows to almost join his hairline. This approach is not reciprocated.

The President is cordial but rather brusque. He makes an opening comment that sets the stage. The Director is clearly put on the defensive and imperceptibly backs up as if to regroup his thoughts. His longtime friend is not friendly. He makes an attempt to answer, but is cut off by several more direct questions. The Director responds with an almost set-piece answer that he immediately notes as he says it, is not being well-received.

The light blue eyes, which can be almost invisible when the President is unhappy, are now sharp and dominant. Though somewhat shorter than the Director, he is at the moment physically dominant. He points a finger at the Director's chest and makes a short statement. The Director brings himself to a casual position of attention and nods in affirmative. He turns around and walks out of the room.

The President then turns to a younger man with dark black hair and continues the conversation they were holding. Both are very intense and very concerned. No words are wasted, and both intent and concern are clearly registered. They discuss dates, options, possibilities, and potential results. Time and options are rapidly running out.

A Plan Emerges

This was an extremely important decision. The task force planners had been wrestling for weeks as to exactly how to bring the troops, the helicopters, the fuel, and the fixed wings together. The result was as much by osmosis as fiat. The solution just became clear and General Vaught made it the concept.

It is obvious now that we can't overcome the laws of physics and motion. We can fly the helicopters the distance required or we can try to haul the troops in the helicopters, but we can't do both. We will fly the helicopters with nothing on board except our jury-rigged internal fuel tanks to a designated refuel site and fly the troops to them aboard the C-130s, which will also have the additional fuel bladders for the helicopter force. This location will be called Desert One. Desert Two will be the final larger site for the helicopters near Tehran.

At Desert One, the troops will offload the fixed wing, wait until the helicopters have refueled, and then load on the helicopters for Desert Two.

As always, the devil is in the details.

The Plan

Over time, the parts and pieces began to come together through a combination of common sense and achievability flavored with the odds of probability. Coming to a final conclusion as to how the raid would be managed was perhaps the most crucial of all pre-deployment actions. This would be the skeleton that would finally integrate all the parts. This narrative is a recapitulation/recast from the official journal entry I maintained for the task force. (See Appendix F.)

They had all gathered in the planning stages and are now seated around a long wooden table. On the side facing a map were the Chairman, General Vaught, and the intelligence officer, Lieutenant Colonel Lenahan. On a short side was an army officer with a long green notebook with a hard cardboard cover. Across from the Chairman was the Chief of Staff of the Army, General Meyer, with a smaller map in front of him. Both versions had a small scale map of Iran, a large-scale map of the embassy and a National Geographic map of the Middle East. Across the various maps were a number of different colored narrow tapes. The Operations Officer, Navy Commander Maynard Wyers, conducted the briefing. His words were few and to the point.

The assault force will forward deploy to Egypt. The helicopter crews will deploy to (site X) and thence to Diego Garcia where they will be flown by fixed wing to the carrier. The tankers will scatter to (site Y).

The helicopters, with all available fuel cells full, will launch from the U.S.S. *Nimitz* and cross Iran at this point. They will proceed along this route to Desert One. Concurrently, the MC- and EC-130 aircraft will launch from this point with the assault force and fly along this route to Desert One. There, the helicopters will refuel and take on board the assault force to Desert Two. The fixed-wing aircraft will then return to this location.

The helicopters will depart Desert One along this route to here. They will drop off the assault force and proceed to their laager site here where they will camouflage themselves and go to sleep.

The assault force will be met by trucks led by Major Meadows and drive to this location in the city where they will rest and conduct a reconnaissance of the objective.

The next night, the assault force will move by truck to the embassy and the foreign ministry. They will breach the buildings on the 27 acres, rescue the hostages, and move them to the soccer stadium across the street.

Concurrently, the helicopters will lift from their laager site and orbit until they receive a message from the Assault Force Commander, Colonel Beckwith, to proceed to the stadium. Simultaneously the egress airfield at Masirah will be seized by Rangers coming from this location along this route.

Once the hostages and assault force have been extracted from the pickup site, they will proceed along this route to the egress airfield. There, they will transload all personnel on board the C-141s and depart. The helicopters will be destroyed in place by the Rangers prior to boarding the exit aircraft.

The Chairman carefully follows the pointer of the briefer and refers to the chart diamonds and rectangles matrix on a second board. The same matrix is reproduced in the book in front of General Meyer. It outlines in detail the exact timing of the mission for each unit and the critical decisions or actions that must take place as the operation unfolds. The Chairman is very detail conscious. He looks at the pointer, examines the timing chart, and then places his fingers of his right hand on his chin as he weighs the issues at each critical point.

He asks several questions as each stage is briefed. His comments are usually related to the feasibility of a given step or the ability of that unit to do the task. Toward the end of the briefing, he asks several questions about the light and dark periods. He appeared particularly interested in the entry and exit flight routes and asks pointed questions about the Iranian radar coverage. Lieutenant Colonel Lenahan presents a short précis of the radar profile and recent intelligence concerning Iranian radar practices. He seems satisfied with the answers.

At the conclusion of the briefing, General Vaught makes several key points regarding intelligence and training and what he needs in the way of resources— especially time—to make it work. These are tough requirements and will require the Chairman to talk directly to the President. It is obvious to all that this plan is the only solution. Unlike professional military school solutions, there are no three courses of action and the best choice. There is one requirement and one capability. The task force now had to make the capability a fact.

General Meyer noted, after the meeting broke up, that the amount of available darkness in Iran was diminishing daily. The pressing mission now is to make the force capable of performing the mission before the amount of darkness became insufficient to execute the entire program at night. It is 6,308 miles to Tehran from Washington, and the relative position of the Earth to the sun is changing daily on a predictable basis. The ability to force a decision on execution within the right light data requirement is much less predictable.

PART 2

Training and Adjusting

Converting Ideas into Reality

Initially, we were consumed with developing a paper plan of options and possibilities and winnowing them down to probables with subject matter experts. In time, there was a clear necessity to actually physically test our ideas using the entire force. General Vaught was clear he could not recommend an attempt until he was satisfied that all the parts worked.

The plan has many parts and pieces and we have not progressed beyond ideas and concepts. General Vaught is very concerned that the bright ideas everyone has are or are not workable. We need to prove the truth by actually doing something. We have progressed far enough along in terms of the concept that we need to do some serious physical testing.

At the latest meeting, attended by all elements involved (Delta, the Special Operations Wing [SOW], staff), it was agreed that we would deploy the various players to actually test their respective operational parts. Once those are deemed viable, we know they can be plugged into the plan.

Key participants are Delta and the helicopter forces in the desert and the Air Force SOW aircraft between Hurlburt Field and someplace out west.

Where Do We Play?

General Vaught has tasked us to figure out where we should do the ground training. We know it has to be a desert-like environment, be relatively isolated from view, and offer long-leg options for the helicopter force that match operational altitudes, weather, and distance. It also has to be supportable in terms of basic logistics—food, fuel, accommodations, etc. Above all else, the locations have to be supportive of the OPSEC concerns.

This becomes "I know of this place" discussion amongst the staff. We reject Fort Bliss/White Sands due to the OPSEC issues that would exist. The players would be exposed to simply too many people even though it fitted every other criteria.

Fort Irwin is rejected because it has a mixed National Guard/active element and is so small that any sudden imposition would send up a major red flag. Twenty-nine Palms (a California Marine training facility) is equally rejected simply because it has too many people training all the time and the presence of Army types would send signals.

Fort Carson has too many people and the unusual mix of helicopters, fixed wing, and an isolated Army element would also send up red flags.

The several Air Force bases in the West are also rejected for OPSEC reasons.

By chance, we note that Yuma Proving Grounds (Army) is close to Marine Corps Air Station (MCAS), Yuma. Yuma has a history of classified experimentation and has the logistical wherewithal to support the force. MCAS Yuma also has a footprint for the RH/HH-53 helicopter, a Marine bird as well as an all-weather runway. The combination seems ideal for the task.

General Vaught talks to General Meyer and Lieutenant General Shutler (the Marine Ops Deputy) and gets conceptual approval. Vaught then asks Colonel Pitman, with myself as bag holder/Army liaison officer, to visit and gain local approval.

We are strongly admonished regarding OPSEC. We cannot inform the base commander's as to the real mission other than to say "This is an important national initiative." The Chairman approves the initiative and arms Pitman with a letter: For Whom It May Concern requesting all possible support. We are to fly to MCAS Yuma tomorrow to get the lay of the land.

The Training Concept

To this point, each of the participant elements has developed plans and concepts for its piece of the puzzle, as best we know that puzzle. But none of the ideas have been tested in the real world under real time conditions and constraints. Time to do so.

Vaught holds a commanders and staff meeting and searches for a consensus on how to work all this without violating our OPSEC envelope. After less than 15 minutes of discussion, a plan develops.

Each element will initially train on its own at Location X to work its internal parts. In time, elements will then coalesce to work out joint issues—helicopters and ground troops, helicopters and fixed wing, joint re-fueling and force transfers, etc. Each stage of the evolving plan will be exercised with the relevant players until we are confident that the piece will work.

- In time, the entire sequence will be worked to ensure timing is correct.
- All operations must be halted/grounded by daylight.
- No operation will be undertaken during a Soviet satellite passing.
- 1st SOW will work out of Hurlburt Field initially, which is their home base. No OPSEC issues.
- Delta and the helicopters will train independently at Yuma Proving Grounds and MCAS Yuma. They will come together as training dictates. The helicopters will do their flying over Yuma Proving Grounds, which is isolated and has the requisite environment for field beddowns.
- Vaught and staff will rotate between training sites as events dictate.

The Chairman approves the plan.

Pitman and I pack our bags to go west to verify and coordinate the plan.

The Planners' Selection Process

Finding suitable locations to train as simulated objectives was a constant test. To preserve security we could use a location once but not twice. Over the course of weeks of repetitive exercise, site and route selection became an increasingly daunting test. The two key route planners were myself and an Air Force major.

Two men ponder the map. One is wearing Air Force blue, the other army green. Their job is seemingly simple but is absolutely critical to success. They must find training locations that correctly duplicate the distances, altitude, and geographical areas that the real mission will be flown against. The map has a color code marking for every federal piece of property or military post in the United States. This map is placed next to the coast and geodetic survey map of some areas they have narrowed down to as duplicates of the mission profile.

The Air Force officer measures the map distance with a large ruler and refers his measurements to a piece of paper in front of him. The Army officer makes small circles on the map and carries the conversation. He is a big picture man with the blue suiter doing the detail work. When they mutually agree upon a given direction and ground location, they confirm their opinion with a piece of acetate tape. The tape is colored and represents a number of things—helicopters, tanker aircraft, assault forces, truck routes, etc. The officer in green peers closely at the U.S. map and notes the altitudes at the terminus of each piece of tape. He refers that altitude to the one marked on a similar scale map of Iran. If the altitude is not generally the same, the planners erase their circle and look for a new location.

After about an hour, they lean back and review the new map like artists examining their work. The new map looks very similar to the map of Iran they have pinned to the wall.

The general sits down and talks to them. The Air Force officer follows each trace of the U.S. map while the army officer follows the same trace on the Iran map. The general nods his head in agreement and leaves the table.

Helicopters are mechanical tools. They are bound in a completely predictable way to winds, altitude, and temperature. Any variation in those elements, and there's a significant variation in the machine's performance: it flies faster or slower with more or less power and carries more or less weight. Flying on the margin of the performance demands a great deal of experience. The colored tape will provide that experience.

calls back to his headquarters, we took off. Occasionally, it was a pleasure to do that sort of thing to some people.

A minor problem is that the T-39 taxi service changes rental agents at the Mississippi. If you transit the river, you have to switch planes. The T-39 does not have a trans-continental range and operates on a regional basis. All aircraft west of the Mississippi were operated by 12th Air Force and those east of the Big Muddy by the 9th Air Force. This meant that long flights usually took longer than necessary due to the swap-out requirement, particularly if a relay bird could not be prepositioned. In these cases, it probably would have been quicker and possibly cheaper to travel commercial, but we have no travel funds. Our solution was to bring along several thick books, ear plugs, a snack lunch, and extra work.

Civil Servant

As we work through a myriad of isolated military locations, we are invariably faced with dealing with the civil servants rather than uniformed personnel. They are the heart and soul of these far-flung places and truly have Go or No Go capability regarding what we do with their piece of the world.

Tucked away all over the country are hundreds of military posts and stations ranging in missions from preparation for direct combat to routine supply and administration. The heart of each one seems to be a body of civilians who keep the place going. Last night, we encountered such a place.

We have a requirement for 300 night vision goggles for the force. They cost about $8,000 apiece and are absolutely invaluable for our work. The problem is that they are very scarce and hence, tightly controlled. Normally the requisition and shipping process, assuming approval, would take 45–90 days with no guaranteed delivery date. The JTF logistics folks got the requirement last night to dredge these things up in time to make a night mission rehearsal in 36 hours. We researched the Army stock depot locations and finally found the place that had them. Naturally it is Saturday night when all the hard-working little old ladies in tennis shoes are elsewhere, as they should be.

After weaving his way through a maze of people over the phone, Lieutenant Colonel John Barkett, our J4 (logistics officer), found the person with the keys to the kingdom at 2300. John talked to this person—a genuine little old lady—for some length of time and basically said "We need 300 of your NVGs by tomorrow night. I can't tell you what for, but only that it is crucially important and call this number in the Pentagon if you want to verify my authority."

With that, he asked her to take the NVGs to the airport and put them on the next plane to Tucson via counter-to-counter service. No paperwork, no messages, no approval from the boss.

We learned this morning that the woman personally went to the warehouse after the call, signed for all 300 sets and then with the help of the night watchman put all 300 sets in her station wagon and drove them to the airport and after processing the shipment papers helped load them on the next plane to Tucson.

God bless America and its little old ladies!

Flying Leathernecks

A key task for me at Yuma Proving Grounds was to locate places where the force could rehearse out of sight and be gone by daylight. This required that we template the altitudes and distances on the real mission profiles. At my request (a major) the post commander (a colonel) granted me unlimited access to his Korean War-vintage aircraft the post used for filming experiments. The plane came with a pilot, a warrant officer 4, who was both extraordinarily capable as well as circumspect.

I have at my disposal an A-1E Skyraider that is used here to photograph aerial experiments. I use it daily to scout training sites and landing areas. It's great. A two-seater with lots of visibility. We begin the day by selecting several old World War II training strips on the map that are a logical distance away. We then take off and scout them out. Most are either overgrown or have unrecorded obstacles such as wires or junk. Many are part drive-in movies or a desert store complex. Some are OK and noted for future use. Without the aircraft, we would never be able to put together a credible program for training with the response time needed.

Extra benefit is that I get flying lessons. I can climb to 10,000 feet, dodge through the mountain passes, and play tag with the clouds. For an infantryman, I am being captured by the lure of aviation.

Heaven

Sometimes I was able to do a brain dump and put the stress away. This is one of those times.

I slide behind the wheel of the old pickup truck and drive slowly out of the gate, savoring the scene. The floor of the desert and the surrounding mountains fills my vision as the rising sun begins to make its effect felt throughout the view. A movable and ever-changing feast of pinks, yellows, oranges and mauves, dance and shimmer in front as the truck picks up speed along the flat desert floor.

The rocks and mountain peaks are bathed in purple and indigo. Occasional streaks of pink and magenta cross through the atmosphere in prisms of sunlight against the arid objects of the ground.

The air is fresh with sage and a hint of rain. I drink in the smell with deep breaths, close my eyes and allow my mind to wander back to my hometown. It is scenes such as this and also the smells that indelibly imprint themselves on my mind and give me an abiding love for such an environment.

The small towns shimmer in the distance as the view begins to transform from small black streaks into discernible shapes. The scenes begin to waver and shimmer as the density currents rise toward the clear blue sky.

About a hundred yards in front, a fox dashes across the road in futile pursuit of a roadrunner. I reach down and extract a package of potato chips and a cold Coors breakfast beer. Traveling brunch.

For a moment, and only a moment, I wonder how the folks in 2C840 are doing.

Cotton Gin Rendezvous

Most of our logistics and personnel support came through civilian airfields and other facilities. I usually wore civilian casual as I went about my business. Near Yuma, we used the local cotton gin as the universally recognizable linkup site for arriving support.

The local cotton gin is one of our key landmarks. It stands out dramatically on the flat tableland. It is the height of the picking season and trucks are lined up 24 hours a day getting weighed and dropping their cargo. The trucks are hauling multiple trailers with tall grated sides. The roads for 50 miles around are strewn with loose cotton tufts that have blown free. If it weren't the desert, a casual observer would think we had just had a snowfall.

We tell all newcomers landing at the airport to drive to the cotton gin and wait under the "pepper tree" for a pickup. Tonight I am picking up 55 sets of PT clothes, flight suits, gloves, and running shoes. It's coming in by a commercial delivery van and the driver will transfer it to my vehicle under the pepper tree at about 0200.

The gin is going full blast. It is 0115. The scales are being run by a grizzled old coot wearing a $500 silver and turquoise Navajo belt buckle. The trucks all look the same, but each driver is different. I have made the rendezvous many times before. I have seen mothers with babies, grandfathers, scrawny teenagers, and M1-A1 ranchers. They all have one thing in common—they are damned careful about the final weight and watch the old coot like a hawk.

The process is quite simple: the loaded truck rolls up onto the scales, the weight is recorded and the truck weight is subtracted. This is big money arithmetic. Tonight I wait inside the weigh station and drink coffee and socialize about the weather, the Rams, riparian water rights, and Carter. Most people seem to favor nuking Iran.

I have a hard time coming to grips with the fact that a country that can produce such bounty, as in evidence here, and such honest hard-working people, has to create a capability, almost from scratch, to bring home some of its citizens incarcerated in a foreign land.

Hungry Wolves

Absent a budget and official status, we had to slide everything under the table. This ranged from the very large to the trivial. Something as simple as feeding the troops became a major exercise.

The immediate crisis for me in dusty jeans and a sweaty t-shirt was to find a way to feed Charlie Beckwith's starving horde. The Army bureaucracy requires a signature for each meal issued along with social security number and unit identification. Any of this information, particularly all of it wrapped up into one neat package, would blow the cover story and open the doors (and telephones) of this isolated desert outpost to all sorts of speculation. To compound the problem, Charlie wants a double ration for all his people. I anticipate having a hard enough time trying to BS my way through a ration per man with the post mess.

I duck into a nearby open bay World War II barracks and do a Superman act in the shower area. Now wearing U.S. Army fatigues without any unit insignia, I purposely head for the back door to the mess hall, avoiding the Spec4 with the sign-in sheets sitting inside the front entrance. Once inside, I ask to see the mess sergeant, the true guardian and ultimate dispenser of consumable nourishment.

As soon as he presents himself, I wring my hands, roll my eyeballs, say several magic incantations and invoke the potential wrath of "The Colonel" on me and plead the case for the empty stomachs of the overworked, dirty soldiers whose day will be immensely brightened by the taste of good, hot food. They have not had any in 24 hours and they will enshrine the memory of the mess sergeant in the unit history if they survive the next few weeks. My effort is successful.

Mess sergeants are a cross between a "supply sergeant" and the consummate chef. The first rule of the supply sergeant is whatever is on his shelves is his, and if he gives it away he has lost part of himself. This contradicts the artistic temperament of the chef (which all mess sergeants believe they are, and many are) which wants to receive recognition and accolades for his culinary creations. The chef wins over the supply sergeant.

Now stripped to a dark brown t-shirt, I quickly back up my dented and springless CJ-7 rent-a-bomb jeep to the loading dock and out comes a dozen 10-gallon marmite cans chock full of the best the "chef" has to offer. A quick three-man fire brigade loading line and the jeep is ready to roll. Only one signature required and the notation "for EDRE (Emergency Deployment Readiness Exercise) support."

The jeep rattles off down the bumpy road at speeds sometimes hovering around 50 miles an hour for 45 minutes, racing the setting sun the last half of the way. Charlie's hordes quickly descend on the food without control. The first 10 people at each of the hot food containers digs deep and absconds with the majority of the meat, while the rest complain. Too late to do anything about it. I think to myself, if this was a CIA op, I'd take a shoebox of money, drive another hour, buy three cases of Big Macs and shakes and everyone would be happy. Well, at least for a day or two.

Port-A-Potty Pilots

Outside our home-away-from-home, a giant wooden and metal structure built during the Big One (World War II) and periodically recalled to serve another generation, stand a line of about 20 port-a-potties. They are routinely used for their intended purpose. Several times a day I check the levels.

The floating matter resting on a bed of Downy toilet paper exposed only a small portion of itself above the waterline in a manner typical of icebergs. However, that exposed portion clearly was equal to or slightly above the level of its original point of origin. Clearly, this is a case for SHIT SUCKER SIX!

We all have Motorola "Brick" radios to keep in contact and each has a call sign that identifies him. Lieutenant Colonel Pete Dieck, the Communications Officer after consultation with Charlie, has appropriately dubbed me "Shit Sucker 6." Not only am I required to feed and water this crowd, I'm also tasked with policing the end result. The problem becomes complex because we can't have the troops seen by the port-a-potty contractor when he brings his truck to the site. He works only during the day. I work out a deal where at a precise time, I escort the sucker truck to the "row" and we keep the troops inside. The suckerman does his thing and then leaves under escort.

Our greatest crisis, however, is when the need for the sucker services becomes unavoidable on a Sunday afternoon during the height of the pro football season. No contest. Football 1: Pentagon 0.

Hopefully, it will be a long time before the desert reveals its secrets.

A Better Idea

There is lots of justifiable nervousness about the blivit refuel concept. The Air Force has come up with something called Harvest Bear. The Bear is simply a huge fuel bag on the floor of the aircraft with several large hoses running out the back end. A flying gas station.

Plan now is to fly the gas station to the helicopters, refuel the helicopters and transload the troops from other fixed wings to the helicopters. This will reduce the strain on the assault troops and provide a much better refuel means.

The blivits will be kept in case something gets screwed up and we have to run an emergency refuel for an isolated bird.

The Pilot

During our rehearsals, midair refueling was a key requirement. I was invited to see one of the tankers in action. This was in a far distant land.

The navigator quietly told the pilot that the tanker aircraft should be about five miles ahead. The entire compartment became very still as all eyes strained forward into the black to pick out some sign of the target. The pilot adjusted his night vision goggles with his right hand and quickly picked up the faint light in his upper left quadrant. It was higher up and farther to the east than he had anticipated. He rapidly made adjustments to the wheel and power to compensate. Rapidly, the nose of the MC-130 drew even with the tail lights of the tanker as it rose slowly to the same level. The navigator could see nothing with his naked eyes but watched the amber cursor on his radar outline the sister object. At the center of his screen, the bright dots became almost one.

The bottom of the tanker refuel probe had a series of infrared lights that blinked synchronously like a cheap neon advertisement. To the naked eye, nothing could be seen from the MC-130 cockpit except for the occasional blue flash from the tanker's exhaust. The huge refueling aircraft, even at a distance of less than 200 feet, was felt more as a presence than clearly seen. If a cloud or bright star mass happened to pass over the mother ship, a momentary glimpse of the fuselage could be discerned. Other than that burst of sensation, the overall feeling was of great tension as the pilot slowly maneuvered his craft under and below the fuel probe. In spite of the noise of the rotating propellers, it was not difficult to hear the labored and intense breathing of the flight engineer as he had his hands on the refuel door lock and fuel intake pump switch.

The MC-130 pilot was carefully listening to the sergeant flying the probe and concentrated on its dim lights as they moved toward him. Come in too fast and he could ram the rod through the fuselage or the window. Too slow, and he would run out of fuel, and he was near that point.

The probe moved slowly down and then out from the tanker, like a mantis deliberately settling itself before it strikes its mate. The pilot had his left hand on the wheel, and his right hand on the throttles and exerted slight, almost telekinetic movements to the connection point. In spite of the altitude and the air conditioning, the pilot compartment was humid as sweat sprung on foreheads and the backs of hands. The pilot's eyes nervously danced between the probe and his instruments as both the navigator and the co-pilot made critical readings.

Over all of this conversation was the soothing voice of the sergeant flying the probe and coaxing, as if by voice, the two huge objects together in a binding copulation. Altogether, this minuet went on for several minutes, first passing too high, then too low, then too fast. The sweat beads began to pool from small to large drops and then fell on the waist portion of the flight suits from the larger pools gathering on the bottom of each chin.

The boom with its boomerang wings at the tip passed slowly by the cabin window. First left, then right, and then out of sight like a time lapse movie of an emerging grass blade. An audible "thunk" was heard and immediately a green light went on and the flight engineer's gauges began to move as his hands flew across the board like a pianist. The navigator breathed a deep sigh but both the pilot and the co-pilot remained as tense as before the joining. The pilot continued to make slight fingertip movements as he struggled to keep the tension between the two aircraft expressed through the probe to tolerable limits. The flight engineer quietly called out the poundage of fuel as it surged through the piping above their heads into the tanks inside the wing structure. As each tank reached its capacity, the engineer closed its gate and opened another as the mother ship slowly fed nourishment to its sky-borne orphan.

The flight engineer began to count down to the pilot as the last few pounds of fuel were coursing aboard. The pilot passed some terse instructions to the co-pilot, fixed his eyes on the probe and at the zero count heard the sergeant flying the probe tell him that he was retracting. Concurrently, the flight engineer informed him that the probe was free. A thousand messages went from the pilot's nerve cells to his brain and back as he reduced throttle and broke the aircraft to the left and down in one simultaneous gesture of coordination. The tanker began to rapidly fade out of the pilot's goggles as he once again saw only stars and clouds in his field of vision, and far below, the erratic twinkling of water and starlight on the ocean. The pilot placed the aircraft on course, steadied its altitude and for the first time in a quarter of an hour, drew a full breath. He slowly pulled off his goggles, stretched his arms fully forward pressing his fingertips at a sharp angle against the cockpit glass and slowly got out of the seat as the chair glided to a halt on its runners.

The Navigator

The navigator of the tanker laid out his map on the small darkened workspace. He was facing the left bulkhead of the cockpit and so caught a constant streak of light as the stars flew across the window of the compartment and registered on his right iris. At the moment, his pupils had concentrated on the barely perceptible pencil line he had drawn on the map over the uniform blue of the Indian Ocean. The red of the safety light glowed dimly as he made out each tick on his map that outlined the heading and course changes to and from his destinations. He noted each tick mark, referred to a pad and mechanically punched in data on the internal navigation system which sat at eye level to his front. It was the only white object in a wall of black. It would permit him to place the aircraft within one tenth of a mile of its intended destination. If the aircraft requiring fuel had an electronic system that didn't malfunction, both planes would rendezvous together in a sea of black velvet, accomplish their coupling, separate, and return home.

Marked on the navigator's map were several elliptical marks; these were the "tanker tracks." They marked the route the tanker would take during its mating flight with the exiting assault MC-130s. Also marked on the track was a hash mark where a rendezvous was intended to begin and to terminate. To the left of the navigator was a piece of paper of equal importance to the map. It marked in Greenwich Mean Time when the rendezvous was planned to begin and end. Also marked was the time when the tanker would begin its own refuel load and when it had eaten so much of its own load that the object of the exercise would not have enough fuel available from the tanker to make it back to home base. Tonight, the times were very close together.

The navigator looked outside the side window and saw the Indian Ocean moving slowly by in all directions with no break in the overall visual effect. The ocean was a very large place that required a great deal of fuel to move across. He placed his trust in his training, his calipers, and the on-board computer. Several thousand miles away, moving on a tangential course, were a similar body of people with similar thoughts and prayers.

Silver Bird

As we progressed, the JTF expanded to examine options for insertion and extraction. This is one of those.

The requirement had surfaced more than a month ago. The technical feasibility analysis said substantial improvements in performance could be attained. Permission was granted and funds approved to do the engineering design, bend metal and make the modifications. The skunk works had done a magnificent job. In terms of time they had beaten their U-2 record of 100 days. Of course, with the U-2 they had to essentially start from scratch. Our challenge was in some regards both greater and lesser. They had to start with a specific airframe and modify its lift and drag. The advantage: they knew the airframe intimately, they had built the original and the numerous variations and upgrades since then. The challenge was to make it do things it had not been designed to do with only external changes.

We were now in the operational test phase. The test had been conducted several times before in the previous 10 days, but always in daylight. The results had been positive. But tonight we were entering a new phase. This was to be the first nighttime test. Much depended upon a positive outcome.

As we stood there in the dark, along the unlit runway, I was reminded of a similar experience almost two years earlier. That time it was a glorious clear Florida afternoon and we were standing at the end of the MacDill Air Force Base runway at the invitation of General Hennessey. He had rounded up seven members of his JTF cadre on short notice without explanation. As we stood basking in the warmth of the mid-afternoon sun, our attention was directed to a silver transport that was approaching the runway at an altitude of 8,000 feet. We expected it to fly past, make a swooping slow turnout over Tampa Bay to the south of us and make the normal letdown approach.

This was not to be. As the aircraft reached an invisible spot in the sky, an extension of a vertical 90 degree angle from the end of the runway, it began a tight descending circle. The circle continued until its descending flight pattern was that of a corkscrew. As it came within clear recognition range, we recognized it was not a plane any of us had ever seen before. It looked like a fatter, slightly longer, more streamlined version of a C-130 Hercules, or a miniaturized version of the oversized C-5 Galaxy. Its wings had a moderate sweep with the ailerons and flaps moderately extended. While making its next to last spiral, the trailing edge of the wings slid out and down substantially extending and shaping the wing surface until it resembled the definitive downward curve of the wings of a giant bird just before it alights on the tree branch.

The new silver bird we had been watching did not land on a tree branch, but it did touch down on the approach end of the tarmac and came to a complete stop in less than 60 yards. The crew then retracted its extended aluminum feathers. After doing a 180-degree spot turn, the pilot taxied the aircraft back to its original touchdown location and re-extended the feathers moderately, brought the engines to maximum power, released the brakes and in less than 300 feet the giant silver bird was airborne. This aircraft was one of two built by competing companies to meet the Air Force requirement for the next generation tactical airlifter. Neither aircraft was procured, however. The need to replace and strengthen the wings on the relatively new fleet of C-5s consumed the program money earmarked for the NGTA.

Here we are nearly two years later about to witness the first nighttime landing of a C-130 with extensively modified wings and a braking system using rockets to assist in bringing it to a quick stop, and another set to assist in a rapid liftoff in a short distance.

The delicacy was one of timing and inches. At what altitude, measured in less than 10 feet, should the retro-rockets be fired? Once fired and with the wing flaps already fully extended, the aircraft will virtually stop in mid-air and fall to the ground. The airframe cannot sustain a drop of probably more than 6–8 feet and expect the landing gear, particularly the nose wheel steering mechanism, to function correctly.

The aircraft comes into view. It is in a steep 45-degree approach as if clearing substantial vertical obstacles (trees or buildings). Just after clearing the artificial obstruction, the aircraft changes its angle to one more parallel to the ground and we hear the pilot pour the coal into it. It is two seconds into the predestinated and very abbreviated landing zone. It looks to us that the wheels are 10 feet above the ground. The suddenness of light and noise from the retro-rockets shocks the obscurity and stillness of the night. The aircraft is immediately suspended in mid-stride, and hits the ground hard with no forward motion.

No one is hurt but the aircraft will not to move again on its own for a long, long time. The big blue god back in the building declares the development effort at an end.

I ask myself, where are the aircraft that were flying (and landing) so successfully 2 years ago?

Mr. Wonderful

The AC-130 gunship was assigned to the force very early as it was one of the few Air Force fixed-wing aircraft with a mid-air refueling capability. This was written at the first demonstration for us at Eglin AFB.

The AC-130 is a great aircraft. It is a flying gun platform. It's got a 105mm howitzer, 7.62mm miniguns, and 20mm Gatling guns in addition to a great searchlight with infrared and thermal visibility. It is designed to bring very accurate fire from above. For this operation, it is our Ace in the Hole.

We set up some barrels in the desert last night to give the troops an idea of what it can do. The barrels were marked by a strip of white engineer tape 50 feet around it. We all stood off about half a mile.

The aircraft was unseen. It began to fire. We could see the rounds impact one after another, dead on the barrels. Not a single miss. Next came the miniguns, they opened up and we could follow the red stream from the aircraft to the ground as the aircraft circled the point. The spiral was large in the sky but precise at the point of impact. It was a moving DNA molecule in a design of exquisite death.

Truly awesome!

I hope someone tries to screw with us.

The Wall

One of my subtasks was to find and support training sites at Yuma for the assault force. Part of this was to construct replicas of actual known sites to be cleared or crossed. After careful analysis by Lieutenant Colonel Lenahan, we received the precise dimensions of the wall that separated the embassy from the street. We built a portion in order to practice breaching/crossing techniques.

It stands alone and is congruent to the desert floor. It is about 40 feet long and 2 feet wide. It is astride a wide dirt pavement roadway. On both ends of the wall structure are guy wires holding it in place. The entire effect is surreal against the pinks and mauves in the arid horizon. This is the Wall. It is an exact duplicate of the wall on Roosevelt Avenue that the rescue force will have to breach. It perfectly matches the real thing in size, composition, and design.

Routinely, but only at night, the assault force works with this wall. All manners of mobility and penetration are discussed and demonstrated. Conclusions are reached. The wall is exercised over and over again.

At first glance to the casual observer, this wall is useless. This wall is priceless. This is the Wall. Fail here, and all else that is planned fails.

Each dawn, we cover the wall with a desert camouflage net to discourage the Soviet satellites tracking overhead.

The Midnight Massacre

*Knowing we would use the RH-53 helicopters onboard our carriers, we initially
identified the crews from the to-be-deployed* Nimitz *as the assault force crew.
Accordingly, we arranged for their deployment from the East Coast to Yuma.
There we sequestered them in barracks and underwent a conversion to night time
ops. The crews, like us, were isolated from the local civilians and post personnel.
It was Colonel Pitman's task to guide them into the necessary training modules.*

Last night was a disaster. What the senior Marine aviator, Colonel Pitman,
has feared all along is now painfully obvious—the Navy pilots simply can't
hack it. From the very beginning they have been an undisciplined bunch with
a collective bad attitude. They are not used to living under "field" conditions
and do not like the extended night work and the long-range, multiple-hour
mission profiles required. The officers keep fairly quiet but the enlisted guys
bitch openly. While they fly the missions, more or less, it is plain their hearts
aren't in it. I soon come to the conclusion that I would not want to place my
life in the hands of these guys in the middle of Iran.

Pitman is on the phone to Marine Lieutenant General Shutler in the JCS,
aviator-to-aviator, Marine-to-Marine. Changes have to be made. There is
much heavy conversation about where alternate pilots can be found on such
short notice. Army pilots really aren't an option as the Army has no RH-53
helicopters of any type and hence no 53 experience. Marines have several
squadrons of 53s and will provide the new blood.

The "Old Boy" net is in full swing. Pitman and Shutler have been on the
phone all night talking over names and possibilities. I gather the Navy is less
than happy over the situation, but one Navy pilot does have the "right stuff"
and makes the team. The helicopter force will still be mostly populated by
members of the Corps. One Navy officer, and all the rest Marines with the
exception of one Air Force captain who managed to move himself from the
training cadre to the operational team by dint of competency.

The swap-out of the Navy crews is well-orchestrated. The old crews will not know what is happening until it happens. They are brought in for the standard evening briefing and told beforehand to bring all their bags as a unit move will take place following the brief. After the brief, they are put on a bus and driven to the airfield where they are loaded on a sealed C-141. The Navy commander is handed a packet of sealed orders to be opened upon aircraft touchdown. They will get off the aircraft in Diego Garcia under sworn silence, then continue to the Carrier Task Force underway in the Indian Ocean.

Even if they break their vow of silence, there aren't many ways to talk to the outside world once onboard the carrier.

Finding Pilots

Now that the Navy had been fired, Pitman had to find replacement pilots. He naturally turned to whom he knew in the Marine Corps.

If one fires, one must hire. We went to the Marine base and met with a friend of Chuck Pitman's, who runs the flight program. Most of the evening is spent in his BOQ quarters going over old acquaintances and their various aviation capabilities. Chuck compiles a list and gets on the phone to Washington.

Marine rooms fall between the Navy and the Army in terms of quality and class. Heavy into oranges and plastic early Holiday Inn décor, with several mass production drip paintings of improbable scenes on the walls. Will this be the scene of the most crucial decisions of the Iran rescue? We have gathered about six people in the room. As the lowest-ranking widget, I am delegated to buy pizza, beer, and snacks while the great minds deliberate over the fate of the nation. It takes me 10 minutes to find a place open that meets all the requirements. It might be easier, but I insist on Coors and one of the members demands smoked almonds. Where do you find smoked almonds at midnight?

By 0130, Chuck has his hit list and Marine Personnel Bureau will begin cutting orders tomorrow morning. There are several people on Okinawa about to get a big surprise. I hope they have trained their wives for extended periods of absence.

A Matter of Money

The lack of an overt Department of Defense fund cite was a huge issue that would plague us throughout our tenure. It was impossible to have one as that would create major OPSEC/security issues. The fact we had no fund cite was our de facto cover. But we had to persuade a myriad of non-cleared Department of Defense providers to assist solely on future promises. We were not always successful. This is about the issue of refueling our training mission birds at MCAS Yuma.

Chuck Pitman and I have just returned from our support base. The comptroller, a Navy-type, wants up-front funds or he shuts off the fuel. Our guys are in a small quandary; they have no funds and no fund cite. They can't tell the local folks what we are doing or why. They have messaged the Office of the Secretary of Defense daily but that has not helped the local situation. For some strange reason, there is resistance in the joint staff and the service staffs to cough up money. If there is a budget, we must exist. And for purposes of OPSEC, we don't exist. Maybe the institution is afraid a budget will legitimize us.

We call back to the "Building" and talk to General Vaught. I draft up a message that everyone wants to retool. It is called the "there is no such thing as a free lunch" message. General Shutler and Colonel Pitman talk one-on-one, one Marine to another on the phone but the problem remains—no fund cite. The helicopters burn fuel and the Navy is guarding the tap. It's lights-out tomorrow.

We are informed the "free lunch" message is not well received. For want of a nail, etc. Eventually this instance is covered by the Navy, robbing Peter to pay Paul, but the problem of funding continues to plague us throughout the operation.

Thanksgiving Surprise

We were asked to drop by the logistic support building today. It was quite moving. The "Little Old Ladies" of Fort Apache, as we have affectionately named our home-away-from-home, have a Thanksgiving surprise for us. The head LOL met us at the door and escorted us inside. She made a little speech.

"We are not sure what you are doing here or where you will be going but we know it is important. We weren't sure if you would be with your families over Thanksgiving so we thought we would put one together just in case. We wish you good luck, and hope you come home safely. You will all be in our prayers."

It was very hard not to cry.

Visit to the *Nimitz*—
Disappointment One—December

General Vaught was extremely sensitive to the state of the helicopter force aboard the Nimitz. *He was mindful that the crews on the* Nimitz *had basically been fired and might foster obstructionism. Denied his request to personally visit the carrier, he detailed Colonel Chuck Pitman as his representative. Pitman was a highly decorated Marine aviator and was brought in to assist the rotary wing program. Colonel Jim Kyle, Air Force, was his counterpart for fixed-wing lift.*

Colonel Pitman has returned from visiting the carrier. His primary task was to provide the on-board organic mine sweeping squadron with the flight profiles necessary to duplicate the actual mission. We want to make sure the birds can hold up under the extended flight required. While the mission crews train on like birds in the desert, the actual mission birds are on the carrier. The feeling is that if there are to be mechanical failures, they should show up during the requested prolonged flight routes.

An added advantage is that the mine-sweep helicopter crews are largely composed of the people that were moved out during the initial mission training. At least they have a clear understanding of the critical nature of the mission and should make an extra effort.

Chuck says the admiral aboard has a nice cabin and wears white all the time.

Slippage—Disappointment Two

Based on the earlier visit results, General Vaught asked Colonel Pitman to return to the carrier in January 1980, which he did.

Chuck Pitman has returned from visiting the carrier. They have not done what they were told to do. They still haven't stressed the birds. General Vaught is fit to be tied. Chairman is nervous but not willing to drop the hammer.

A message is being prepared. Knowing who the recipients are, it's doubtful it will make any difference if they don't want it to. Some people just don't want to believe that this option will ever be used. When it goes down, it will be too late to recapture the lost opportunities and real people will get hurt—but none of the people responsible for the problem will be near the action so it will be easy to disavow responsibility.

I know the maxim: when in doubt diffuse responsibility, and for God's sake, don't assume any authority.

Death by committee.

Navy Pictures

The general had to pass the same picture several times a day as he went from his workspace on the Army stuff to his office and the Joint Chiefs of Staff area. The picture was one of many in what is known as the Chairman's Hall. The walls are lined with pictures of each past Chairman, their staffs, and organizational diagrams of how the joint system "works." The general muses that there is quite a gap between myth and reality. However today, his eye fixes on a particular man in one of the first frames of the hall closest to the inner ring.

The picture is a black-and-white photo of a Navy admiral who was then the Chief of Naval operations under President Truman.

The general noted the history of the man, allowed a slight smile to cross his face and then continued on his way to his planning cell laboring 40 feet down the hall.

The general had just returned from a brief and heated meeting with the Chairman. The result was inconclusive and almost as frustrating as the cause of the meeting in the first place.

The general had been recently informed by his helicopter assault force liaison officer that the helicopters aboard the *Nimitz* had not complied with the training flight profile they were directed to execute. The admiral aboard the ship had been informed in detail about the training requirement but to no apparent result. Unless the helicopters were mechanically stressed to the same degree they would face on execution night, there was no assurance they wouldn't break down.

The general knew from long personal experience that all things mechanical have no soul. They would not respond to pep talks or fly beyond their limits for an idealistic notion. They had to be treated like machines and forced to do what they were required to do or they cannot be depended on or their mechanical issues discerned. Locker room speeches would not work on mission night.

The General Was Vaught

Initially, when informed of the mission shortfall, Major General Vaught went to a senior Navy flag officer. The naval person listened closely, but not with much enthusiasm. A commitment was made to do several things. Now, it was clear that the commitment had not been fulfilled.

The general had asked the Chairman's permission to visit the carrier. Perhaps his presence and direct involvement might impress the leadership with the necessity of accomplishing the trading priority. The Chairman took his request and discussed it with the Navy in the form of the present Chief of Naval Operations.

The general was informed by the Chairman that he could not visit the carrier.

Now the general looked at the old black and-white photo of the old CNO and noted that he had been fired by the President for failing to obey instructions. He wondered if lightning could strike twice.

Two Brave Men

Selection of Desert One would require an actual visit to ensure the ground could hold the weight of the C-130s. This would have to be a joint CIA and Task Force operation. The Chairman was very hesitant to authorize it for fear of discovery. Finally, when it was apparent that the mission had a high probability of proceeding, he authorized the flight with Secretary of Defense and White House concurrence.

Once the authority had been granted to go to the optimal Desert One, a rather unique aircraft, its pilot (Bud McBroom) and its passenger (Air Force Major John Carney) assembled on a darkened strip in a desert area contiguous to Iran. The pilot, Bud, had been flying for 30+ years over many bad places. He was very calm, practiced, and professional. His passenger, Air Force Forward Controller, John Carney, was equally mentally and physically prepared and equipped. As part of his minimal gear, he carried a penetrometer to measure the ground firmness. He also had a couple of covert infrared beacons he had designed and built in his garage. Assuming the ground was firm, John would bury these beacons along the desired runway alignment. They would be activated by the lead MC-130 by transmitting a signal.

The aircraft lifted off into the emerging dark, took a sufficiently low altitude to evade known radar and proceeded on the determined course. The low green light aligned with the electronic navigation map and way stations steadily wound its way into the nothingness of the southern Iranian wasteland. They continued this for several hours, saying very little and occasionally sipping coffee.

In time, they approached their target area as indicated by Bud. With night vision goggles, John scanned the area and could easily see the main paved highway. It was about 0200 and no vehicles could be seen. Bud throttled back and made several low passes over the area checking for obstacles or issues. Signaling to John, he took a long leg out to approach his landing spot. There was no discernible wind. He dropped the landing gear and in almost dead silence dropped on the dirt and began coasting. He throttled back, halted and did a 180-degree turn, selected a spot about 200 yards off of the road and idled the engine.

John immediately got out of the aircraft with his bag and a weapon and offloaded a small motor bike. He began to traverse his imaginary rectangle. Every few yards, he would insert the penetrometer, read the gauge and move on. In less than an hour, he had walked the required area. His final act was to walk the centerline and bury his IR beacons. He walked back to the still idling aircraft, climbed in and signaled ready to go. Bud revved up the engines, turned onto the runway area and in a cloud of stirred dust, lifted off quickly into the night, turning south but still quite low. In the entire time there, not a single vehicle transited the highway. This place was good to go.

Pierre and the Pause

We completed our largest single rehearsal in early March. Vaught was prepared to tell the Chairman that the force was ready to go. Almost simultaneously, the Chairman told us to "stand down." There was a pause in our program ordered by the White House. In the view of most JTF members, this pause was a key contributor to our failure on launch. The ultimate failure of this initiative forced President Carter to re-start the task force—but a month later. The crucial issue was that the pause moved the force more and more into the light envelope, exposing forces moving in or out of Iran. When the decision to go a month later was made, the forces were 2+ hours in daylight coming and going.

We are dumbstruck. We have just returned from the desert and are ready to go for real. Everyone has a high degree of confidence in the sequence and execution, and most importantly, we have darkness on both sides of the program—entry and exit.

The Chairman tells us that he and the Secretary of Defense had a meeting at the White House regarding the progress of the task force. Apparently after considerable discussion, they were informed by the President that Pierre Salinger, the Press Secretary, had opened up a huge opportunity through the French to start serious negotiations. We are to stand down.

None of us believe this will bear fruit but we don't get to vote. Everyone is getting very tired of this constant yo-yo-ing of our forces.

PART 3

Execution and Events

Cash and Carry

Once it was clear the decision had been made to execute, we began to develop the nitty-gritty details essential for mission execution. Key among these were the creation of individual escape and evasion packets. The core of these were some form of useable currency.

The long table in the planning room was covered with money. Money in many shades, denominations, and nationalities. Two people were stacking funds by denominations and placing the stacks in front of cards carrying the name of each assault element: MC/EC-130 aircrews, helicopter crews, Delta Force, MFA Force, driver monitor team, communications element, and command group.

The money was primarily Iranian. There were also stacks of fresh Belgian francs, Swiss francs and German marks. The quality of the minted paper almost reflected the quality of their society. The intelligence officer had said that Belgian francs were the most prized by the Iranians—possibly because they liked the pictures.

Some of each stack had gold coins. The two officers enjoyed dividing these up, weighing and feeling each coin in their hands as they moved them from the large box to the smaller stacks. Junior grade Midas's.

Altogether, there was almost a half million dollars on the table. It had been brought to 2C840 in several cardboard boxes which were gathered from a local supermarket. The contents were from another office in Northern Virginia that was used to dealing with such matters.

Once the pair had separated the money into neat stacks, they banded them, then placed each stack into a cardboard box, and sealed the box, which was already marked with the appropriate unit identifier.

The pair then briefed each of the waiting unit representatives on the contents of these boxes, and the others which carried the escape and evasion packets. It was a formidable task and carried a great deal of wishful thinking. People thousands of miles from friendly territory were supposed to seek shelter in a land that was overtly hostile, among people that they didn't look like and who spoke a language they did not understand.

Each man who would go "in country" would receive a packet of money, a small-scale map of Iran with certain notations printed on it, and a small English-German-French-Farsi phrase book with key questions and answers. A separate sheet of instructions was included that provided directions for the user to include radio contact plans and movement directions.

The kits (and the money) were all signed for by a proper military hand receipt. This would be a bureaucratically correct rescue attempt.

Small Miracles

Supporting the force is a wide array of Air Force aircraft and support personnel. They do not know of the mission itself but only the requirements to service the task force fixed-wing aircraft. How to do that while maintaining worldwide OPSEC is a huge endeavor.

The Air Force has a real Sisyphean task. The rescue fixed-wing aircraft and the supporting AC-130 gunships, as well as on call fighter aircraft will require a considerable tanker fleet. The aircraft will also require extensive maintenance and support assets at several locations. None of this is yet positioned, but must be very quickly. They are the linchpin of success. How to get this vast fleet of planes, people, and equipment in place is a huge undertaking. This must be accomplished in less than 10 days with no visible footprint.

The assault aircraft must be individually infiltrated and fueled so that they appear to reflect the normal traffic pattern for those aircraft in that part of the world (Egypt, etc.) No small feat as the Air Force doesn't usually frequent some of those parts.

In addition, there has to be a required level of base support when they arrive, now identified as Wadi Kena, Egypt, such as food, fuel, spare parts, living accommodations, etc. That mass of material translates into a requirement for numbers of vanilla Military Airlift Command airlift, which must appear to be on "normal" logistical missions. Air Force planners, unaware of the true nature of the operation, tell us it will take about 10 days to get everyone set in place if things go well which they rarely do.

It's 6,000 miles from here, so things are bound to go bad. Colonel Kyle, with an assist from very high sources, develops a cover plan using a major joint exercise as the reason for our Egyptian footprint. We hope ...

Pallets

Deployment of the Air Force gear has to begin before the assault force arrives. Task Force personnel are dispatched to Egypt with planners and supporters for a joint exercise. They are unwitting as to the actual purpose. Regardless, they begin to receive the log aircraft and establish a standard forward operating base. One of the tasks I inherit is to ensure the flow and tracking of all the pallets. This would normally be an Air Force task but it has no cleared personnel in Washington. I became an "expert" in Military Airlift Command (MAC) logistics very quickly. The state of the flow to include specific pallet loads was a daily question by the Chairman to me in the morning and afternoon brief.

Our great crisis is unfolding—how many pallets will be allowed to fly forward? Will they all be in place before we launch? Too few means inadequate stockage. Too many may create an OPSEC issue. We have a daily meeting on the subject. We are trying to infiltrate all the unit requirements forward in time to launch the mission. However, it is taking some time for the system to warm up and we don't have a firm handle on precisely what is where.

The morning pallet meeting usually has Lieutenant General Shutler, Vice Admiral Johnson and Major General Dyke and several of the JTF staff. One of us will phone Mother MAC in Germany with pallet numbers and they will track their locations and the expected arrival time forward. Part of the problem is prioritizing cargo. Some folks want the air conditioners and others would like ammo and spare parts. Spare parts will win, but we have no guarantee that is what will arrive. There are too many people along the chain who can make unilateral decisions. We are not allowed to assign any priority other than *high*—which is tagged on the bulk of all pallets.

Army guys managing Air Force MAC loads is a challenge. But there is an advantage when I identify myself as an Army major as that seems to trigger lights and I usually get affirmative/will do answers.

Upon investigation, I uncover the issue. Air Force does not usually fly pallets from Point A to the ultimate destination. That is only for special cargo with very high priority and we are not allowed to ask for that. Hence, a load goes to Point B and awaits a plane to go to Point C and then awaits another plane to get it to its ultimate destination. I do not have a good solution and the Chairman won't budge.

We have uncovered an extra problem. Seems that General Vaught mentioned in a casual conversation with the Chairman that we would need 90 pallets forward. He is now stuck on this figure. People have attempted to tell the Chairman that the figure was preliminary, but he chooses to feel it is final. No problem, but it isn't enough. After the Air Force special ops folks got through their load planning, it is clear that the magic number is an additional 40.

I received a strangled phone call from Florida for more pallet space. The SOW left a flare kit behind. We have our guidance, which is dumb but restrictive. The local commander is told to do what any commander would do under similar circumstances.

We have managed to ship 94 pallets forward. Hopefully everything got there but the air conditioners.

The Chairman instructs me to provide a list of the "frustrated" pallets and their locations to his deputy, Lieutenant General Pustay. Pustay will call the senior commander at each location and "suggest" those pallets be expedited. The Chairman is starting to budge.

Waiting and Wondering

Upon executive orders, the JTF forward deployed to Egypt. This force and Major General Vaught's command group located themselves in a bunker on an Egyptian airfield.

Bunker 13 is stifling. More than a hundred people are inside 13. They are the assault security force. It is hot. Too hot to do much more than watch the lizards on the cement ceiling. Troops sleep half-heartedly, read a paperback or indulge in small group conversations. Things are slow, but there is an intensity in the air. Hot as the air is, the weight on each man's mind is worse. After a time, the minds become blank and the eyes fix in a torpor.

The men are generally average in height and appearance—no giants and no dwarfs. Hair ranges toward the long side and many have unmilitary-like beards. Dress is uniformly casual, largely jeans and t-shirts. Skin is pale white to deeply-tanned to coal black.

Inside each man is the same organic composition with system plumbing. Yet, these people are markedly different. While each human being theoretically has an equal distribution of chemical elements, valences, and automatic particles, each person uses them in a different way with a different result. That is what makes humans what they are. Each person sends and receives internal messages thousands of times a minute and causes reactions to be performed throughout his body in response to these messages. How well those messages are sent, received, and reacted upon depend in large measure on how effective that person is in doing the task at hand.

At this point, most have worked very hard to make sure their particular chemical and electric messages perform in a flawless manner. If there is any measure of a man's heart, it is in his eyes. Chemistry and electricity have been very favorable to this group. In each iris can be seen, can be felt, to the observer, a certain hard flinty aspect of this walking chemical soup. Nothing is said, but a great deal is understood. At this moment, the United States government has a great deal tied up in this experimental organic chemistry shop.

Now they are all waiting. Nothing in a soldier's burden is worse than waiting. Waiting for the inevitable and for the unknown. Everyone knows they are going but no one knows if they are going back. At this time, these men are just a little bit better than the rest of us; in a short time they will be a lot more important.

A Mistake

21 April

Panic! One of the SOF birds failed to bring its flare canisters. The crew believed the cover story—training mission only—and left the gear behind. They are now "forward."

We have been on the phones all night trying to locate not only the canisters but also a basic load of flares to go with them. Then we have to marry them up with a C-141 that will expeditiously haul them to the forward operating base, and all without violating OPSEC restrictions regarding airflow into the forward base.

Success. We locate flares. Army Major Airborne Ranger in the attack with no overt authority other than energy. A C-130 is flagged to pick up the canisters from Hurlburt Field and the flares from Warner-Robins Air Force Base and take them both to the C-141 standing by at Andrews Air Force Base.

We can't take much more of this. The normal requirements of staging the operation are overwhelming enough without added crises.

But the Chairman appears relieved, which means I am also.

Responsibility

The cover joint exercise has drawn a normal amount of support personnel to Wadi Kena as well as the assigned liaison to the Egyptian base, an Air Force colonel. He is not "read on" as to what is really happening. He and his people operate with a casual peacetime attitude.

22 April (Forward)

There is a large oil spill under the engine of one of the MC-130s, our most priceless asset. In the words of the aircraft crew chief, the number two engine is tits up. Small problem, no cherry picker crane for an engine change and minimal interest from the locals in obtaining one. Fortunately, we have a spare engine.

General Vaught has ensured that there is a very worried Air Force Colonel who is responsible for support to U.S. assets here. Several direct conversations have taken place. However, the colonel does not have a broad imagination and dithers aloud to anyone who will listen. He is not at all optimistic about finding a crane. A tour is made of the base and a perfectly fine Soviet crane is located belonging to the Egyptians. Because it is not an Air Force crane, the colonel doesn't think we can use it and most certainly won't take responsibility. He isn't responsible for launching all the birds either.

General Vaught is located and briefed on the problem. He takes the colonel to the crane and briefs him on the situation. The colonel is still unsure. The general shows him the magic letter from the Chairman telling all readers to "render whatever assistance is in your powers to respond to the bearer." The colonel still isn't sure. Vaught's patience has worn out. The colonel is steamrolled, the crane taken under control, and the engine changed—within an hour of mission takeoff.

How do such people exist?

Disappointment Three

Colonel Pitman deployed with the helicopter crews to the Nimitz. *One of the first things he did was examine the log books of the RH-53 birds. Recall Vaught had been promised by the Chairman, Commander in Chief, Pacific (CINCPAC) and the task force admiral afloat, that the desired profiles would be flown. This discovery resulted in an emotional TacSat discussion between Pitman on the carrier and Vaught at Wadi Kena that I monitored.*

Pitman has called Vaught. Review of log books of the RH-53s indicates that the Navy had not flown the flight profiles as had been directed on three separate occasions. Birds have simply not been stressed to the degree the mission will require. Chuck asks for guidance, Vaught does the only thing we can do at this stage: press on and hope for the best.

This will be a data point the post-raid Holloway Board, which investigated the failure, will assiduously avoid discussing or acknowledging.

Nimitz Issues

In the 48 hours between when the mission crew on the carrier landed and mission execution, all were involved in detailed mechanical dissections of the airframes to ensure all possible mechanical issues were fixed.

On 22 April, the carrier fire suppression system is accidentally activated. The mission birds below deck are drenched in foam. Frantic efforts are made to clean up the mess before launch. The helicopters are being independently examined three separate times. Once by the Navy crews, once by the Sikorsky tech reps, and once by the Marine mission crews. Everything has been researched to the nth degree. Each bird's log book was analyzed by Sikorsky from the moment it left the factory production line to this moment. Every item on every bird that indicated a prior problem was replaced. Every key component that had reached its projected half-life was replaced.

The sand filters are removed. They are essentially useless and cause a 10 percent loss in power and increase fuel consumption.

The sea is like glass. It gets dark very suddenly. It is almost impossible to find beer on this ship. I don't know how these people survive.

Demarche

Just prior to our helicopter entry into Iran, the U.S. Government, through one of our JTF members, presented a demarche to several countries we thought might be a threat to our program.

I am learning something new. Apparently, a demarche is a clear, unequivocal statement by a government to another government that something is about to happen and not to interfere. At the morning brief, this became a hard requirement from the Secretary of Defense.

We are to deliver a plain language text message from the U.S. to several potentially unfriendly nations that if they see something and attempt to interfere, they will be very painfully wish they had not. This will be couched in reasonable diplomatic language but still sufficiently clear to make the point.

One of our members has been chosen as the messenger. The problem is how to work the timing so he is in the right place halfway around the world. Not too early and certainly not late. Shades of the Japanese embassy message on 7 December 1941. He has been given a very fast asset and several key code words he can use on a public phone for final verification.

Didn't get this class at Fort Benning.

General Vaught's Office

While Vaught and the force were forward deployed and ready to launch, 2C840 was converted into a VIP ops center so the heavies could monitor the progress of the operation in real time.

Tonight is the night. All the heavies are here. The Service Chiefs and the Chairman are sitting in Vaught's office with the Secretary of Defense. Inside next to General Vaught's desk is the red phone patch to the White House and Wadi Kena and a small radio loudspeaker on the TacSat link with the operational elements. They can both connect Vaught with the President should there be a need. A small map has been placed on the wall outlining the sequence of events and the flight route.

The chiefs do not look happy. Everyone is quite tense. Probably because they feel they were invited for the crash but not allowed on the take off. General Meyer asks several good questions. The Air Force listens, the Navy grumps.

The mission is under way. I as well as others shuttle from our room to the chiefs with traffic as it comes in.

The Carrier

The ship is very corporate. The people talk in generally hushed tones. They move with great seemingly deliberate purpose. Each person has his place and is sensitive to it. Maps and signs point to various locations as if to ensure that no one wanders astray or interferes in someone else's area. The spaces are both very great and very small. The hangar deck, the heart of the operation, is mammoth. Godzilla could hold a picnic. The crew living area is cramped with each man having to sleep on his "closet," which is about three square feet of storage space for his cruise.

The management moves around their space in a predominantly white motif. They speak slowly with great personal assurance. There is little hint of either anxiety or enthusiasm. The physical geography of the management spaces seems to lend itself to separation from the blue collar sector. The discussions and responses seem to be well scripted and the scenes well-rehearsed. Everyone knows their places and steps on their marks. The "star" sits high above the mass of the ship and appears occasionally on the bridge to view activity and to ask several questions. Satisfied, he returns to his cabin to compose thoughts and messages, in that order.

The carrier has an atmosphere of energy somewhere between noise and vibration but not clearly discernible between the two. The mass is so large that the state of the sea is almost irrelevant to programmed progress. The atmosphere, whatever the cause, is steady and unchanging.

Meals are served to the crew on fold-out tables in the passageways of the hangar deck. It is a hurried affair. The food is uniformly excellent as institutional food goes. Abutting these tables against the bulkheads are outlined rectangular frames. These frames outline the maw of the ammunition elevators. Behind them are endless chain belts that hold ordnance for the aircraft to be serviced on deck. It is impossible to serve a meal and operate the belts simultaneously. At present, the crew doesn't know that it may miss dinner.

The Combat Information Center

The heart of the carrier is the CIC. This is where the staff and commanders digest all the information available, plot it on Plexiglas boards, and make decisions regarding the disposition of the fleet. The problem at hand is how to drop the Soviet "tattle tale."

The CIC itself is rather small horizontally, but large vertically. The room is framed on two sides by Plexiglas panels with compass roses embossed on them with sailors writing in reverse print the various flag plots and directions they receive. On the opposite or interior side of the room, stand several officers with a chief petty officer reading data, making low comments, and noting the ship locations as they are marked in white china marker pens. The room rises two stories, much like a chimney. It takes the information from the bottom and passes it up to the bridge above for digestion. The room is bathed in a soft amber light with small green reflections of cathode tubes supplemented by red highlights as portions of panels alternately light and grow dim again.

The quiet, confident man in all white looks at the piece of paper in his hand. He asks several questions in a low tone and nods his head in affirmative. The officer who brought the paper goes back down to the CIC. He issues several statements. Everyone stops what they're doing, listens intently, and when he concludes, they immediately begin doing things.

The Plexiglas panels begin to change their ship dispositions as the chronometer marks the passages of the hours and the volume of water beneath the keel of the *Nimitz*. Particular attention is paid to the small green dot on the radar screen as the electric wand passes back and forth over the same intense spot. This is the Soviet AGI.

Two people approach the chief watch officer with separate paper. He reads one, initials the other. A message is sent and another adjustment is made on the Plexiglas panels. Shortly, another adjustment is made to the flag plot. The bridge signals over the telegraph to the engine room.

The engine room on a nuclear carrier looks nothing at all like an engine room of a conventional propulsion system. It is more like the inside of a laboratory with banks of dials, wheels, buttons, and graphs. Several adjustments are made. Imperceptibly at first, but then slowly and with increased intensity, the ship begins to pick up vibrations and a sense of forward motion is clearly felt by all aboard ship. The wake begins to roll and then becomes almost a small mountain several dozen yards wide as the stern settles down and the bow picks up. The amount of inertia generated and the volume of the water displaced is reaching impressive proportions. Further and further to the rear, the small intense green light of the radar drifts beyond the cursor limits. The plan is working.

The piece of paper in the CIC was very important.

Relative Value

We became quite familiar with carrier ops out of necessity. We needed to ensure that whatever profile we presented once aboard would match that of a routine carrier op and to also understand what a typical carrier profile looked like so we could select the best time and location for a final launch.

The entire day the carrier has been moving effortlessly through the Indian Ocean, initially facing into the wind and then against it as it launches and recovers aircraft. The flight deck is a maelstrom of activity as people in a rainbow of colors handle the aircraft as they rise from the bowels of the ship. The massive elevators raise each aircraft to deck level, sailors hook the plane to a tow, turn the craft, attach it to its launch catapult and then move quickly aside. The pilot looks at the launch chief to his right front. The blast deflector flap arises like a snapping hand with gouts of steam emerging from the opening in the deck. The launch chief signals with a whirl of his hand and the jet is sent hurtling down the deck amidst a cloud of steam. In less than a second, the aircraft is airborne and speeding toward its intended destination.

This pattern goes on all day broken only by the return of the aircraft. The flight deck and the hangar deck are filled with a constant snap and hiss as the catapult launches and later restrains the aircraft. The vibration of each extension and retraction is transmitted throughout the ship to the point where, in time, the crew is sensorially oblivious to the rhythm of operations.

The return operation is done in reverse. In trail from higher to lower altitude, the incoming aircraft line up on the deck and then seemingly float toward the ship. Beneath the aircraft, a small steel rod with a hook on the end descends. The tailhook catches one of the restraining wires—arresting gear—that rise above the deck about 18 inches. The restraining gear catches the aircraft and with another burst of steam and a tremendous amount of directed inertia, brings the aircraft to a sudden halt. The arresting cables drop and the sailors push the aircraft towards the elevator floor while it is neatly folding its wings. The plane quickly disappears below the deck like a bee disappearing into the hive.

Throughout the day, this pattern continues. Millions of dollars' worth of aircraft come and go as the ship and the task force radiate its power and protect it beyond the horizon as a magnet projects its force field. On the hangar deck, underneath and off to the side, as if observing this, sit eight RH-53 Sikorsky helicopters, the assault force.

The carrier was not designed with them in mind. It was built to accommodate something much faster with different performance tasks. These helicopters are adjuncts to the normal task force mission. Their routine job is to fly mine sweeps or anti-submarine duties, not rescue missions to Iran.

Standing aside from the helicopters and observing the day's activities are the helicopter maintenance crews. They have oiled the last part and examined the last functioning piece. It is now just a matter of waiting.

As dusk settles over the fleet, the noise of the carrier abates as the last operational aircraft are recovered. Now in darkness, the helicopters are slowly moved toward the elevators and brought individually and quietly to the flight deck. Their moment is about to begin. The intrinsic worth of these aircraft is dramatically less than the stars of the afternoon show but for the next 24 hours, they will be at least as valuable in the interests of the United States.

The AGI

A major on-going concern was to ensure the Russians had no inkling of the rescue. Major steps were taken to consider Soviet satellite tracks as well as the ubiquitous AGIs (intelligence gatherers) trailing the carrier. Spoofing this ship before launch of the raid was a critical necessity. It was believed that the Soviets would inform the Iranians if there was any hint of a rescue operation.

The ship sits about half a mile astern of the *Nimitz* and is directly astride the carrier's wake. It is fairly wide but reasonably graceful in appearance. It appears to be very clean. It is painted a very light cream and green combination with a red border running along the top deck railings. It has a single funnel and a fairly large bridge area. Between the bridge and the funnel is a forest of antennas of all description. Some look like TV antennas, others are spirals, others are long whips. Some are fractionated and bent over the side. Over them all are several long wires facing both parallel and perpendicular to the direction of the ship. This is a Soviet spy ship, or "tattle tale," assigned to trail the carrier task force and report on its operations.

From ships in the carrier task force, it is possible to view the trawler, commonly known as an AGI. It is possible to spot the Soviet crew as they walk or work along topside. They are wearing a variety of dress and headgear and either ignore the U.S. fleet or take pictures and point as they all collectively make their way across the face of the Indian Ocean. Inside the AGI, things are a little different. The atmosphere is slightly heavy with the odor of cabbage, sausages, and tea. The bridge and communication spaces are air conditioned. The rest of the ship is subject to the variances of the outside temperature and the ventilator system. As a result, the ship's brain trust in the bridge area tend to wear smart looking uniforms, actually well-pressed civilian clothing, while personnel in other work areas appear rumpled to the outside viewer.

The woman is the watch officer in daylight. She is quite intelligent and has a great deal of experience. But she is somewhat cautious and not willing to enter closely behind the carrier during more important operations such as launches and cross decking operations. The twilight and first evening watch is taken by the captain himself. He has taken this turn by experience because he knows that the U.S. Navy does the majority of its significant operations at this time. He usually maneuvers his ship to within a half mile of the carrier and occasionally cuts across the bow of an escort frigate. His policy is to ignore the signals of protest and put on the innocence or the stern appearance of having the freedom of the seas. In a playful mood, usually coincident with his birthday or a state event, he will attach himself directly over a picket submarine and trail in its wake until the sub grows tired and shakes him off with a 10-knot burst of speed.

The captain is very good. His requirement is to always stay within visual range of the carrier. His opposite number is required to make him fail that mission for a one-hour period.

The Sea

The sea is like glass. Obsidian black glass. Nothing is moving but the great carrier and its escorts throwing up a large white wake that ripples where seconds before not the slightest hint of contour existed on the surface of the sea.

No lights show. Each vessel is tentatively outlined against the dwindling Straits twilight: EENT in the military lexicon or End of Evening Nautical Twilight. Barely noticeable among the great bulky silhouettes of the fleet are several slowly rotating blades parallel with the flight deck of the carrier. The noise is virtually impossible to hear in the distance. The overall image is one of great serenity.

Venus is now identifiable, but stands almost alone in the darkening aquamarine dusk. It's time to begin.

The Audience

The carrier crew, less the helicopter squadron, was never informed as to the real purpose of the helicopters or the sudden appearance of the primarily Marine crew. But they understood something important was happening in their presence and they wished to be part of it.

As night descends on the ship and the artificial lights begin to take effect, they start gathering. First in individual movements, later in small groups, they begin appearing. They move to places on the hangar deck and stand against the bulkheads watching, hoping they won't be spotted as being too obvious and being asked to leave. Some find places on the stairwells and ladders overlooking the hangar deck when they can see but not be seen. Their focus is on the eight helicopters which are being slowly wheeled from their anchor points to the elevator hoist.

The eyes follow each move of the aircraft and observe each move of the pilots and crew as they walk around their craft and climb aboard. The observers say nothing but watch intently as if they were for the first time ushered into a church service mid-ceremony.

They have come from all over the ship to watch, from the galleys in mid-meal so they wouldn't miss this; from their bunks deep within the ship; from the reactor spaces far below the waterline; and from their relatively comfortable accommodations in officer country.

Until a very short while ago, they had no concept of what these helicopters, these space users, would do. As if by some unseen messenger, the carrier crew has individually received notice as to what is happening and each man wants to be a part of this moment. Sailors stand with hands over their mouths and anxious eyes. Little human sound is heard. The only noise is the ceaseless vibrations of the ship itself and the whir and clank of machinery that is making things happen. Much is thought, but little is said. All sense something important is about to happen and they want to be part of it.

As the eight helicopters are aligned on the flight deck, the audience moves slowly to gain a vantage point. However, on topside, controls are much more stringent. Most still remain standing on the hangar deck and search for a vantage point up the elevator frame to the deck opening. Only ingenious placement or those with a job can directly see the task at hand. Two sailors squat behind a fire extinguisher between two large horizontal antennas, hoping they will be obscured from critical view.

One by one, the helicopters launch into the darkening sky, turn perpendicular to the flow of the ship and slide off into invisibility. The audience stands transfixed through the last launch. When the final dark shape recedes beyond vision, they move slowly to their normal places. No one is talking. Only thinking.

My Kingdom for a Cook

At the point of boarding an EC-130 at a classified location, Colonel Beckwith and his deputy, Lieutenant Colonel Lewis (Bucky) Burruss are called back by a representative of the CIA. He pulls them together and informs them that a chance meeting occurred on a commercial aircraft flight between an Agency employee and a Pakistani cook. The cook alleges he was in the embassy and was intimately familiar with the locations and guard routine. Colonel Beckwith thought of this for a minute and then determined the scenario was too contrived to be credible. Further, any adjustments would postpone the operation and he was not prepared to do that based on a clearly questionable source. We, in the task force, always later wondered if this was an Agency subterfuge to cover the fact they had this info for some time but failed to share because they never really believed the operation would occur and did not want to reveal a deep source. No legitimate answer was ever forthcoming.

On the day of planned execution, the Suits from the Agency suddenly appear in both 2C840 and the takeoff airfield of the Delta Force for Desert One. The most important man in this entire operation has just allegedly been revealed at the eleventh and a half hour—a Pakistani cook who claims to have worked in the embassy. He is posited as the key to the golden door regarding the hostages' exact location. So we are told.

The story is that he was just released by the Iranians and is being spirited back by CIA for interrogation. He has been cooking for the hostages since their initial incarceration and is intimately familiar with every aspect that goes on under the roof; where each hostage is; where each guard is; what the guard routine is and what internal changes have been made to the floor plan. This is all potentially absolutely vital when we consider that the Delta operatives have about 10 minutes to clear the whole place. Knowledge of what compound can be ignored and what rooms need to be cleared and what way to approach a door is critical information.

To this point, we have not had anything even close to the potential information this man has to offer. Thanks to Standstill Burner and his crowd, we do have a good idea of the Embassy shrubbery.

Gunga Gunga Gunga Din!

Agency reports that their man just coincidentally sat down next to him on a plane. And pigs fly. Charlie has no choice but to ignore the data before he gets on the airplane.

FLIR

Night vision equipment was a very new technology in this period. Very few systems were available and most of them were prototypes and classified. The task force had to be highly selective in equipment distribution to maximize effectiveness.

The electric wand quickly shifted from the 9 o'clock to the 3 o'clock position as it painted the desert floor. The features of the terrain were clearly discernible to the trained observer. Each rock, hill and gully showed a distinct impression for a split second on the round green screen. It was a constantly changing movie in one color but it outlined a very important script.

The screen had to exactly duplicate the pre-programmed flight route or Desert One would not happen.

The lead aircraft was equipped with FLIR (forward looking infrared). It would "paint" the way to Desert One for the "dumb" birds that were following loaded with the fuel that would be expended under perfect conditions to barely within safety margins. Navigational errors at this range and in this place would have strategic consequences.

The man in charge of the mission took his place in front of the screen. He closed the small curtain between the screen and the pilot so as not to disturb the cockpit night vision. The constantly sweeping electric wand reflected in his eyes and off the soft sheen of his forehead, bathed in light oil and sweat. The cockpit lights were a very soft blue, because the traditional red was the worst of all colors for use with NVGs, which the pilots alternately wore and hung down around their necks. They had all worn goggles so long that each averaged an extra inch and a half around their necks from when the training first started. The pilot spoke in low tones to the man at the FLIR and to his copilot or navigator.

The compartment was very crowded and hot. There was a great deal of tension in the air and anxiety in everyone's voice. While it was just like the training missions, it really was not. Though the physical exertion and requirements were the same in training, this flight was not. The coast of Iran had just passed below them and they could barely make out the white surf line of the Indian ocean in the rapidly building dusk. Ahead of them lay a dark cream-colored landscape, a black sky, and muddied shapes on the horizon. The FLIR continued to show where they were in relation to the earth that they were no longer able to see. The job was simple but the task was very great.

Flying the Hood

The helicopters followed a route from Bandar Abbas to Desert One, where they would be refueled and take on the rescue force. We followed their course through a variety of means.

After five months of planning and preparation, the *Eagle Claw* participants are deployed for mission execution. Just after 1900 on 24 April 1980, the eight helicopters (called "Bluebeard") departed from the *Nimitz*, nearly 60 miles off the coast of Iran. They had been preceded by the EC-130 refuelers ("Republic") and the MC-130s ("Dragon"), carrying Delta Force, from Masirah.

Less than two hours into the mission, Bluebeard 6 has an indicator light warn of a main rotor blade spar crack. The crew lands (followed by Bluebeard 8) and decides to abandon the helicopter after inspecting the rotor blades. The two crews fly back to the carrier.

Penetrating deep into Iran, the fixed-wing contingent runs into a phenomenon called a "haboob," a wind storm of fine dust particles that obscured vision. A short time later they encounter another haboob that is much more intense than the first one. Colonel Jim Kyle attempts to warn the RH-53s, but had no luck with his communications gear. While these dust storms presented minor obstacles to the airplanes, they upset the cohesion of the helicopter flight, which had to disperse in order to avoid collision.

The remaining six helicopters are spread in a traditional aviation V formation. They have flown this way for about 20 minutes since the other two aircraft broke off. The flight lead pilot is scanning the desert floor and looking for the pass through which they will have to traverse in order to descend underneath the Iranian radar profile. Suddenly, he becomes aware of an all-encompassing condition.

He is seemingly immersed in absolutely nothing but it has an overwhelming effect. His night vision goggles (NVGs) can't pick up any definition. He looks quickly to his left and right and can barely sense the outline of his wingman. The group is moving left and right, up and down, and with jerking movements,

Delta for *Eagle Claw* (U.S. Army)

trying to stay aligned. They are sailing through something—the haboob—but it has no discernible substance.

The commander, Lieutenant Colonel Seifert, orders his aircraft to turn on the outside red safety light. This helps somewhat but primarily causes six small suns to glow in the NVGs as they fly through the abyss. Inside the aircraft, a creamy dust begins to penetrate from everywhere and settles silently on the flat surfaces. The air is stifling and sweat beads emerge on everyone. Some of the sweat is from the fetid intense heat, but a great deal is sweat that is generated from deep within when adrenaline and rationality work together to force the brain to maintain its assigned task.

No attempt is made to use the radios. Radio silence must be observed. What is this stuff and how big is it? The C-130s must have already flown through it.

Quickly, Seifert refers to his co-pilot who is acting as navigator. Where are the mountains and when are we past them? Have we stayed on course?

When is our next critical turn? Have you been keeping an accurate watch on the time and airspeed?

Suddenly, the six suns become four, which become three, which become one. Each helicopter is now on its own, having separated in the haboob. The giant nothing has captured each and it is working its effect on each crew's brain. The pilots, well-trained in instrument flight, turn to the only option they have. The blue panels beside each critical dial and gauge give off a steady reassuring light as each pilot makes notations with pencils, judges air speed, distance, and direction and reaches independent conclusions about the passage point through the mountains and the route to Desert One. They have done similar practice flying missions under the "hood" hundreds of times but they have never had nature place a hood on everyone. In training, one pilot flies blind while the other sees. The pilot always has the option to remove the hood in training. Here there is nothing to grasp and nothing to raise. The hood is all-encompassing. It sifts silently through the spaces in the airframe and accumulates as the sand in an hourglass. In time, the fine loess-like powder builds on the panels until it has to be brushed aside to see what is underneath. What goes on in the mind of a pilot however cannot be brushed aside.

Desert Crossroad

Once the location of Desert One had been established, the air mission commander, Colonel Jim Kyle, established the command group location (himself, Colonel Beckwith, and Lieutenant Colonel Siefert) relative to the fixed- and rotary-wing parking plan. Here, the decisions would be made as to the next phase of the plan.

The senior leadership moves to a predetermined place on the desert floor based on the aircraft landing pattern. This has been rehearsed several times. The first to arrive is the air mission commander, who is fairly large with a clearly recognizable physique. Standing next to him is the leader of the combat control team. He is of average height, solid body mass, with sandy hair, blue eyes, and a light tan.

His lips are naturally thin but are closely pursed to almost non-existence. Looming out of the dust is the ground mission commander, who is only slightly shorter than the other two, but stockier. He strides with a rolling purposeful manner and begins talking at a very rapid, almost breathless rate of speed. He looks anxiously around and in the course of a single sentence makes a 360-degree reconnaissance. The taller man bends down and in a gesture either of control or assistance to his own listening, grasps the speaker's shoulders and puts his forehead almost on top of the other man's head. Both are talking at the same time. Standing slightly to the side is the combat control team boss. He is far enough away so as not to physically interfere but close enough to make out what is being said.

The four engines of the first C-130 aircraft are beating up a huge and continuous wall of swirling, fine desert powdery grit. The ground is composed of soft, loose, floating particles. Over the course of minutes, other engines are added to this vast noise and wind machine. The cumulative effect of all the aircraft engines creates a background noise sensory that dominates everything. The engines can't be shut down for fear that some may not start again. Visibility is severely restricted to less than 50 feet. Movement outside of the dust tunnels is clear and unrestricted.

Finally the helicopters start to arrive. The air mission commander looks into the dazed eyes of the helicopter force commander pilot. Something tells him that this man is psychologically wounded as well as physically tired. Various mechanical problems had developed, plus two horrendous dust storms. Broken machines.

Six helicopters out of the original eight made it into Desert One. However, Bluebeard 2's secondary hydraulic system indicated failure, and Lieutenant Colonel Seifert made the call that it was "no go" for that helicopter. One short for the mission!

The stocky man grasps the canvas cover of his pistol holster and speaks anxiously to the air mission commander. We had a plan. We have to follow it. Facts are facts. I'm getting my boys. I recommend ...

The air mission commander takes a quick poll and confirms the pre-agreed scenario, then grabs the radio to make his report. Things are definitely beginning to fall apart.

Rationality

There had been considerable discussion regarding the minimum amount of helicopters necessary to mount the operation. Below is the background that Colonels Kyle and Beckwith were painfully aware of when Lieutenant Colonel Siefert reported the helicopter status. The inability of the CIA to accurately identify the location of the hostages on the 27-acre embassy compound forced a continuous worst case requirement for manpower and lift.

Long before this moment, they had reached a decision. The answer was six. There had to be six flyable helicopters at Desert One or the mission could not proceed. It would take five flyable aircraft to lift everyone, hostages and rescuers alike from the embassy and foreign minister's office in a single lift. It would be impossible to leave any personnel behind for a second lift with the potential for several hundred thousand emotionally charged Persians surging toward the compound walls, filled with hate and intensity. Six was the answer.

Because it was assumed that one would break down at the desert hide sight, five would be left. So six had to be at Desert One. If six had to be at Desert One, then seven should be launched from the carrier. But the generals are paid to be prudent, so eight were ordained. Six had to arrive in flyable condition to Desert One.

Kyle, Beckwith, and Siefert stand amidst the swirling noise and dust in the center of the air fleet. They all are acutely aware of the numbers, and Siefert's message of only five flyable helicopters signaled a mission change. There was no reason for decision discussions. Six was the agreed upon plan well prior to launch and now there were only five.

The Timing Map

When the Chairman gave the execute order, he required that a direct communication node be established between 2C840, the forces in Egypt, Desert One and the White House. He and the Secretary of Defense would monitor events from 2C840. We built a map and timing chart for the event.

Back home, we have shoved the table back and spread our chairs around the map. The map is covered in plastic and we have put the operational graphics over it and taped the chart next to it. Off to the side are a bank of radios and the red phone with FLASH OVERRIDE installed. The radios connect each element with the JTF Operations Center and the phone goes to the Pentagon and then the White House. We have made one small error. We didn't get enough clocks. One of our resourceful naval types scrounged two old aircraft instrument clocks that we taped above the map with masking tape. The tape doesn't hold very well and Iran always requires adjustment and additional reinforcement.

We know from the start when something should happen and track the action from that or the sporadic radio messages. NSA is our best source—if they ever really target the Mafia, Sicily will dry up. As traffic comes in, it is logged in the ledger. Our Chief of Staff moves from our room to the Chairman's room with the information. A red mark is made on the flight route indicating our best guess as to the forward progress of the flight.

The monitoring indicates a gendarmerie station picked up the sound of some C-130s along the coast at about the time ours were going feet dry. It's a long coastline. They got the directions wrong. Not our birds or if they were they have been discounted by the police as Iranian.

Reports are received of the launch of a pair of fighter aircraft. Moments later we are informed that it is in reaction to a border incident to the north with Iraq. Adrenalin recedes.

A helicopter is down. Not sure where or why. The Chairman comes in. We give him our best guess based on airspeed predicted. All units are on radio silence. Adrenalin returns.

Report that a second helicopter has picked up the downed crew and is moving on. Anxiety replaces concern.

C-130s should be down at Desert One now. No signs that the Iranians know what's going on. Emotional pause.

NSA reports Bluebeard 5 (helicopter) is trying to raise the *Nimitz*. One of the RH-53s has turned back. That leaves only six heading for Desert One—the minimum essential to continue. Anxiety and adrenalin.

Colonel Kyle reports that one of six helicopters to make the refuel site has hydraulic trouble and can't go on. Vaught asks him for options. Kyle reports consensus is to go back and come again another day. Vaught advises the Chairman we have an abort condition. He recommends to Chairman for relay to the Secretary of Defense and President that mission be aborted/postponed at this time. National Command Authority approves.

We are stunned. We stare at the map. After all this effort and devotion it's all over. It's just not fair. We all go blank and speechless.

The Mishap

The events at Desert One were more complex than reported. The assault force was transported there on board the EC-130s.

The EC-130 has been rigged as a combination gas station and troop transport. The floor of the cargo bay is covered with a single large black bag. It is filled with several thousand pounds of JP4 aviation fuel. Projecting from its topside at several places are hoses connected at 90 degree angles to the bag itself. The hoses are about 100 feet long and about 2 inches wide. They are configured to be pulled out neatly behind the aircraft and aligned directly behind the ramp where they would be relatively free of the rotor prop wash for refueling. While it would be very hot and dusty handling the hoses, the refueling operator could at least stand up.

On top of the fuel bladder reside elements of the Delta Force. They lay on top of the bladder with their rucksacks and specialized equipment propping them up so that they could see outside the ramp. They have no function here other than to wait for the order to move out and board the helicopters after the refuel phase. Because they are so disciplined, and in spite of their natural curiosity and desire to exercise after the flight, they remain stationary on the bladder and do not leave the aircraft. Underneath their rucksacks, laden with explosives, ammunition, and scaling equipment, individuals could feel the vibration as fuel surges and flows into the pipes into the extended hoses and then to the thirsty helicopters.

Outside, the helicopter pilot pressed his right finger over his earpiece to aid his hearing. He said something to his crew and then focused his eyes on the Air Force ground guide. He moves his dual controls and the aircraft begins lifting off, moving to where he thought he wanted to go. To an outside observer, where the pilot wanted to go and where the helicopter was going were poles apart. The gas station was about to become a crematorium.

The tip of an RH-53 blade is about 6 inches wide and 1 inch thick. It is tapered like an aircraft wing with the contoured end up. At the very tip, it often shows white and green or yellow where sand and dirt have abraded the factory protective coat.

On top of the C-130 is a refuel probe receptacle. It is about 2-feet square and grey green in color. It has a large angled entrance in its center to receive the fuel probe from a tanker. When everything is working well, the receptacle will lock on the probe and take on several thousand pounds of fuel. It is connected by pipes to the main aircraft fuel system. The entire apparatus sits directly over the crew compartment.

The helicopter pilot grasps the collective and the cyclic simultaneously and makes a sequenced move—much like rubbing your stomach and patting your head. This movement of the controls causes the helicopter to lift from the ground into a controlled hover, working its way out of ground effect caused by the downwash from its own rapidly swirling rotor blades. The helicopter pilot's intent is to move past the C-130 to its left and then set down behind it and take on the fuel necessary for a return to the *Nimitz*.

The mechanical computers onboard the RH-53 are working perfectly. But an error occurs in the human computer, and without a red light to warn him. The helicopter drifts steadily to the right, rather than the left, and begins to creep discernibly forward. The extreme tip of the rotor blades slices into the high, thin, but rigid piece of the C-130 called the vertical stabilizer—the tail. The combination of extreme rotational speed and the physics of a hovering object drives the helicopter forward and down into refueling plumbing of the slumbering C-130. The interior piping is catastrophically severed and the pressurized fuel released to mix with the fetid desert air and sparks of crumpling metal.

People outside, their hearing deafened by the outfall noise, begin to look toward the bright light emanating from the crippled C-130. They stand stock still for a moment as their private computers analyze the information.

The fire spreads but is initially localized. The shocked soldiers and airmen that are packed in the belly of the injured aircraft discern, not the cause, but the results of what has happened and after their initial shock, begin to move rapidly toward the exits of the aircraft. The flames grow in intensity, surging backwards from the punctured roof, then charting their way down the shattered wing root toward the floor where the flames flare up the bulkhead wall and lick the rubber bladder of the fuselage.

The crew chief is passing people out. They squeeze out violently and fall to the ground like paste out of a tube of toothpaste, some with their outer clothing on fire. Some feel the fire before they feel the relief of the hot Iranian desert air and gasp as their bodies begin to recover from what their minds had recently registered. Then it happens.

The fire creeps its way along the fuselage wall where it finds a large aluminum vessel the size of a basketball. This is an onboard oxygen container. It explodes like a great burst appendix and flings its metal skin in hundreds of lethal metal darts. The combination of heat, oxygen, and fuel ignites the abandoned rucksacks and their explosive contents in a sporadic string of explosions that shreds the thin aluminum skin of the disintegrating C-130.

The command group watches in stunned silence as a large white ball arches from the flame into the rotating blades of a stationary helicopter. The white ball fragments and disappears as the rotor blade shudders and begins to tear apart, sending more debris toward more rotor blades. What had become a conscious, rational decision to abort for a later return now becomes an act of salvation.

Report from Air Mobility Command

Report by Colonel Jim Kyle: accident, explosion, fire, many hurt and killed, catastrophic.

Kyle requests authority for *Nimitz* to destroy abandoned helicopters. National Command Authority disapproves. Survivors begin flight out of Iran. We are beyond emotion now.

We are tracking the return. We have several crises. The most pressing is the refuel track for the exiting MC-130s. The rendezvous of the tankers and the MC-130s must be perfectly timed. The distances are so great that if the timing is off by even 30 minutes—tankers early, MCs late—the tankers begin to eat their load and either them or the C-130s don't make it home. The other emergency is getting a medical burn team to the Oman recovery field in time to meet the lead MC-130 with the burn victims. The third and continuing concern is the potential for a military reaction if the Iranian Government discovers what's going on. We got in without tipping our hand. Hopefully we will be as successful coming out. So far all's quiet in the Iranian Air Defense network.

We watch the KC-135 refueling tracks constantly. We are within 20 minutes of marginal fuel for somebody.

Aerial refuel is now taking place. This particular crisis is over. My partner comes in to replace me. I'm not about to leave.

The room is now filled with people of all rank and description discussing future plans, reaction and how to handle the situation. I move from group to group, taking notes and compiling it to brief back to the chief.

I feel like a hollowed-out shell. In the course of 12 hours I have migrated from the highest to the lowest point of my career.

The Iran clock has fallen off the map.

The Request

The decision matrix for the operation was well-detailed and the plan and its options thoroughly understood by all participants. What was not part of the plan had just occurred. The chaos of explosions and the necessity for an immediate departure necessitated a departure from the plan.

Jim Kyle, standing amidst the chaos of wind, dust, noise, and burning aircraft calls General Vaught just prior to loading on the last C-130 to depart. He makes a short request that an airstrike be flown immediately against the remaining helicopters left at Desert One to ensure their destruction along with the sensitive communications gear left on board.

Vaught relays the request through the radio net to the Chairman and the President. A short consultation between the President and Jones is held. Several issues are raised: the distance required for aircraft to fly from the carrier to the desert landing strip; the possibility of Iranian alert and an encounter deep inside enemy territory; the difficulty of pilot rescue should one be shot down; the ability to actually hit the targets at night; and the necessity to place three fuel tankers in Iranian airspace and the ever-diminishing period of darkness remaining in the mission envelope.

The Chairman recommends the strike not be flown. POTUS concurs. The disapproval is passed to Vaught at Wadi Kena. The entire process from Kyle's request to disapproval took less than 15 minutes.

Kyle only briefly concerned himself with the issue. His eyes were fixed on the navigators map and the computed fuel remaining onboard to reach the mid-air refuel rendezvous point. By now, fuel was at its marginal limit. He knew the tankers were sitting in their orbit point waiting for him. Could he and the remainder of his flock make it? As a history buff, he knew luck was always an important factor in outcomes. Tonight there was very little luck.

The Bunker

General Vaught and his command group were in Bunker 32 at Wadi Kena during the initial helicopter transit to Desert One. It was Vaught who announced mission failure to the group.

Someone has told everyone to pack to go home. Mission canceled. Accident at Desert One.

The moment in history has passed and nothing could be done about it.

The Retrograde

The Army Chief of Operations, Lieutenant General Glen Otis, was asked by the Chief of Staff of the Army to visit the force on its return. Otis was a solid combat soldier and grimly faced the task. I accompanied him.

There is nothing to be done. Recovery is not possible. There are no second chances.

Someone has told everyone to pack their gear and police the area. The mission has been cancelled. Nothing is to be left behind. Nothing.

The C-141s broke ground in Egypt about 0700 Egyptian time, swung West and continued that way to a height of 30,000 feet and a speed of Mach 0.7. It was both too fast and too slow. On the aircraft was the command group and the survivors of Desert One. Each wanted to return and do it again. And each also wanted to put it far behind him.

Blankets were passed out and people tried to sleep in the narrow, portable airline seats that go with Air Force-installed economy class, without much success. The crew offered hot food but no one wanted to eat. There was so much to think about and so little to say.

The aircraft touched down in Virginia about 2200 EST and rolled to a halt at an isolated spot on the tarmac. That spot was normally reserved for the receipt of dangerous or quarantine cargoes.

A senior Army general officer stood outside at the bottom of the steep set of mobile stairs waiting for the crew door to open. As it was being swung open he stepped briskly up the stairs and stepped inside. The air was palpably thick with a hidden dark atmosphere. He was immediately reduced from his normal vibrant energy to a state of momentary paralysis. As his eyes adjusted to the semi-darkness that was the interior of the aircraft, he was able to make out separate faces, eyes, arms, and detached forms. Some wore eye patches, others had bandages on their arms and faces. Most had a vacant subdued look like just-slapped puppies. He went from man to man shaking their hands and thanking them for trying. Charlie did some minor posturing but was definitely not up to his typical standard. The entire visit took about 20 minutes. The visiting general escorted General Vaught to the small brown and white Army C-12 that was waiting nearby and headed toward Washington. The real war was about to begin.

Later

Colonel Paschall is about to open the door to General Vaught's office but is almost bowled over by the Secretary of Defense, Doctor Brown. He makes a very audible "Oh shit," and strides out the door.

The chiefs are silent as they depart. The Chairman remains and gives Paschall some guidance. The Chairman then leaves.

I turn out the office lights.

The backroom is chaos.

Where Is Fred?

One of our recruited Iranian assets, Air Force Staff Sergeant Fred Arooji, performed some exemplary tasks covertly in country. When the mission failed, we could not contact Fred and hoped he could independently leave the country. His situation became a specific subject at each daily briefing for the Chairman: "Where is Fred?"

Fred went in early to help set up the support. No one is sure if he got the word to get out when the operation went bad. We hope that Fred had the sense to go to his family home, obtain some support, and make his way out but we don't know for sure.

If anyone individually deserves a medal for this operation, it is Fred. He had a choice to take the safe way and stay in the States. Instead he chose to risk it all for the mission.

I wonder if we would do the same if we were in his shoes?

All the U.S. intelligence assets went into full throttle to "find Fred." "Where is Fred?" was the daily lead to the Chairman's briefings. Everyone from the President on down wanted to know.

Within a few weeks, Fred emerged. He had transited by ground and with family connections to a small Iranian seaport. There, he hired on as a boat hand. In time, the boat landed at a friendly port and Fred made his presence known to the U.S. Embassy. With miraculous speed, he was returned to the States where he met with the Secretary of Defense and Chairman who thanked him profusely for his service.

The Chairman then allowed me to drop that item from his daily briefing. We all sighed a giant gasp of relief. A good man who did great things. And he still serves.

If I had the power, I would commission another face at Rushmore.

This is an immigrant more than repaying his debt.

A Royal Debt

Due to issues of range and OPSEC, we had to disperse the fixed-wing fleet to several locations, some of which are still classified. In order to gain access, we had to make some commitments to the local leadership. In this specific case, the local ruler was asking us to repay what had been promised.

The prince demands his payment. We arranged for the use of the great man's island through the Old Boy network. We also arranged to use his jet fuel, which we did in copious amounts. Payback was to be a large tankerload of fuel to replace that which was consumed. We managed to suck up most of his nation's fuel reserve and left him and his subjects barely breathing fumes.

The problem of the moment is that the monsoon is about to hit the area and the ship hasn't departed for the place. Once the season starts, the ship will probably not be able to close due to high seas. Reports indicate that the place has ground to a halt. Several of the leader's subordinates stand to lose their heads if the fuel doesn't show up ASAP.

Shell Oil now seems to have a handle on the issue but it is very complicated, especially when the original reason for the fuel shortage cannot be disclosed. Right now we have a Chairman problem and have begun tracking and reporting the tanker traffic to a higher degree than Grand Admiral Erich Raeder ever did.

PART 4

Aftermath and the Path Forward

The Face of the Enemy

The men were silent, tense, and yet distracted as they fixated on the object to their front. They were military even though some were in civilian dress. Their rank ran the gambit from plebeian to proconsul. At this moment, regardless of position, they were equally helpless and frustrated.

The television was on a small cart that raised it to an uncomfortable viewing level if you were standing. It was just as well, as this was not a moment of relaxation.

The picture quality was poor. The lines of resolution, actually the tiny arrays of color and in their various shades, waxed and waned as the television sought to convert its electronic pulses into an understandable presentation.

The color shifted from red to green to black and white further distorting the ability of the mind's eye to properly comprehend the image.

The audience initially seemed frustrated by the poor reception. Then frustration turned to exasperation. Then to disbelief. Then to silent and embittered rage. The picture and the mental image had to come together in perfect focus.

The small screen was filled with a face. The face was bearded and crowned with a turban. The turban was loosely wrapped with a left turn, the end tucked under the topmost fold. The mouth was rapidly moving, revealing short, well-gapped teeth that were partially obscured by the tendrils of a stringy black moustache. No sound was heard. The scene spoke for itself.

The camera had pulled back to reveal a much larger scene. The man was gesturing to a large crowd. In one hand he held an old bolt-action rifle which he was using as a makeshift cane. The people around him were similarly dressed and were intently listening to his every utterance. To the speaker's front, several large mounds lay on the desert floor. Occasionally small pieces of paper would trace a path across the mounds, past the speaker and onto the feet of the audience.

The speaker extracted a long bayonet from his belt and bent down over one of the black mounds. Without breaking the stride of his rhetoric, he impaled an object with the top of the blade and thrust the object toward the unblinking and now perfectly focused eye of the camera. Instantaneously, the identity of the object was recognizable.

The speaker was Hashemi Rafsanjani, a senior Iranian cleric and the speaker of the Iranian Majilis. The object on the end of the bayonet was the charred wrist and watch of one of the American aircrew that died at Desert One.

Hammer Captures POTUS

16 May 1980

It has been not quite three weeks since the abort. The President meets Charlie and his boys within 72 hours after they hit the States. They deserve it. That was where Hammer receives the new mission order, "Get ready to go again." This order morphed into Project Honey Badger; more on that later.

It takes a little longer to round up the two groups the President will meet today. The aircrews had taken their aluminum steeds back to the various corners of the world over a period of days. The advance scout team is still in Tehran when Charlie touched down on American soil. It will be almost ten days before the last man would leave Iran.

The President "dropped in" today at the Pentagon to thank two very important groups of people. Group One is very small. Their identities need to be kept secret because they may have to return to Iran quietly again. Group Two is the overt crowd: aircrews and the JTF staff. It's OK to know most of them.

Unknown to the vast majority of the larger group, with the exception of seven members of the JTF cadre, the small group is assembled in the Secretary of Defense's office. The four men, three enlisted, two Army, one Air Force, and one retired Army officer, himself a prior enlisted man and recipient of a battlefield commission in Vietnam, come to attention when the President enters the room. They are wearing conservative civilian clothes. They had little warning and no precise information on the events that would transpire that morning. The President personally awards each a very high-order medal for their bravery and courage, and engages each in personalized small talk. The President, an ex-military man himself, realizes what these men actually did for their country. He is clearly moved by their efforts. There is some give and take but the President is subdued and the group is somewhat in awe. The meeting takes ten minutes. He closes the private ceremony by thanking them again and wishing them "God Bless."

Group Two has been assembled in the Secretary of Defense's conference room, just next to the Secretary of Defense's Office. It is large enough to hold the more than 120 military personnel assembled there. All are in Class "A" dress uniforms. Most do not know the precise purpose of why they were called to town or assembled here on the third floor of the "E" ring. The President enters from the left via a side door from Secretary of Defense's office along with Secretary Brown and the Chairman. The President is shorter than the other two men, but flashes his famous radiant smile. He is clutching some rolled-up notes on white paper. The Chairman introduces the President and General Vaught. General Vaught takes over as MC. He makes a few comments: Thank you, Mr. President, for taking time out of your busy schedule to meet with us today, etc.

The President steps up to the podium and gives a short speech straight from the heart without referring to the white papers. He thanks the assembled multitude and is about to leave when Hammer catches him by the elbow and propels the Commander-in-Chief to the first row of standing officers. This group includes the air mission commander, Colonel Jim Kyle, and the JTF Chief of Staff, Colonel Jerry King. Hammer then proceeds to guide the CINC down the five rows of standing men, introduces each man by name to the President, all 120 plus, one at a time. Perhaps less than ten seconds is spent with each while a picture is taken by the White House photographer. The last man to be introduced is the JTF J2, no picture is taken. The photographer ran out of film!

The entire program takes less than 15 minutes. While we don't feel better about the outcome, we feel better about ourselves. Whatever impressions we previously harbored about the President, this is a class act.

Homecoming

27 January 1981

Several of us receive an invitation to the White House to attend the welcome home of the hostages. A few of us are chosen to attend. Some such as the J2 team can't. They're still in Europe integrating the mission debrief into one coherent picture.

The lawn is massed with people and media. The steps are covered in soldiers and flags. Daniel Schorr is on top of a TV platform carrying on—as usual—in the clouds. A newsperson traipses across the lawn wearing a coat of patches composed from almost all the endangered species. Lots of noise and pushing. I get the feeling we are window dressing. Charlie is dressed up for the occasion in greens, and Hammer has put on his most gripping jaw set. It has been so long in coming it will be anticlimactic.

The new President arrives. Hostages arrive in a sea of flags and an ocean of noise. We are directed inside to a large state reception room with bare wooden floors and federal furniture lining the walls: Williamsburg redux. The former hostages are on one side of the room and we are on the other; it's almost like a junior high prom. We are encouraged to press together. Each element is unsure about the other or what to make of the encounter or know what to say.

We are polite, say little, lapsing into polite whispers and as quickly as permitted, break off and go home. They appear uncomprehending. They will never know the price that so many paid on their behalf.

Reflections and Conjecture

This book has traced from a single perspective a number of instances where some people and some of the uniformed services and agencies did not provide what could be called full cooperation and support. In that this was one of the most important things the nation was doing at the time—rescuing our citizens—why did this occur? What follows is personal speculation on my part, but I believe it is reasonably accurate.

Overall

From the beginning of the planning there were five obstacles to the success of the operation:

1. Most of the service principals, less General Meyer, were convinced that the plan would not be approved and were convinced that if approved, the operation would be a failure. As such, they were not willing to commit resources and risk beyond the very essential and directed. This was particularly egregious and harmful on the part of the CIA.
2. There is a culture within most bureaucratic organizations to zealously protect their own turf—with minimal sharing of personnel and assets or assumption of responsibility. No senior flag wanted to expend efforts and assume responsibility if the operation was either not approved or failed. The exception was Army General Shy Meyer.
3. The logical and correct great concern regarding OPSEC severely limited the ability of the JTF to acquire assets or train. Lack of a formal budget line was particularly limiting.
4. There was a failure of leadership at the top of the civilian side. Secretary of Defense and POTUS, knowing how the bureaucracy was reacting, as well as the daily impact on the JTF efforts, could have taken a more active role in forcing compliance and support. By not doing so, there was an impression that this was Major General Vaught's program, not that of the United States writ large.

5. The constant start-stop of the program throughout its existence marred credibility and attracted a non-supporting attitude. People outside the JTF just did not believe the raid would ever be approved. Hence, they felt free to selectively ignore or lowball support and assets. There is considerable evidence to support that view, even within the JTF.

We were always on a "Get Ready to Go in Ten Days" to a "Stand Down" roller-coaster ride. This condition was continuous from the creation of the JTF to just before mission launch in April. Morale was on the same roller-coaster ride. Support elements, senior services, and others were continuously directed to go ramming speed followed by a STOP signal.

The Central Intelligence Agency

When Stansfield Turner, a close friend of President Carter, became the CIA Director, he entered his position as "Christ Cleansing the Temple," a term provided by several agency employees to me. One of very first acts was to examine the HUMINT (spies, local experts, etc.) aspects of the agency with an eye for reduction. This was concurrent with a more laudable goal to bring the emerging technical world into the agency programs, specifically satellites and a fuller cooperation with the National Security Administration and its broad capabilities in the SIGINT/ELINT world.

HUMINT is not just spies and glamour. It can be a person who will be used only once on a specific task due to unusual access or placement. It could be a long-term asset routinely tapped. It could be a person of significant value at the national level or simply a janitor in a building. Finding, vetting, hiring, and managing HUMINT is a crucial art and skill with extraordinary potential or potential irrelevance. In our case, quality HUMINT was the only solution to the base question: Where were the hostages?

That answer would drive the number of assault personnel really required and the concomitant helicopter lift required. Without that data, we had to plan for a 100 percent worst case regarding personnel and lift.

Within a relatively short period of time, Turner had accomplished two major initiatives.

The varied and broad HUMINT capabilities were greatly reduced. Many sources were cut off and employees either transferred or retired. Turner viewed HUMINT as fraught with risk, prone to provide unreliable non-verifiable data, and too expensive for the return. As a result, the extensive HUMINT base the agency had built over the postwar period was reduced by a great degree. Part of that loss was Iranian assets. This was told to me by agency sources much later. In sum, the agency had lost much of its previous capabilities, but was not prepared to reveal that to outsiders.

The key piece of data we desperately needed was the reasonably precise location of the hostages. Only HUMINT could reveal that. This is what not knowing those details meant:

The entire 27 acres and its three discrete building complexes would have to be searched and cleared. We could not afford to miss any hostages.

We needed to secure/isolate all 27 acres. This required considerably more personnel than required for a single building complex.

The end effect was that we had to plan for a worst-case scenario of clearing the entire compound. This, in turn, drove the head count and the minimum required helicopters. Had we known the hostages were all on the ground floor of the embassy building, with the exception of CIA hostages in the "Mushroom Factory" (secure buildings used by CIA on embassy grounds), we could have proceeded with one less helicopter and a reduced Delta force at Desert One. In sum, we could have continued the mission as originally planned.

Post raid, we had several private discussions with some agency personnel on this issue. They independently corroborated the same story; "We never thought the raid would actually go. Therefore, we were not prepared to risk an asset."

To this day, we (the JTF) do not fully understand the "Pakistani cook" engagement. As Delta was literally loading onto the aircraft at Masirah, an agency representative came planeside and briefed Burruss and Beckwith on information "they had just gleaned from a Pakistani cook." Allegedly, this cook was sitting next to an agency rep by chance on an airplane and said he was cooking for the hostages. He preceded to outline the hostage location and the security situation in some detail. This information was then passed to Delta ramp side.

Neither Beckwith nor Burruss fully believed it and it was too late to make major adjustments to the operations plan and was thus ignored. In retrospect, the details passed were corroborated as being true when the hostages returned and were debriefed by Lieutenant Colonel Lenahan. The validity of the agency story is anyone's guess. Only the agency knows and it is not talking.

The U.S. Navy

The personalities in charge of the Navy during this period presented an organizational attitude of significant parochialism, defensiveness, and pursuit of unfettered autonomy regarding the other services. We briefed the Chief of

Naval Operations on an almost daily basis and he was abundantly aware of the requirements on the Navy and their significance within the entire plan. I can say personally that he consistently presented an unhappy, combative personality on most of all these discussions.

After we reviewed all helicopter options, the deploying *Nimitz* RH-53 squadron was tasked to send its personnel to Yuma for the necessary low-level night training. Initially, the Navy was asked to send its entire RH-53 squadron destined for the *Nimitz*. Colonel Pitman "acquired" 12 USMC CH-53s from MCAS Tustin for the training, which minimized the Navy manpower and equipment requirement.

The Navy crews, led by a Lieutenant Commander, arrived and were placed in an isolated portion of Yuma Proving Ground in World War II-type barracks with some modifications, e.g. air conditioning, bunks, showers, etc. Colonel Pitman then met with the squadron commander and established a training routine. Part of this was converting to a reverse cycle as well as laagering in the desert, a key requirement.

Very quickly, the Navy crews became quite restless, argumentative, and manifested a number of personal and organizational discipline issues, particularly the enlisted men. A key issue in their mind was the inability to go downtown at night and the reverse cycle schedule.

In less than two weeks, it was clear to Colonel Pitman that these personnel would never work out. Accordingly, after long discussions with the JCS Director of Operations, the Navy crew, less several deemed of good quality and interest, were shipped to Diego Garcia and then to the *Nimitz*. They knew exactly what was intended and the role their helicopters would play.

Major General Vaught was always quite sensitive regarding helicopters and their varied mechanical predictabilities and failures. The Sikorsky RH-53 was known to be acutely difficult to maintain. Accordingly, he met with reps from Sikorsky and using Mr. Tom Seaman as his issue manager, they, Pitman, and several helicopter experts designed a gradual exercise profile for the *Nimitz* birds. The idea was to gradually stress the birds for increasingly long legs to identify any mechanical issues that might arise; these were the actual mission birds. Flight profiles began with one hour and finished with eight hours. The times to be accomplished over a one-month period. This concept was briefed to the Chief of Naval Operations and passed to CINC Pacific Command (CINCPAC) and the force afloat.

On two separate occasions, Colonel Pitman visited the *Nimitz*, noted the lack of exercise and conferred with the *Nimitz* command group and squadron commander, all of whom promised compliance. Colonel Pitman was so concerned after the second visit that he visited CINCPAC and personally briefed Admiral Sylvester Foley, CINCPAC.

General Vaught requested permission to visit the *Nimitz* and was denied. However, Chairman Jones wrote a clear language letter to CINCPAC requiring compliance and CINCPAC acknowledged compliance. When Pitman arrived in April for the mission launch, no profiles of more than 90 minutes had been flown. No explanation was given.

It is the strong belief of most JTF aviation personnel that several of the mechanical issues encountered on mission night would have been revealed had the birds been stressed.

When the Navy inquiry members, arriving less than 8 hours after the failure, learned of the profile issue, they ensured it would not be part of the Holloway Board agenda. (The Chairman, Air Force General David Jones, announced the establishment of the Holloway Board immediately following the failed rescue attempt. Its announced purpose was to investigate the issues that inhibited success and to recommend a future organizational concept to ensure better results.) The Navy inquiry board also took steps to ensure I would not be called. Why?

Conjecture mixed with data from participants. The Navy elements involved from the squadron commander up the chain probably harbored serious doubts that the mission would ever be approved. Hence, why do what we don't have to do within the normal deployment profiles and tasks?

There undoubtedly was considerable resentment regarding the "firing" of the squadron at Yuma harbored by many if not all involved.

As conjecture, I believe the Navy, wearing its "Autonomous Service" cloak, just did not want to subordinate its forces to non-Navy elements. I would be very surprised if this was not a subliminal part of the makeup of Admirals Hayward and Foley. They amply demonstrated that attitude toward me on numerous occasions when as Action Officer, I had to bring a number of issues to them personally. This attitude was also quite consistent in the many Tank briefs: barely concealed disdain is a reasonably accurate description.

Post-raid and during the Honey Badger build-up, the Navy understood that it had to get on the emerging SOF train or lose both control and resources. While it created SEAL Team 6 as the Delta equivalent, the commander, Captain Dick Marcinko, underwent a painful growth and a clear message that he was playing in a very small playground and under tight control. I would also note that when the CINC of Special Operations Command (SOCOM) attempted to work procurement for an Underwater Swimmer Vehicle as well as "brown water" naval assets, he was strongly rebuffed. Only when MFP-11 (the new SOF Funding Line) came into being, were these equipment needs satisfactorily met.

In sum, the Navy did not believe the raid would happen, it resented non-Navy engagements, and it viewed SOF as a potentially dangerous sideshow placing Navy's reputation at risk.

The Air Force

Unlike the Navy, Air Force had a SOF capability in existence: the First Special Operations Wing (SOW) at Eglin/Hurlburt Field, Florida. The unit had the RH-53 Pave Low Sea-Air rescue helicopters as well as the AC- and MC-130s. The unit was a subordinate command of Military Air Transport Command (MAC): the supply and transport side of the Air Force

At the time of the Iran JTF, the SOW was basically populated by very low-priority airframes, many dead-lined, manned by less than Air Force-anointed superstars. Life was good. The weather was warm.

However, the SOW gave 100 percent of what it had and then some to assist the cause. Their problems were more endemic higher up the chain. Mother MAC was not prepared to grant the SOW a spare parts priority to put them on a war footing. This would be very expensive and done at the cost of other assets. CINCMAC, General Heyser, continuously voiced support yet the resources, both material and human, did not follow.

The SOW had several mid and senior grade officers that our Deputy, Major General Richard Secord, identified as needing quality replacement. This did not happen with few exceptions and then only after General Secord either went to the Tank or threatened to.

Even after Honey Badger was well underway, senior Air Force foot-dragging was endemic. Two examples would be the use of the C-5 heavy airlifter for the second attempt and the parts priority for the SOW.

When Honey Badger began, the MH-500MD and the OH-6 Loach helicopters were new and important additions. Delta and the Rangers also had developed several vehicles for airfield seizures (a key task) and cross-country movement. Lift of these assets into Iran became an issue. There simply were not enough aerial refuelable C-130s and C-141s for the force. Vaught directed we look at the C-5 as an option.

Tom Seaman, General Vaught's aviation expert, went into the original language of the C-5 procurement as written by Air Force in its justification to the Hill. It specifically said the C-5 would be designed to operate on "expeditionary (dirt)" airfields and in very austere environments. In the Tank,

General Vaught pointed this out and formally proposed the inclusion into the force. This had been previously staffed with Air Staff with acknowledgement but no commitment.

Air Force Chief of Staff demurred. He then went to the Chairman. The Chairman, in turn, went into our spaces and told General Vaught he could not have them. Vaught directed us to brief the Chairman on the lift issues and shortfalls. The Chairman went back to Air Staff. Vaught was then informed he could use the C-5s "for planning" but not exercise. At mission execution, the aircraft would be provided.

The 1st SOW was largely populated with broken airframes or about to be dead-lined airframes. Spare parts were non-existent and the needs so deep and dire that General Secord estimated it would take 6 months of a war priority to repair the force. He went to General Heyser, the head of MAC, the "mother" of the 1st SOW, and asked for help. Heyser promised support but it was not forthcoming. Day after day, the deadline rate was shown to Vaught and the Chairman. A Tank session was held with the Chairman, Vaught, Secord, Heyser, and the Air Force Chief of Staff. It was agreed that the SOW would receive an unprecedented Wartime Priority One. On paper, this would flood the SOW with parts. It did not happen.

Several weeks later, Secord and I visited the SOW and toured the hangar queens. Records within the SOW did not reflect the new priority. It was business as usual. Secord took the unprecedented step of openly messaging Vaught, the Chairman, Air Staff, and Heyser regarding the non-compliance. Within a day, General Heyser got Secord on the phone and demanded to know why the message was sent. Secord simply said that was what General Heyser had requested and agreed to and was ignored by his own staff for whatever reason. In time, this was fixed.

Why? Again, among the senior Air Force flags, there pervaded an attitude that the mission would never happen and that "all this Spec Ops business" was a flash in the pan and a deviation from core Air Force interests. I personally heard this from both three- and four-star Air Force personnel.

The CINCs

The Iran rescue took place during a period before "Joint," Nunn–Cohen, and Goldwater–Nichols were on the books. The military commanders in chief (CINCs—a term now no longer used except for the President) were pretty much the local gods on earth and they were not going to allow usurpers to play on their ground. Of equal import was that no CINC possessed the capability to do what needed to be done from the perspective of kidnap or hostage barrier scenarios. Hence, a major joint conundrum existed: the Chairman was creating a unique force that would operate independently in CINC territory, but oh, wait: Iran is not part of any CINCdom. It might fall under RedCom or Eucom or CINCPAC or NoCom.

Add to this mix, the very territorially sensitive European Commander in Chief, Bernie Rodgers, and the highly parochial Admiral Foley and the OPSEC violation-prone Readiness Command at MacDill AFB. No force other than the new JTF could do the job, so the task could not be passed to a CINC and his in-being forces—the traditional resolution.

OPSEC was of such a concern that existing large conventional force engagements would quickly violate presidential mandates in addition to being unqualified for the tasks. The Chairman became the balancer in charge. He initially decreed that the CINCs would be informed but not prior engaged. General Rodgers insisted on being informed before execution which was agreed to.

In the interim, the JTF established liaisons to keep the CINCs informed and to continuously stress the need for OPSEC. As soon as the post-raid Holloway Board met, the engaged CINCs chimed in that they were not fully briefed, kept in the dark, and success may have been achieved had they only been part of the plan. They were also unanimous, behind-the-scenes in lobbying, to ensure that future issues would not include a private military force of the Chairman. It's all in the attitude.

State Department

From the beginning, the JTF was an open book to State. Lieutenant Colonel Lenahan spent considerable time there gathering dossiers on each hostage and more mundane items such as architectural drawings of the embassy structures. Very quickly, it was apparent that shields were raised by State and support was halted. Several senior State personalities made it clear to the Chairman, Vaught, and Lenahan that State was opposed to any rescue attempt and would not cooperate out of principle.

Within a month of the embassy takedown by the Iranians, we were directed by the Chairman to cease all discussions with State and have no communications. Simply put, State could not be trusted not to leak what they didn't like and thereby undercut President Carter's options.

Why didn't State cooperate? Conjecture falls into several areas:

The Secretary of State, Cy Vance, was adamantly opposed to a rescue and this could have had a trickle-down effect. In fact, Carter later told Brown to keep State isolated from the program.

State has always had an historic antipathy toward "things military" and that reinforced the internal negativism.

There was genuine fear that a rescue attempt would hazard the lives of the State employees and that negotiation was the best way to seek release. A military option negated that possibility.

The Bottom Line

Today, we enjoy Special Operations Forces and their extraordinary capabilities as a matter of course. In 1980, there were no proven capabilities but a dire requirement. The JTF had to plow the hard original ground, expose the issues and have Congress later create a quality playing field for SOF using the scars of Iran as the building blocks.

The Phoenix Rises from the Ashes—Barely

The birth of our highly lethal, effective, and well-publicized special forces today was almost aborted at its birth. The parents, the military services, largely disavowed the child and strove mightily to keep it hidden in the attic away from the more favored children. The child was created out of whole cloth under the stupefying pressure of our hostages held in the U.S. Embassy in Iran in 1979. In a moment of rude awakening, the senior members of the services agreed that no force on the shelf was capable of extraction of our citizens without a major conventional assault, which was not a viable option.

Accordingly, a small force was cobbled together from parts and pieces of sidebar capabilities to resurrect U.S. honor and resolve. This force, named Joint Task Force Eagle Claw, began its work in November of 1979 and ended its existence in April of 1980 with the failed attempt.

Rather than immediately spend effort ascertaining how to make the once-failed capability better, the institution undertook a number of independent service investigations primarily directed to right perceived internal wrongs and to protect specific services from receiving blame for the outcome. It was not until the Grenada Invasion in 1983 and the unraveling of this residual force and its attendant problems that the U.S. Senate finally forced a variety of reforms and organizations that bore the public fruit, symbolized by the assault on Bin Laden as well as the extraordinary work the SOF community has accomplished since Senator Nunn and then retired General Shy Meyer forced the Department of Defense to endure the unendurable. The course of events began virtually immediately before the Eagle Claw force returned to the United States.

The Chairman, Air Force General David Jones, announced the establishment of the Holloway Board immediately following the failed rescue attempt. Its announced purpose was to investigate the issues that inhibited success and to recommend a future organizational concept to ensure better results. However, the sub-rosa intent of the Commission quickly became apparent.

This was but one of three separate "investigations" that dissected the rescue attempt. There was also the initial Navy inquiry as well as the Gast Review (named after Air Force Lieutenant General Gast, our erstwhile deputy commander). All three were essentially parochial interventions designed to ferret out any issues that could negatively reflect on a specific service or service establishment as opposed to actually improving future operations.

The Holloway Commission had several high level institutional objectives. First was to reign in the Chairman in order to preserve the influence of the specific services and to prevent him or his successors from using the newly emerging special operations capabilities as a private force circumventing the geographical "war fighting" CINCs.

The second was to ensure these new forces came under service-specific controls and not have the capability for independent operations as the Chairman's private army. The commission outcome ensured both objectives were met. The basis for that outcome was pre-ordained and lacked real integrity.

The commanding general of the attempt, Major General Vaught, was never called to appear and was not permitted to make either a statement regarding the investigation conclusions or to publicly comment.

The commission cherry-picked specific items and issues and built their conclusion on those items, which they viewed as negatives, absent any balanced testimony from the operators. It specifically chose to ignore what most task force members considered a crucial shortfall: the failure of the Navy to fly the requested and agreed-upon helicopter range profile legs leading up to the Desert One helicopter mechanical issues.

The Holloway Board was determined to keep the special operations genie in the bottle and retain a firm grip on the emerging forces. It (and many senior leaders) saw special operation forces as a threat to their traditional control and management. From the viewpoint of traditional "form," what the Chairman and Vaught did was unforgivable and they piled on as hard as they could. Real world issues plus a Carter/Brown directive forced them to accept that new capabilities were required, but would be "managed." The Joint Special Operations Command (JSOC) was established, but intentionally emasculated from an operational viewpoint.

General Meyer and Major General Vaught, immediately after the rescue attempt, created an organization within DAMO-OD named the Office Directorate Special Operations (ODSO). It was to invent, build, maintain and manage the myriad of emerging Army SOF elements as well as to be the

Army face for JCS SOF issues and operations. Within six months, ODSO went from a zero budget to $180 million and growing.

Soon after its creation, General Meyer paid a surprise visit to the ODSO spaces in the Army Operations Center. He began by outlining his view of the world, its threats, and the necessity to create capabilities to effectively meet these threats. No service had much of anything to offer and he intended to fix at least the Army side. Concurrently, the nature of the governing statutes as law, as well as operational issues, dictated that the Army and the CIA work much more closely and develop joint capabilities. Very soon, we began to accumulate several new and unique organizations as well as necessary capabilities, all under the constant pressure of world terrorist events. In the absence of a true counter-terrorist capability, Meyer directed that ODSO wear both a staff bureaucratic hat as well as an operational management hat.

Army Chief of Staff Shy Meyer was the lone, strong voice at the senior services level for the "brave new world." When he left, his successor, John Wickham, had no interest in the forces and was uncomfortable with the Army direction. Hence, he told Lieutenant General Max Thurman to create an organization—Technical Management Office (TMO)—specifically to investigate where the Army was "off the reservation" and to control the force.

At that time, I was in the Army War College working on a sub-rosa cover program system for then Brigadier General Downing and the newly created SOCOM which I dutifully and naively briefed to TMO. The action officer sent me a copy of the note from Vice Chairman of the Army General Brown that said: "This is not the sort of thing the Army should be doing." Clearly, this was indicative of the internal perception and bias by the new Chief of Staff and his deputy. Only Secretary Jack Marsh's intervention (he was both Secretary of the Army and Assistant Secretary of Defense for Special Operations/Low Intensity Conflict [SO/LIC]) kept the Army from killing the critical intelligence support element (the Field Operations Group—FOG) and Task Force 160, the newly established helicopter force. Further, the effect of world terrorist events forced the Army to build its SOF resources contrary to what it really, institutionally, wanted to do.

Generals Meyer, Vaught, and his successor, Major General William Moore, believed it was essential that SOF have a four-star spokesman to work with the CINCs and tasked ODSO to build a joint proposal for a special operations CINC.

Lieutenant Colonel Bruce Mauldin, from DAMO-ODSO, wrote the bulk of a paper entitled Strategic Services Command (STRATSERCOM) that would create a four-star SOF CINC. We (ODSO) briefed it in the

Tank to the Service Chiefs and Chairman at the request of General Meyer and were directed by the chiefs to take it to all the CINCs for their input. The proposed CINC would be a non-geographical CINC responsible for maintaining the various SOF elements as well as developing their logistical and intelligence support apparatus. It was specifically not to be a deployed war fighting headquarters. STRATSERCOM would simply pass forces to the engaged geographical CINC.

The CINCs unanimously trashed the concept, with Army General Rogers (Supreme Allied Commander Europe) and Navy Admiral Foley (CINCPAC) being particularly vehement in opposition. As a result, no SOF-centric CINC would exist until after the Grenada operation. After Grenada, this became today's United States Special Operations Command (USSOCOM) based on demonstrated need, which at least was demonstrated to the U.S. Senate.

General Meyer was very sensitive to establishing and resourcing these emerging forces strictly within institutional guidelines. As the resource/budget officer, I was required to get all the funding lines straight and with proper approval. I briefed both General Meyer and the then Vice Chief of Staff of the Army, General Vessey, weekly on progress, issues, and resolutions. This included classified briefs to the House Armed Service Committee, Senate Armed Service Committee, House Internal Security Committee, and Senate Internal Security Committee by Bruce Mauldin and myself with the respective Chairman's and Ranking Minority members for reprogramming. The Hill gave us everything we asked for and more and signed formal classified documents for the record.

Mr. Frank Keenan, the Army Comptroller, was my key supervisor in this area. All our funding documents had his and General Meyers' initials; a point that drove the later Project Yellow Fruit investigators and prosecutors crazy. (See below.)

DAMO-ODSO, per guidance from the Chief of Staff of the Army and Major General Vaught, managed several elements including SeaSpray (a joint Army-CIA aviation element), FOG (intelligence support) and the Army Delta force. Office Directorate Special Operations (ODSO) was also the liaison to/for JSOC with Army and joint staff.

A crucial issue we encountered very early, as a result of the Beirut kidnappings and related terrorist events, was a problem with maintaining cover and keeping operational funds for operators from being traceable back to Department of Defense by the bad guys. This was an issue richly appreciated now but less so then.

The emerging internet now allowed deep dives into personalities and business entities. It was no longer possible to hide personal or organizational trails from a diligent investigator. Personalities could not be posted to Location X as a commercial business owner without a credible commercial/traceable background. A person under cover could not survive cover if he or she did not have a traceable history of that cover. Funds could not be passed to an entity or person unless its sourcing was credible as a commercial sourcing. Department of Defense was simply not organized or competent enough to establish such cover.

Colonel Jim Longhofer, head of ODSO, after extensive discussions with CIA, developed Project Yellow Fruit as the overall system for such cover and finances. Unfortunately, one of his key field operatives went too far and exposed the program with his acts of bad judgment. The timing was such that TMO and Chief of Staff of the Army Wickham were anxious "to make an example" and they were aided by Mr. Greenberg, the ambitious Assistant U.S. Attorney in Washington who threatened the Army if it didn't pursue the Yellow Fruit membership. In sum, all top cover enjoyed under General Meyer had vanished and Longhofer was thrown under the bus by the new Army leadership. He was later fully exonerated by the Military Court of Appeals.

The Army pursued several trials, in all of which I testified. The key issue, inter alia, was this: why was the money hidden and how was it hidden? Prosecution just could not accept that none of us dipped into the till. I had been the primary bagman during my tenure in ODSO, hauling thousands of dollars in cash around the world. At the last trial, when concluded, the prosecutor, a captain, took me aside and said:

"OK. Now that the statute of limitations has expired, how did you guys hide the money you took?"

I responded, "We didn't take any money."

He turned around and left the room.

The Joint CIA-Army aviation element, SeaSpray, was a bright idea between General Meyer, Colonel Longhofer, and Lieutenant Colonel Mauldin. Meyer saw Army integration with the CIA as a very logical necessity based on the emerging world. He wanted to start the process of mutual support. Both had a lot to give the other. ODSO knew that aviation was probably the best and most achievable answer within existing capabilities. ODSO would buy the aircraft and provide some pilots, but the Agency would "own" them and provide the necessary legal cover and support.

We visited what was then known as the Clandestine Operations Branch to develop the concept, resources, and operational guidelines. This capability, once operational, provided significant benefits when exercised in the real world. Colonels Longhofer and Mauldin rounded up some experienced pilots from previous tours and combined them with Agency pilots into a single entity.

I traveled to Hughes helicopters with an Army aviation procurement representative, Major Ken Jacobs, and bought the first series of "Little Birds," the just-modified Hughes MD 500s. These were taken to a covered location mod shop where they underwent final modifications that provided some unique capabilities.

Concurrently, Colonel Longhofer, in a very creative way, changed Major Wayne Moomjian, U.S. Air Force, to become Lieutenant Colonel Moomjian, U.S. Army. Wayne became the first SeaSpray commander and led the unit on a number of highly successful operations at the national strategic level, the key public example being the return of President Jamal of Lebanon to Beirut after a covert visit to the United States.

At this point, certain frocked Air Force officers assigned to Clandestine Operations Branch-CIA viewed SeaSpray as a threat to Air Force interests and attempted to sabotage the program several times. When General Wickham became the Army Chief of Staff, Lieutenant General Thurman tried to kill SeaSpray. However, the Agency, recognizing its value, took over the entire element less the Army members. Lieutenant Colonel Moomjian and several ex-Army aviators were transferred as full civilian operatives.

During this period and to outline the significance of the events and the necessity for USSOF engagement, some of the issues to be dealt with included the Dozier kidnapping, seizure of the *Achille Lauro*, multiple Beirut kidnappings, arms swaps with Iraq (then at war with Iran), covert acquisition of Soviet helicopters in Africa, elimination of Radio Venceremos (the clandestine voice of the Nicaraguan attempt to overthrow the government of El Salvador), support to the mujahideen in Afghanistan against the Soviets, and several counterfeit currency issues in Western Europe emanating from Southwest Asia.

A final move was to fully integrate the Army Rangers into the SOF structure as Tier Two forces. They would be the security muscle for the Tier One forces, securing airfields, putting together the Little Birds, and securing the external perimeters of raid sites. For these tasks, the Rangers were given specialized equipment such as night vision goggles, laser sights, and MP5 submachine guns.

The inclusion of Rangers in this program was not uniformly accepted by the light infantry community. Some feared that the "SOF stuff" would degrade the Ranger infantry excellence and keep them apart from the rest of the "real army." Over the course of several somewhat resistant regimental commanders, the use of Rangers within the SOF community became an integral and continuing part.

No Greater Love

On 23 or 24 April every year since 1981, a small group of people meet on a rise of ground in Arlington Cemetery in Northern Virginia. In the early years most wore the uniform of their country, usually Air Force blue, mixed with Army green or Marine green. Now it is rare to see a uniform in the gathering. Civilian clothes dominate.

They gather near two headstones about 150 yards behind the Tomb of the Unknown Soldier which is guarded by Army sentries every day of the year, 24 hours a day.

No one guards these graves, but they are remembered, just as are the surrounding thousands. These are the resting places of the eight aircrew members whose lives were cut short by flames while performing their country's duty on behalf of other American citizens. The other six rest at other locations throughout the United States. However, all are remembered here each year, and every day in a small memorial chapel at Hurlburt Field, Florida.

The chapel is built around a full-length stained glass window that tells the story of their collective sacrifice. The chapel and the education fund that was created on behalf of the children of all eight airmen came both from donations from members of the Air Force Special Operations Community and private American civilians—particularly H. Ross Perot—who within days of the mishap at Desert One had created the education fund and gave it its financial foundation.

PART 5

Congress 1: Bureaucracy 0
The Nation Wins and
SOF Becomes a Capable Force

Introduction

Part of what follows is a first-person account of the development, defeat, and then resurrection of an attempt by then Chief of Staff of the Army, E. C. Meyer, to create a new special operations organization despite intense opposition within the Department of Defense. Part of it is a personal reflection of the events surrounding the creation by Congress of a special operations organization that closely paralleled General Meyer's proposal. And lastly it is an historical review of the military establishment's opposition to significant change within the SOF area and its forced inclusion within the Department of Defense structure.

There are two purposes to this chapter. First, to provide a first-person historical record of the evolution of strategic services command (now United States Special Operations Command [USSOCOM]) as proposed by General E. C. Meyer. And secondly, to outline personal observations regarding the military bureaucracy's approach to significant, innovative concepts they dislike.

Control and risk management perceptions appear to be the overriding rationales for opposition. It is also very hard for the corporate military body to rise above parochial issues and respond to visionary needs in light of their traditional associative history.

Within the 20th century, there have been six attempts to significantly restructure how the defense establishment did business. In each case, the changes were seen as necessary by the civilian leadership and were bitterly resisted by the military leadership. Three of those adjustments were attempted within the last 40 years and two of the three were attempted in the last 20 years. Between 1900 and today, bureaucratic style regarding reaction to reform remains largely unchanged. In particular, it did not willingly accept change in its Special Operations (SOF/LIC) programs. Only since the several desert wars has that attitude significantly changed.

During the last 25 years, there have been two major Department of Defense SOF reorganization plans: the Strategic Services Command (STRATSERCOM) proposal in 1980 by General E. C. Meyer, Chief of Staff,

U.S. Army and the USSOCOM mandated by Congress that was almost a duplicate of the STRATSERCOM proposal. I drew several conclusions from my personal experience with both issues:

a. The military establishment is naturally resistant to significant change regardless of the logic for that change. The early 20th-century Elihu Root Reforms and the Department of Defense Re-Organization Act of 1947 are proofs of this. The similar condition on the eve of World War II encountered by General George Marshall is well discussed by Forrest Pogue in his book, *George C. Marshall, Organizer of Victory*.
b. The military establishment, in the formative period, was particularly resistant to changes in its SOF/LIC structure.

President Kennedy's enhancement of special forces was a precursor to this, albeit on a smaller basis. On this specific subject, I had personal exposure with many of the principals. Their unanimous independently offered comments are quite clear:

c. The military establishment would continue to resist implementing changes it does not support well beyond the level of resistance it would accept from subordinate organizations.
d. The overall effect of this attitude is a diminution of military efficiency, capability and credibility.

I would be remiss if I did not state that this condition regarding SOF elements has dramatically changed to the positive. It was not so then.

The discussion in this part is divided into two parts. Part One is the rationale for General Meyer's STRATSERCOM proposal and why it was not adopted by Department of Defense in spite of the clear need. Part Two is the congressionally mandated USSOCOM and the resistance by Department of Defense to executing the intent of Congress as expressed by binding legislation.

Project Honey Badger: In the Beginning

Immediately after the failed rescue attempt, President Carter directed that the force be prepared to return to Iran, under extreme conditions, to rescue whatever hostages could be rescued if the Iranians began an execution scenario. Initially, this was a continuation of the ad hoc JTF structure. This was quickly adjusted in the light of certain realities.

OPSEC was somewhat of a lesser requirement in that it was now public knowledge we had some form of capability. The need for specialized elements and capabilities was clear. This included refuellable aircraft, more appropriate helicopter elements, several service-unique forces dedicated to these sorts of missions, night vision equipment, and a variety of secure communications equipment.

Perhaps most important, within a bureaucracy, was a formal budget. Nothing in Department of Defense happens without a line item dollar figure approved by Congress. This formal budget process underpins all personnel costs, procurement contracts, and operational expenses. This became known as Project ELT, the classified funding title for all Honey Badger initiatives.

This budget formalization would reduce much of the service's angst regarding funding their contributions as well as the significant costs associated with specialized procurement. Concurrently, it was recognized that operational costs associated with building a quality special operating force structure would be significant, a cost the service leaderships did not wish to eat.

In the Chairman's "Blank Piece of Paper" review, a number of service-specific force requirements, specialized equipment and operational capabilities were identified. These were turned into specific service action items by the Chairman and fed back to each service for review and comment. They were all collated under the term Project Honey Badger under the administrative management of General Vaught and the JTF staff acting as his joint office for the program.

After considerable discussion with General Vaught and a recognition of the varying but strong opinions of the senior services leadership, the Chairman decided that the entire project and its proposed requirements be briefed in the Tank for a decision. This program was closely monitored by the Secretary of Defense, Dr. Harold Brown, who requested a pre-brief.

I prepared a series of briefing charts for the Tank presentation that General Vaught told me to bring to the pre-brief. The pre-brief members would be the Chairman, General Vaught, Colonel Paschall, the new JTF Chief of Staff, and myself.

The charts I displayed outlined the proposed resource allocation by type (people, equipment, operational time, etc.) for each service. It also outlined the suggested specific budget line items by service to be included in their annual budget submission. Honey Badger was proposed as a Department of Defense level Research and Development Office reporting directly to the Secretary of Defense through the Chairman. It would hold the highest classifications and be briefed to Congress as a classified program with an overall budget line item titled Project ELT.

Dr. Brown took the briefing charts and went to his desk. He presented General Vaught with a signed document. It was a simple sentence that said the Secretary of Defense approves the force recommendation and directs the services to support it. The decision brief in the Tank was converted to an information brief. With a signature, Secretary Brown obviated all the anticipated services' antipathy to the program and its needs. In the parlance, they had to eat it.

Honey Badger/Project ELT became the overarching program to resource the equipping and training for the entire potential rescue force as well as in support of other emerging operational requirements for the new forces. These included the many Beirut-area kidnappings, Baader-Meinhof and Red Brigade events in Europe, and other problems in the world not manageable by conventional forces.

Much of the following discussion on standing up SOF elements was conducted under the auspices of Honey Badger/ELT as were all the service-specific upgrades and adds to their internal capabilities, much of which was done under duress and the decidedly negative view by the senior leadership.

Honey Badger/Project ELT would fund all costs associated with rescue scenario training as well as other SOF-centric training scenarios. The services would fund their internal procurements and manpower adds. However, those forces and resources would be identified within the service budget as support of Project Honey Badger/Project ELT as a congressionally approved high priority program.

As the project budget officer, it was my responsibility to account for the ELT costs and reimburse each service for their costs associated with a Honey

Badger exercise. This role also allowed me to assist General Vaught by assuring each service, primarily the Air Force, provided the maximum forces required. It was a "free lunch" in that regard.

Army "adds" included rotary wing and intelligence capabilities as well as expansion of the Rangers and Delta forces in both equipment and personnel. The Navy established Seal Team 6 and the Air Force rebuilt the 1st SOW and procured additional refuelable aircraft.

The JTF Eagle Claw organization remained as an operational headquarters while JSOC was being stood up. Numerous operational scenarios were conducted throughout the United States with both control headquarters. General Vaught's Army staff organization, DAMO-ODSO (more later), assumed an operational role and conducted/oversaw significant real-world tasks abroad. These were resourced by Honey Badger/Project ELT.

Acting as the Joint Action Officers for ELT, Major Bruce Mauldin and I made routine trips to Congress to brief Honey Badger/ELT ongoing operations or resource/re-programming needs. The briefings would cover each service's aspects as well as joint operational issues.

These were closed-door discussions with the appropriate committee chairs and the ranking members with no staff. In all cases, no information was compromised and all requests approved on the spot. General Meyer was fully aware of the process and received routine memos regarding financial activities of the Army within the Honey Badger program. Status briefings to the services were provided in the weekly Tank sessions for the principals and their operations deputies.

Within the Army, this resulted in a combination of anger and incredulity on the part of some of the Army aviation procurement bureaucracy. The helicopter procurement and the creation of Task Force 160 were strongly opposed by many Army aviation elements, both within the procurement structure as well as uniformed aviators in the field. Their concern was that the creation of the Task Force would siphon off limited aviation funds, but more importantly, attract the best pilots to man the organization, diluting conventional aviation forces.

Project Honey Badger/Project ELT permitted the establishment and growth of all Department of Defense special operations capabilities. It provided the initial funding programs for all services' SOF development and covered the expenses of the many joint SOF scenario training and rehearsals for potential real world events. In time, these resource programs were imbedded in each service's budget to the point where they are now priorities and are fully self-sustaining today. In the beginning, that was not so.

How SOF Got Started
on a Very Rocky Road

Two roads diverged in a wood, and I—
I took the one less traveled by,
And that has made all the difference.

—Robert Frost, *The Road Not Taken*

Since the creation of the Iran rescue task force in fall of 1979, I have been directly involved in a great many SOF-startup issues. These include Deputy J3 (Iran Rescue Force, JTF 1-79, Office of the Joint Chiefs of Staff); Chief, Special Operations, Army Deputy Chief of Staff for Operations; Commander, TF 2-505 (Grenada); Commander 1-75th Ranger Battalion, and as a student at the Army War College (AWC) studying the relationship between Congress and Department of Defense on SOF issues as well as assisting then Brigadier General Downing, Washington Liaison for USSOCOM, and General Lindsay, the first CINCSOCOM.

For the great majority of this period, I worked closely with many of the principal military leaders of the SOF and Department of Defense community as well as being deeply involved at the operational level. I had the unique experience of participating in SOF planning at the highest national level as well as executing SOF programs at a tactical level.

While at AWC, I became acquainted or re-acquainted with several members of Congress and their staff that were deeply interested in SOF issues. This relationship began on the basis of professional discussions on a subject of mutual interest and grew into a cooperative effort toward outlining the nature of the relationship between Congress and Department of Defense on SOF/LIC issues. As a result, I was given access to documentation, conversation and attitudes that was unique for a professional military officer.

As part of the AWC program, I conducted an oral biography of General (Ret) E. C. Meyer. I had worked closely for him on SOF/LIC issues. Specifically, I had been one of two action officers that worked with him in developing his proposal to create a SOF/LIC Unified Command, Strategic Services Command. Throughout the conduct of the oral history program, I was struck by how closely General Meyer's vision and concepts dovetailed with that of Congress on the need for a unified SOF/LIC command. I thought his vision and Congress' efforts would make the basis for an interesting study on one aspect of Congress-Department of Defense relations.

The history of the initial development of SOF is counter to the vision of both Meyer and Congress. The Service Chiefs, now including General Wickham as Meyer's successor, viewed the rise of SOF as both a burden and inappropriate imposition on their traditional roles. My view is that they saw the "new SOF" as a high-risk, low-payoff, loose cannon on a rolling deck with great potential for risk to the respective service reputations. What is now viewed as "normal" and expected/desired, was then viewed as a cup of hemlock.

This is that story.

The views and opinions expressed are strictly my own and are based as much on experiences and perceptions as academic research. This is not intended to be a richly sourced documented academic reference, but more of a first-person narrative and my interpretation of events and personalities.

PART 6

The Strategic Services Command Proposal

The Problem Begins

The Iran rescue attempt failed for many reasons, some mechanical, some organizational, and some political. But it did have one major long-term success: it focused national attention on developing a competent ability to organize and execute Special Operations/Low Intensity Conflict operations. The methods proposed to resolve the emerging SOF/LIC issues became as contentious as the emotional aftermath of the raid itself and still remain unresolved.

The failed Iran rescue was a national embarrassment. It galvanized the nation and the military into public introspection and criticism. The attempt was contrasted with the successful operations conducted by the Israelis at Entebbe and the British at Princess' Gate.

Wellington's comment that Waterloo was "a close run thing" certainly applied to the Iran program. The military successfully trained over 500 men for eight months, deployed them in total secrecy halfway around the world and failed only because the machinery had some unpredictable failures. Clearly, what was broken had to be fixed. What was needed must be provided.

By the time the Holloway Board reached its conclusions, solutions were being translated into capability. A collection of intelligence and operational units began to emerge on the government books. Names like Delta, SeaSpray, Rangers, Field Operating Group, 1st SOW, SEAL Team 6, SOLL II, Task Force 160, DARISSA and the DARCOM Special Projects Office began to appear at briefings. Every service soon had some part of the special operations pie.

Missions and requirements flowed into the Pentagon as the National Command Authority was assailed with continuous requirements to fill the needs of this emerging form of nebulous warfare. Still, there was no central management of the requirements, the money or the programs.

The Holloway Commission had spawned the creation of the Joint Special Operations Command (JSOC) ostensibly to fulfill the management need. However, the commanding general did not own his forces and only used them within the limits prescribed by each service for its component elements. In many cases, internal service special operations units operated independently from JSOC and could take equipment and personnel from their sister elements in JSOC without coordination or JSOC approval.

The budget for special operations grew dramatically. In 1981, the Army special operations budget was $32 million. By 1983 it had risen to $440 million and by 1988, the total SOF budget was approximately $2.5 billion (though it represented only 1 percent of the total Department of Defense budget).

Almost immediately after the Iran hostages came home, SOF elements were operating around the world. Units found themselves in Afghanistan, the Philippines, Laos, Thailand, Mexico, El Salvador, Honduras, Bolivia, Jamaica, Italy, Egypt, Oman, Lebanon, Crete, Panama, West Germany, Iraq, and Saudi Arabia. Significant accomplishments were made in problems that heretofore were impossible to address.

Other Federal agencies were equally pleased. The military had filled some embarrassing gaps in their capabilities and they were happy to both train, sponsor, and in some cases underwrite military programs to fulfill national objectives.

The National Command Authority, State Department, and Department of Justice were happy. Ambassadors sang the praises of SOF actions abroad. Theater commanders, particularly those in Third World areas, clamored for more support. The Joint Chiefs of Staff were both pleased and perplexed.

SOF became a very sexy subject. Congress poured money, almost without question, into anything that had a counter-terrorist tag on it. Still, SOF represented a deviation from the norm of warfare as the senior leadership saw it. It diverted attention away from traditional programs and represented significant risk. The routine employment of SOF elements abroad on real missions placed them, and their service, and the defense establishment, in harm's way.

Contrary to the normal bureaucratic tendency to centralize, the Service Chiefs resisted efforts to place their SOF elements under a single manager. Instead, considerable effort was expended to keep each service SOF unit under service control and to employ a labyrinth of requirements before a force could be employed. Intuitively perhaps, the service leadership recognized the great paradox of special operations programs.

Special operations were increasingly necessary to resolve the peculiar problems of undeclared warfare that emerged in the 80s. The National Command Authority recognized that SOF was capable of great achievements in gathering intelligence, fighting terrorism, protecting Americans abroad and in effecting U.S. political objectives in an increasingly tough, turbulent and uncontrollable world.

Concurrently, SOF had great potential for risk, embarrassment, and disaster. Operational elements can get out of control. They can and do work beyond the pale of "normal" military control. Mistakes by very few people can be immediately reflected on the front pages of the world in the form of national embarrassment. While Desert One may have been unfortunate, Desert Two could be institutionally fatal.

In 1980, then Chief of Staff of the Army, E. C. Meyer, proposed that the services develop an organization that could manage this emergent form of warfare. This proposal, Strategic Services Command (STRATSERCOM) was never approved. Instead, it died the bureaucratic equivalent of the death of a thousand cuts. This despite the clear need for such an organization.

Ultimately, STRATSERCOM was replaced by a congressionally mandated USSOCOM in 1986 that almost exactly mirrored the Meyer proposal. But that too is in keeping with the history of change within the defense bureaucracy.

Had he read his history before tabling the proposition, General Meyer might have taken less initiative. In the process, he learned three bureaucratic truths:

- The services inherently dislike special operations.
- Significant changes must come from outside the bureaucracy.
- Bureaucracies are very good at fighting that which they don't want to do.

The Vision

Bureaucracy. -cracy coming from Greek kratos *meaning strength.*

—Merriam-Webster

If there is one thing a bureaucracy is good at, it's in not doing what it doesn't want to do.

—Admiral (Ret) Thomas Moorer

General (Ret) E. C. Meyer, former Chief of Staff of the Army, once stated that the lowest point of his career was the eight years he spent in the Pentagon. His reasoning was that the system was so dominated by bureaucratic interests, the services so consumed by petty parochial squabbles, and the management system so overburdened that efficiency, vision, and cooperation simply were not possible.

With four years' experience as Deputy Chief of Staff for Operations on the Army Staff and four years as Chief of Staff, General Meyer had more than an average exposure to the conditions that he decried. Perhaps the best proof of the validity of his analysis of the defense bureaucracy lies in an autopsy of one of his most cherished proposals as Chief, the Strategic Services Command (STRATSERCOM).

STRATSERCOM was an attempt to provide a structure within the Department of Defense (DOD) that would be capable of addressing the emergent threats on the low end of the spectrum of conflict—those issues popularly called Special Operations Forces/Low Intensity Conflict (SOF/LIC).

General Meyer's proposition was in keeping with his view of the military capabilities needed to address the threat. The bureaucratic reaction was equally predictable in its absorption and ultimate rejection of something it did not want. Like the starfish on the coral, it moved slowly and softly, yet ultimately destroyed its prey with no visible harm to itself.

What General Meyer proposed was a unique concept with dramatic implications for DOD organizations. The rejection of the proposition by those required to change was completely consistent with DOD's history, particularly its reaction towards special operations issues.

STRATSERCOM was a child of his own vision of the world, a world that would require a form of support that the DOD was not capable of providing without a STRATSERCOM type of headquarters. He translated his vision into a deceptively simple graph that became the heart of the STRATSERCOM rationale.

Form of Conflict

The chart graphically portrayed Meyer's view of the nature of present and future conflict and the attendant costs. Low-intensity conflict is going on now and will continue to do so. Mid- and high-intensity conflict is increasingly unlikely and the costs to sustain capability on that spectrum are gargantuan when compared to the likelihood of force employment. In sum, it appeared

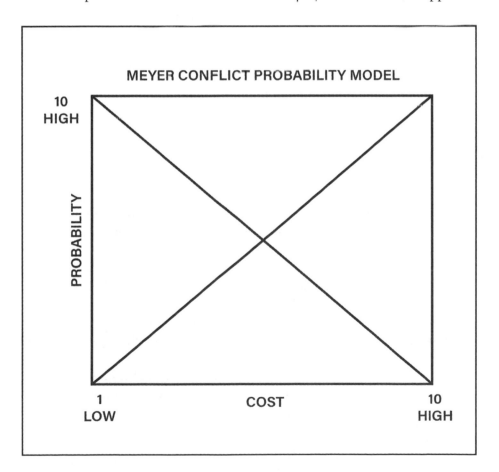

that DOD was spending 99 percent of its funds on an issue with less than 10 percent probability of occurrence while it was devoting less than 1 percent of its resources to the contemporary version of World War III that was ongoing.

The initial chart was hand drawn by General Meyer in Major General Vaught's office and was used to describe his vision in graphic terms. It was subsequently refined and became a basic part of every STRATSERCOM briefing and is still widely used today to describe the rationale and nature of LIC. General Meyer's personal experience with the creation of the air assault concept in the early 1960s served to reinforce the necessity in his mind for top-down direction. He was acutely aware that DOD, as an institution, would not make a radical change to its methodologies without dramatic and continuous pressure from either external sources or from the top down. Accordingly, he made his personal sponsorship very clear. His vision was affected by a variety of inputs.

A contracted study by American University in 1978 found a far different future for the military than the model in which it was then prepared to fight. General Meyer noted that the paper paralleled the conclusions of similar studies conducted by Harvard University and the Brookings Institute. Contemporaneously, the Department of Defense long-term strategy study, "Discriminate Deterrence," closely follows the conclusions of the 1978 study.

In 126 pages, the American University study described future conflict requirements in terms dramatically at odds with those laid down in the Secretary of Defense's Annual Joint Strategic Memorandum, the basis for resource allocation. Its key points were as follows:

- The major powers' nuclear weapons are obsolete. Neither side is willing to use them and will exert insurmountable pressure on less powerful possessors to prevent their use of the weapon.
- The Third World will be the key battleground for power, influence and ideas through the remainder of the 20th century. The mass of conventional forces arrayed in Europe will be irrelevant to the outcome.
- Warfare will consist of low-intensity, low-risk conflict. It is safe and appropriate for the regions involved and relatively cheap compared to traditional conflict.
- Terrorism, both state supported and private, will be increasingly prevalent and will provide major problems in that it does not respond to "normal" military reactions.

- Drug enforcement operations, though legal rather than military problems, will have to be addressed by the military because only it has the resources to successfully respond to the magnitude of the problem.
- General Meyer reviewed the strategy of the Army and DOD in light of the study and reached some broad conclusions. These were based on the intellectual structure provided by the strategic studies as well as his own review of operational issues as they flowed across his desk.
- The services had invested most of their resources in preparation for a global nuclear/conventional war against like structured forces. DOD was unprepared to meet the needs of SOF/LIC and was philosophically opposed to implementing the necessary management structure and funding base. The JCS was being deluged with requests for SOF/LIC assistance and was responding in a piecemeal manner. Critical force improvements such as refuelable MC-130 transport aircraft were not being given the required funding support. The Central Intelligence Agency, which had failed to provide timely support to the Iran rescue force, was apparently unwilling to provide HUMINT support to ongoing SOF operational needs.

Army SOF was not oriented to emerging threats, but was concentrating on obsolete techniques and the leadership was engaged in constant bureaucratic battles over control of operational assets. The Delta Force, operational in fall 1979, and its support elements, were rapidly being victimized by these squabbles and was in danger of losing its quick reaction capability.

Concurrent with his personal assessment, General Meyer was exposed to two external factors. One, a directive from the Secretary of Defense, required formal service support of SOF elements. The other, the Holloway Report, indicated the depth of negative feeling within the service bureaucracies toward SOF issues.

As a result of the disaster at Desert One, the President had directed a major SOF expansion to enable an in extremis rescue attempt should that be necessary. The cover program for budgetary purposes was called Honey Badger and was placed as a DOD Research and Development line item.

Accordingly, the original rescue force was greatly expanded to encompass over 2,000 people with assets ranging from airborne warning and control aircraft to covert helicopter units supported by clandestine intelligence-gathering personnel. Over the course of eight months, the all-service force resolved many of the shortfalls exposed by the debacle in the desert. Clearly, DOD had developed a new and highly potent capability. Now, with the hostages returned, DOD had to determine what to do with this "off the shelf" force.

In May 1980, the Secretary of Defense, reflecting the worldwide realities of terrorism and Third World issues, issued a specific memorandum to each service secretary. The one-page top secret document directed that each service would maintain the counter-terrorist forces it had developed by including that capability in the formal service structure. Included was specific budget guidance that directed SOF dollar floors for each service. What had been ad hoc was now formalized and funded. However, the reaction to the Holloway Report and this directive provided General Meyer with some insight as to how the services would handle Secretary Brown's directive.

The Holloway Board was formed immediately after the Desert One failure. Composed of three retired and three active duty flag and general officers, they were charged by the Chairman of the Joint Chiefs of Staff to determine what went wrong and what was needed to fix the problem. In slightly over a month, they presented their conclusions. They addressed 23 separate issues and made two key recommendations:

- DOD should create a dedicated formal counter-terrorist task force that reported directly to the JCS.
- A Special Operations Review Panel should be created with a body of retired senior officers with extensive special operations background. This panel should act as an independent body to review SOF execution plans.

General Meyer noted that the results reflected several hidden agendas as well as some key omissions. This situation was in keeping with traditional service approaches to uncomfortable situations. Glaringly omitted was any mention of the Navy failure to comply with orders.

On three separate occasions, the helicopter crew on the *Nimitz*, the custodians of the ultimate mission helicopters, were directed to fly increasingly long flight legs, culminating in an eight-hour profile that would stress the machines to their limit, the same limit they would have to fly to arrive at Desert One. This requirement was studiously ignored.

In December of 1979, USMC Colonel Charles Pitman visited the *Nimitz* and provided the profiles to the helicopter squadron commander. He returned in February and discovered that no aircraft had been flown more than two hours. Colonel Pitman rebriefed the squadron commander and the task force admiral on the profile requirements. Additionally, he stopped at CINCPAC Headquarters and briefed Admiral Long, the CINC.

After hearing Pitman's report, the rescue force commander, Major General James B. Vaught, visited General Jones, the Chairman of the Joint Chiefs of

Staff. General Vaught requested permission to visit the carrier as the task force commander and lend emphasis to the issue. After discussing the request with the Chief of Naval Operations, Admiral Hayward, the request was denied. However, the Chairman did send a personal message to Admiral Long, then CINCPAC, outlining the requirement and requiring support. This was acknowledged by Admiral Long.

When the mission pilots arrived on the *Nimitz* on 10 April, the logbooks revealed that no helicopter had been flown more than 2½ hours. None of this was mentioned in the Holloway Report. It was the strongly held belief by many members of the rescue force that had the helicopters been stressed aboard the *Nimitz* during the training phase, that many of the mechanical faults would have been revealed and fixed.

The establishment of the counter-terrorist task force (JSOC), was accomplished, but not without some traditional caveats. These adjustments to force assignments served to make the headquarters less responsive than the Holloway Commission envisioned.

JSOC was established at Fort Bragg in June of 1980 after the Army agreed to be the executive agent (responsible manager) and the Air Force agreed to cede the land to the Army, a portion of Pope AFB.

The Holloway Board felt that a formal joint task force must have readily responsive forces, but only after each service approved the proposed mission and force mix. Forces may or may not be assigned to JSOC. This was an issue to be worked on.

It was assumed by the commission that this would include the majority of the direct action forces created for the Iran rescue. This force was deemed appropriate for most terrorist scenarios that could be foreseen. This included the Delta Force, the Army helicopter unit Task Force 160 and the Air Force SOF element, the First Special Operations Wing (1st SOW) as well as specialized communications support.

The headquarters was given 150 spaces; barely enough to meet its administrative needs let alone its supervisory and operational requirements. (The element has since been upgraded by multiples of hundreds.)

The Army assigned Delta, but temporarily withheld Task Force 160, the key lift and support element. This was reluctantly done by General Meyer as a short-term measure to keep the 101st Air Assault Division at full strength. Concurrently, he directed fund reprogramming that would backfill the 101st and permit Task Force 160 to pass to JSOC control.

The Air Force bitterly battled the Commander of the JSOC on assignment of the 1st SOW. After several heated exchanges in the Tank and a flurry of messages, Air Force provided a small operational control detachment but no aircraft. Air Force agreed to place two MC-130s and one AC-130 on alert at Hurlburt Field for use of the JSOC upon request.

The Navy created a maritime version of Delta with SEAL Team 6 in 1980. This unit was stationed at Dam Neck, Virginia, and was subject to assignment to JSOC for specified missions.

The services nonetheless retained control over forces associated to JSOC. No units could be deployed without specific service authority. Secondary counterterrorism support forces such as Rangers, Task Force 160, the remainder of the 1st SOW, and certain intelligence and communications assets had to wind their way through a labyrinthine approval chain before JSOC could employ them. This was not a responsive system, but it did provide a desirable degree of control and risk management for the service leadership.

Contrary to the Holloway Board vision, the freedom of action and unfettered operational control of JSOC was equally limited. This was partly a reflection of the Service Chiefs' dislike of the Chairman's handling of Iran and partly a normal desire to preserve the well-ordered status quo of the Unified Command Plan (UCP).

The Chairman had chosen to run the Iran rescue program by himself. He compartmented the rescue planners away from the JCS and service staffs and tightly restricted access. He kept the Service Chiefs informed in only the most general way and provided no detail to the U.S. European Command (EUCOM), the headquarters responsible for the geographic area.

Though the services would not be responsible for the operational outcome of the rescue, they would be held liable for the conduct and efficiency of their forces—indirectly so if not specifically. They determined that this would not happen again.

The JCS placed certain roadblocks in JSOC's path that they hoped would cure previous "control" problems. Classified agreements were reached that tasked JSOC to act "in support of" a CINC rather than operate routinely for the Chief of the JCS as was the intent of the Holloway Commission. This kept JSOC from being a private tool of the Chairman. However, bowing to pragmatic reality regarding National Command Authority (NCA) management of sensitive counterterrorism operations, JCS was forced, over objection, to provide a final sentence permitting JSOC "to conduct operations in direct support of the NCA through the JCS when so directed."

Once the Joint Chiefs had resolved the Holloway recommendations concerning JSOC, they turned to the second major proposal. Their reaction again reflected their penchant for control and resistance to the introduction of outside influence.

The commission recommended that a senior panel of SOF-qualified retired officers be established. This panel would report directly to the Chairman and would act as an experienced group of "wise men" regarding SOF/LIC issues. The Service Chiefs saw this as another circumvention of their supervisory role and a diminution of their control mechanisms.

The Chiefs arrived at a classic bureaucratic solution. They developed a control mechanism that provided tight control of SOF assets while appearing to comply with the Holloway recommendations.

The Chairman created an organization entitled the Senior Officer Advisory Panel. It was composed of retired officers of excellent reputation. Among the initial members were Admiral Holloway, General DePuy, Lieutenant General Yarborough, Lieutenant General Manor, General Blanchard, and Brigadier General Blackburn. Though they met monthly, they had neither a specific mission nor authority. As one frustrated member said, "We have been gilded, gelded, and ignored."

Over time, this organization underwent numerous changes of membership and titles. The gelding and ignoring remained unchanged and the Senior Officer Advisory Panel was lost to history.

The JCS replaced the Holloway oversight recommendation with the existing Operations Deputies (OPSDEPS) wearing their joint hats. The OPSDEPS are also the respective Service Operations Chiefs. These officers are three-star generals and admirals charged with the daily operational management of their service. Wearing their second joint hat as the OPSDEPS, they fulfill the same function on joint issues.

The OPSDEPS immediately became the oversight element for SOF issues. Their level of involvement ranged from determining the amount of hours an SOF helicopter could fly to the nature of a VIP demonstration. They very effectively brought control of SOF back to the highest service levels and removed any vestige of independence of JSOC. Commanding General of JSOC was not permitted to exercise his forces in a meaningful manner unless prior approval was granted by the OPSDEPS.

General Meyer saw a consistent pattern from a variety of perspectives that deeply troubled him. Clearly, SOF was the primary form of conflict to be faced by the United States in the foreseeable future. DOD was not well disposed to meet this challenge. Equally clearly, service parochialism would not permit a balanced consensus analysis of the problem in a meaningful way.

He determined to resolve the problem by proposing a unique SOF organizational structure, STRATSERCOM, to the JCS. His intuition concerning bureaucratic attitudes toward SOF was amply rewarded by a plethora of obstructionism, in-fighting, and studied indifference.

The Proposal

During a two-hour meeting in the office of Major General Vaught, held the afternoon of 7 October 1980, General Meyer sketched out a proposed organization that would resolve the majority of SOF problems he had seen over the last two years. Major General Vaught now returned to his position on the Army staff, gave the skeleton plan to two compartmented staff officers, Lieutenant Colonel Bruce Mauldin, son of the famed World War II cartoonist, and myself. Both were members of the Iran task force and intimately familiar with contemporary SOF issues.

The action officers, aided by input from retired Delta Commander Charlie Beckwith and other members of the SOF community, developed some flesh on Meyer's proposal. They quickly learned that the flesh was at variance with the soul of the establishment.

In December, General Meyer approved the draft concept and prepared to present it to the Joint Chiefs for approval. The proposal resolved what he considered the primary existing stumbling blocks to efficient management of SOF/LIC issues.

- The headquarters would be a full four-star Unified Command. This would give it equal status with the other CINCs, separate it from the bureaucracy of the JCS, and provide a capability for both war or the more likely LIC arena of "non-peace." Concurrently, the commander would have comparable status with the Service Chiefs and direct access to the Secretary of Defense, something not enjoyed by the commander of JSOC.
- The headquarters would have all direct action counterterrorism forces assigned to it. Other forces with a SOF or support function would be accessible to the CINC through a unique tiering plan.
- Tier One forces would be assigned directly to the CINC. Tier Two forces would train and work some of the time with the headquarters to maintain proficiency but would spend the majority of their time working on their primary conventional missions. Under Tier Three would be all other

forces that conceivably could be used by the CINC. In this manner, the CINC would be assured of having direct control over forces needed to fulfill his basic mission while still providing quick access to additive forces should they be needed. The responsiveness of this system would be a marked improvement over the existing multi-service layered nature of JSOC's structure.

To control and support the tiered forces, General Meyer developed a service component approach that gave each service a significant role. His intent was not only to provide a sensible system, but also to assuage the other service's sensitivities toward flag and general officer distribution.

The Army component command would be the JFK Center at Fort Bragg, commanded by a major general. He would command all Tier One land forces as well as those Special Forces, Psychological Operations/Civil Affairs and Ranger elements not assigned to a CINC. The air component would be commanded by an Air Force major general. Under him would be all SOF aviation units to include Task Force 160, the Army SOF aviation unit. This was a significant departure from tradition and was done after conversation with the Air Force Chief of Staff. General Meyer was under the impression that Air Force would support the proposal if the Task Force fell under Air Force control. This impression later proved false.

The Navy component would be commanded by a Rear Admiral, Upper Half. Reporting to him would be SEAL Team 6, other unassigned SEAL elements, and a maritime support unit.

An intelligence cell would also be formed with a one-star commander who rotated between the services. He would control the Field Operating Group, later the Intelligence Support Activity (ISA), and other compartmented elements. This unit was critically important in that it fused for the first time both the operators and the intelligence gatherers under a single SOF command.

JSOC would become the JTF headquarters for the CINC. As required, forces from the components would be passed to it for operational employment. The JTF would either report to the JCS or to the supported CINC during its operational life. Only in very special cases was it envisioned that CINC STRATSERCOM would have a direct operational role. Recognizing the great sensitivity by the chiefs and CINCs on this issue, General Meyer went to some pain to emphasize the subordinate aspects of the anticipated control issue.

The deputy commander would be a three-star position. It was proposed that it would alternate between Army and Air Force as would the CINC position. General Meyer's view was that the structure and the command issues successfully addressed the problems experienced by Commander JSOC, the inherent concerns of the services for their forces, and the necessities of operational life. He was to learn that its very efficiency was a foundation for its failure as a proposition.

Satisfied that the basic proposal was where he wanted it, Meyer directed a four-pronged approach to gaining approval. The first step involved developing service credibility and was the opening round in STRATSERCOM's ultimate bureaucratic demise. The first step within the army was to create the future component command and rearrange the army forces to accommodate their ultimate disposition. Deputy Chief of Staff for Operations and Plans, in January of 1981, was directed to fund the backfill of the 101st aviation assets, upgrade the SOF capability of the Rangers, streamline the Delta report chain and determine the long-term needs of SOF in general. This was to be accomplished through a Mission Area Analysis (MAA) sponsored by the JFK Center.

Funds were programmed in the FY 82 "wedge" of the Army budget for the purchase of new helicopters to replace those taken from the 101st when Task Force 160 was created. However, the anticipated passage of the task force soon became an acrimonious debate at the general officer level.

Commanding General, United States Army Forces Command (FORSCOM) and Commanding General, 101st Airborne, both objected to losing control of Task Force 160. They were strongly supported by Commanding General, XVIII Airborne Corps. Their position was that the 101st would be crippled in the short run and the task force would be materially weakened in the long run once it left their control. The task force had been formed from the cream of the 101st's aviators. Its commanders and pilots represented the best the division had in its inventory. To lose this wealth of talent would do irreparable damage to the leading air assault unit in the army. Moreover, the 101st had contingency plans, particularly in Southwest Asia that would require the capabilities inherent to the task force. Once removed from the efficient maintenance system provided by the division and FORSCOM, readiness of the task force would rapidly decline. It was the contention of the corps commander that the ability of the task force to support SOF could be better provided within the existing structure.

Unwilling to lose a key political trump card with Air Force, General Meyer demurred on making a decision. Instead, he directed that the backfill of aircraft and people be executed and held the ultimate decision on the task force to a later date. The STRATSERCOM briefing charts retained the task force as a Tier One unit under the Air Component Commander.

The Ranger issue was hardly easier. The original concept was that each of the two Ranger battalions would rotate as a Tier One unit under the Army Component Commander as it assumed the six-week alert posture for Commanding General JSOC. The remaining battalion would be retained in Tier Two status. The Department of the Army immediately funded both battalions for SOF enhancement after a lengthy meeting at FORSCOM the first week of December 1980. The cost was $32 million per battalion. It included night vision goggles, special weapons and vehicles, and a comprehensive radio package. The Deputy Chief of Staff for Operations and Plans, FORSCOM, formally told the Department of the Army, DAMO-OD, that FORSCOM would not support any proposition that removed either battalion from FORSCOM control, effectively eliminating the possible Ranger inclusion in Tier One.

The FORSCOM argument was based on the worldwide requirement for Rangers. Numerous CINC contingency plans, particularly those in Southwest Asia, required both Ranger battalions. FORSCOM reasoned that execution of those plans would have to take priority over SOF missions. Therefore, the Army could not afford to pass the assets out of control. Further, there was no SOF plan that required more than 350 people, idling half a battalion.

In a compromise between FORSCOM and Deputy Chief of Staff-Operations (DCSOPS), it was agreed that the Rangers would become Tier One only upon specific mission approval by the JCS of a JSOC requirement. The issue of control of Rangers under STRATSERCOM was specifically excluded from the agreement. The Tier One Army contribution was limited to Delta.

The Mission Area Analysis of Army SOF was equally hard to resolve within General Meyer's intent. In November of 1980, he requested that the commanding general, JFK Center, Major General Joe Lutz, in coordination with Lieutenant General Howard Stone, commanding general of Command and General Staff College, present an omnibus review of Army SOF. This study was to address Army-wide SOF needs, forces, resources, doctrine, training tasks, and strategy. This would be the basis for the first material upgrade of SOF since the Kennedy years. It would be the foundation of General Meyer's personal commitment to upgrade SOF to meet the emerging requirements. He knew that he would not be able to sell STRATSERCOM to the other services and CINCs until the Army had made a credible commitment.

The Mission Area Analysis effort was continuously disappointing. The Stone-Lutz proposals aired in January 1981 in the Pentagon fell far short of the desired mark. Essentially, they addressed a need for Special Forces upgrade and barely addressed other SOF forces. Where the Chief of Staff of the Army had hoped for an omnibus review that could be the pillar of a resource and restructuring concept, he received instead a parochial case to restore a single asset of the SOF panoply. He directed a second attempt.

Mauldin and I traveled to Fort Bragg shortly after the first Mission Area Analysis and briefed General Lutz and his staff on the Chief of Staff of the Army's concept. Concurrently, Meyer sent a detailed discussion of his vision to FORCOM, Army Training and Doctrine Command, Command and General Staff College, the XVIII Airborne Corps, and JFK Center. It soon became obvious that it would be impossible to translate vision into reality, at least at this level of engagement.

The second iteration held in March of 1981 lasted less than ten minutes. General Meyer asked for a detailed breakout of the proposals for SOF elements other than Special Forces. Nothing beyond a standard command brief was available. General Meyer dismissed the group and tasked Deputy Chief of Staff for Operations to make a "best guess" of SOF resource needs and fold them into the Army budget. Shortly thereafter, Lieutenant General Stone was reassigned as Chief of Staff, U.S. European Command. The situation got no better as the Chief of Staff of the Army forwarded STRATSERCOM through the approval gates.

The first step was to gain the Chairman of the Joint Chief's approval to formally present the concept. General Meyer knew that General Jones was personally in favor of the concept but was sensitive to the personal animus among the chiefs toward both SOF issues and the Unified Command Plan (UCP) in particular.

Just prior to the STRATSERCOM proposal, the JCS had been directed by the Secretary of Defense to develop a proposal for a Rapid Deployment Joint Task Force that would evolve into a Unified Command. This requirement was very time consuming, emotional, and placed the chiefs at odds with the CINCs. A new issue regarding the UCP would not be well received.

Together, the Chairman and the Chief of Staff of the Army agreed to a sequential game plan. General Meyer would brief the chiefs on the STRATSERCOM proposal the first week of December 1981 and request approval to brief the CINCs. The CINCs would then be asked to inform the Chairman as to their opinion regarding the proposition. After all the CINCs had been briefed, the proposal would be formally introduced into the JCS by General Meyer for a decision.

This approach accomplished several things. Firstly, it kept the JCS from having to formally address the concept, thereby avoiding staff and service road-blocking. Secondly, it kept the issue at the four-star level where issues of contention could be better worked on an informal level. Lastly, by having the initial input informally provided by the CINCs, critical adjustments could be made before it became a formal action.

The two Army staff officers, Mauldin and I, then visited each CINC throughout the remainder of 1981 and into the spring of 1982 and presented the formal STRATSERCOM briefing. Prior to their arrival, General Meyer sent a personal message to the CINC outlining his concept rationale and in some cases included a personal phone call. Despite General Meyer's personal involvement, STRATSERCOM died from an overwhelmingly negative response. This was both internal and external to the Army.

The Proposal Fails

Internally, the Army did not present a uniformly supportive face on the issue. Throughout the 1981–82 period, the Director of Strategy, Plans and Policies, Army Major General John Seigel, who was responsible for handling joint issues, was notably negative to the concept. This attitude affected all Army staff members involved in the STRATSERCOM issue.

While the proposal was never formally "floated" as a formal paper, it was circulated to all service staffs for review and was openly discussed in the Tank during the Deputy Operations Deputy sessions as a pending action. These officers were the 2-star deputies to the Service Operations Deputies, G3s, of each service wearing their JCS hat. They were referred to as the DepOpDeps. Their job was to plough the hard ground on each joint issue and distill it to manageable proportions that their senior, the Operations Deputy, could then translate into a recommended position for the service Chief of Staff to vote on as a JCS issue. Each service representative, as a member of the joint staff in addition to his specific service assignment, carried into the Tank his service's prejudices and desires. The joint staff process was designed to determine what all the Service Chiefs could agree upon. If they could not reach a compromise at the DepOpDep and OpDep levels, that issue would be tabled unless the Chairman deemed it necessary to vote.

General Meyer hoped that by taking an informal approach to staffing, issues could be identified and resolved prior to being formally addressed.

General Seigel looked upon the proposition as a forced opening of the Unified Command Plan issue that was bound to gain enmity from the other services toward the Army. Additionally, he felt uncomfortable with service forces actually being assigned to the CINC and the long-term implications and precedents. The effect was that during the weekly DepOpDep sessions in the Tank, the impression was left that STRATSERCOM was a personal program of the Army Chief and without internal Army support. Externally, things were not much better.

After the formal briefing process, which ended in the spring of 1982, the CINCs maintained a neutral public position but were privately quite negative as back channel communications indicated.

Only the Supreme Allied Commander Europe sent a positive response to the Chairman of the Joint Chiefs. This was a marked change for General Rogers who was now facing multiple issues that only the SOF elements could and did address. Wearing his USEUCOM hat, General Rogers modified his support significantly.

Some CINCs did not respond at all while others routed their messages either to the Chairman personally or to their Mother Service.

Those objections that were raised were very general in nature. The consistent thread was concern that the force would be employed in a CINCs theater without prior coordination and would not work through the existing CINC structure. All agreed that the problems of low intensity combat in general and counter-terrorism specifically had to be addressed. USEUCOM endorsed the concept provided that deployed forces would report to him when in theater. No other CINC formally responded.

Normally the poor response would have resulted in the tabling of the proposal and its formal rejection. However, General Meyer felt that patience might be rewarded over time. He directed the Army staff to do nothing but to allow time and the never-ending flow of special operations requirements to make their point. Though the requirements were constant and the involvement of the CINCs was continuous, the attitude toward STRATSERCOM remained unchanged.

General Meyer paid allegiance to the ancient military maxim Never Reinforce Failure. He did so indirectly by never formally raising the issue. Without a quorum of support from the chiefs and with no support from the CINCs, he realized that STRATSERCOM had no constituency. By not formally raising the proposal, it could not be voted down. Instead, it would be saved for a more favorable time and audience.

In an informal after-action review with his staff officers, conducted in the spring of 1983, General Meyer reached several broad conclusions. These accurately portrayed the traditional bureaucratic reasons for opposing worthwhile concepts for essentially personal or parochial reasons.

There was a strong residual backlash against the Chairman for the way he managed the Iran rescue program. STRATSERCOM was viewed as a potential license for the Chairman of the Joint Chiefs to conduct a private operation in a CINCs area without CINC involvement. The fact that STRATSERCOM had no assigned territory only heightened the suspicion, though the opposite was General Meyer's intent.

There was probably an equal amount of resentment toward General Meyer. As a relatively junior officer, General Meyer had been a consistent thorn in Tank sessions and had generated more dissenting position papers than any other Chief in history. General Meyer was viewed as a service iconoclast who generated concepts that attacked the heart of how the services "did business."

All the services were strongly opposed to opening the Unified Command Plan again. The JCS had just completed a bloody struggle over the Rapid Deployment Joint Task Force separation from Readiness Command and the Secretary of Defense directed designation of a Marine as the CINC. The chiefs had no stomach for a second battle that would be raised to a highly visible public level due to the nature of the subject and the public concern over terrorist issues. There was widespread acknowledgement by staff officers that a public discussion of the issue would require its adoption. Particularly if a terrorist-sensitized Congress got hold of the issue.

Service staffs had expressed great concern over the force assignment issue. The Service Chiefs viewed the "assignment" of forces to STRATSERCOM as a dangerous precedent, the Navy in particular. Service staffs informally recommended non-concurrence based on the possibility that future CINCs could demand the same command arrangements with concomitant loss of service control of component forces.

The change of Chairman over the life of the issue was perhaps the killing blow. In 1982, General Jack Vessey, U.S. Army, replaced General David Jones as Chairman. Though General Vessey was previously the Vice Chief of Staff under General Meyer, he did not view the world in the same terms as General Meyer and General Jones and was inclined to take a much more traditional approach to issues. It quickly became clear to General Meyer that he had no support from General Vessey for the concept. Accordingly, he chose to let the issue die and hope that time would present a favorable opportunity.

This opportunity would eventually appear and General Meyer would be a critical player. In the interim, there would be consistent evidence of the need for a STRATSERCOM structure, General Meyer would be retired, and Congress would take up his torch. This time they could legislate what Meyer was not able to persuade.

PART 7

How We Got to Osama Bin Laden

The Requirements Continue

...but when the hour of crisis comes, remember that 40 selected men can shake the world.

—Yasotay

Throughout the period between the failed Iran rescue in 1980 and the congressional mandate of USSOCOM in 1986, the requirements for SOF employment continued. The National Command Authority, CINCs, and other agencies besieged the military establishment with requests for SOF assistance. The requirements were met as well as the services were able to but not without experiencing the problems that STRATSERCOM was designed to eliminate. Some of these requirements, sampled from the period 1980–83, amply fulfilled the predictions of the Meyer Conflict Probability Model.

1.1980

The ambassador to a vital Central American country does not like what he has been told. A special security team has been briefing him on the necessity of cutting a palm tree on the embassy lawn to permit helicopter landings. The ambassador feels the move would be "provocative" and dismisses the team. Within 60 days, the ambassador is requesting Marine Corps evacuation of his embassy and personally supervises the removal of the palm tree.

2.1981

The Chief of Staff of the Army informs his senior commanders that a personal locator device is available that can either be implanted or placed on some item of clothing. No one is interested. Within a month, General James L. Dozier is kidnapped in Italy. No one knows where he is.

A small counter-terrorist team deploys to Italy to provide technical assistance. The theater commander demands that the team respond to the country team only through his headquarters in Mons, Belgium. The team commander spends the majority of his time carrying messages between the ambassador and CINCEUR as to ongoing actions to resolve the issue. Finally, the ambassador sends a message to CINCEUR, the Chairman of the Joint Chiefs of Staff, and the Secretary of State outlining the authority of the ambassador in his role as Country Team Chief and isolates the team from the theater commander other than by informing. General Dozier is eventually freed by an elite Italian police team.

3. 1982

The ambassador in Lebanon is ambushed along a winding mountain road. Through the bulletproof glass, the ambassador can see both his embassy and the keffiyeh-clad assailants. His security people freeze. Two members of a small Army counter-terrorist team, recently assigned to the ambassador, crash through the ambush and scatter the Arabs. That afternoon, the ambassador urgently requests more Army unit personnel. Soon, other ambassadors are doing likewise.

The ambassador and the Southern Command CINC (CINCSO) desperately seek a means to staunch the arms flow into El Salvador. The CINCSO passes a proposal to the Joint Chiefs of Staff. They inform him that the plan will not work. Not satisfied, he passes the same proposal to the Army Deputy Chief of Staff for Operations, who, in turn, passes it to a small staff section (ODSO) in the basement of the Pentagon. Within three weeks, the Joint Army/CIA element has technical resources and assets in place. The arms flow experiences a dramatic reduction.

A study indicates that a ship would be the ideal platform for both intelligence gathering and operational launching. The Assistant Chief of Staff for Intelligence tells the Chief of Staff that the idea is unsound and won't work. In six weeks, ODSO has purchased the ship, outfitted it and placed it in operation. The program is hugely successful. The Assistant Chief of Staff for Intelligence requests an investigation regarding the procurement, which ultimately validates the methodology.

4. 1983

The Afghan mujahideen rebels indicate that they cannot operate unless the Soviet attack helicopters are kept from the Pakistani border. A method must be found that does not require actual sensitive arms shipments. Army research and development staff requests six months to work on the requirement. Two Army officers draw a concept on a yellow legal pad and take it to a special support branch. In two weeks, the Afghan rebels have an effective weapon. It consists of long Kevlar strings suspended under small helium balloons. The entire system is packed inside a beer can. A Joint CIA/Army team dispenses the cans to the rebels. Three Soviet Hind helicopters are lost to unknown reasons. The Soviets declare a 3-mile buffer zone on the Pakistani border.

Another Federal agency requests the Army to assist in tracking arms shipments into El Salvador. The Army provides a device and certain technical resources. A shipment of M-16 rifles is tracked from Vietnam through Cuba to Panama. From there, they are loaded on an aircraft and flown into El Salvador by General Omar Torrejos' personal pilot. Noted for future action.

Stretched to the breaking point, the El Salvador armed forces cannot defeat the well-organized and coordinated guerilla forces. The ambassador and theater commander request help immediately to stop the pre-election attacks. The Assistant Chief of Staff for Intelligence requests control of the mission but is turned down by CSA when his own staff informs him that they can't meet the need in less than six months. A compartmented Army staff section introduces assets into El Salvador within three weeks, effectively strangling the guerilla control net. The program operates for more than two years and is considered by the regional ambassadors the best investment that DOD made in the region.

Another Federal agency requests immediate assistance in fulfilling a Presidential Finding. Within 48 hours, the Army has assets in place halfway around the world and successfully completes the mission. The team members are awarded the nation's highest non-combat achievement awards. The Air Force requests a formal investigation as to why the Army team failed to request formal support before utilizing a compartmented Air Force asset for covert programs. The internal Air Force investigation concedes the in-place system was rigidly followed.

Satellite photos confirm information that a Soviet-built Hind-D helicopter is abandoned in a North African desert after a crash. Mechanical dissection of the aircraft would be an intelligence bonanza. The Defense Intelligence Agency and the JCS are very pessimistic that diplomatic and military problems can be overcome that will permit access to the crash site. After a week of debate, the JCS, with approval of the National Command Authority, permit an Army element in coordination with another Federal agency to attempt to visit the site (in hostile territory) with technical experts. The Army unit, exploiting personal contacts with a friendly local nation, is on site in 72 hours and returns with a bonanza of critical information.

The Argentines invade the Falklands. The British request extensive U.S. aid which the United States is reluctant to openly provide due to the close relationships that has developed with Argentina. The JCS are tasked to develop a "shopping list" and implementation plan for delivery to the UK. The CSA tasks ODSO to be the central manager of Army assets for delivery. After several meetings at the UK embassy, Viscount Aircraft begin landing at locations throughout the eastern seaboard. Communication links are established with certain British elements. The Army is privately thanked by Margaret Thatcher through the President and a member of the Army SOF community is asked to attend a private thank-you audience with Prince Charles.

A black-and-white photograph taken near the Laotian-Vietnamese border shows a tall, possibly Caucasian man standing in an open field. Scratched out in the earth at his feet is a faintly decipherable sign that could possibly say B-52. Special aviation assets are needed if a rescue attempt is to be made. A compartmented Army staff officer provides the assets in five days, a process that normally requires three months.

During the same operation, a Joint team is prepared to conduct a MIA rescue mission should the intelligence support the risk. Bo Gritz, a retired army officer, attempts to independently deploy his own team into a friendly country and is exposed. The country forbids the U.S. to deploy any forces and expels the adventurer. The mission is canceled.

An ostensibly hostile nation offers the U.S. critical items of Soviet equipment in return for certain U.S. military equipment. The transfer arrangements are complex and involve virtually every U.S. armed service. After extensive debate in the JCS, the Army volunteers to take the mission. Success requires the Marine Corps to give up equipment, the Army to replace it from its own production line, the Army to reduce its NATO war stocks, the Air Force to provide a C-5, the Navy to provide a commercial freighter and the CIA to establish the control mechanism. The Army ODSO division pulls together a complete package in two weeks. With the ship almost in port and the C-5 loaded, the proposal is withdrawn by the foreign nation.

Evolution and Revolution

Those who have opposed these efforts will be strengthened in the arrogant conviction that nobody can make them do what they don't want to do or stop them from doing what they do want to do.

—Mr. Noel Koch commenting on the Department of Defense resistance to implementing SOF reforms

The requirement to "fix" SOF, while it may have died with General Meyer's retirement, did not die as a matter of public interest or congressional involvement. Rather, the pressure continued to build from obvious failings and DOD ineptitudes until Congress passed binding SOF reorganization legislation in 1986. However, that did not settle the problems; it merely fanned the flames and reinforced the military establishment's resistance to externally directed change.

General Meyer knew instinctively in 1980 that SOF needed a drastic reorganization if the United States was to successfully wage the form of warfare that was clearly emerging. Counterterrorism, low-intensity conflict, and peacekeeping missions required a form of organization and a degree of priority that the conventional military structure was not capable of providing. The validity of his conflict model was being proved on a daily basis as the intelligence Black Books made their rounds of the defense leadership.

Recognizing this, Meyer presented STRATSERCOM as a gesture toward needed DOD adjustments. He failed for lack of an internal DOD constituency.

As an internal proposal, STRATSERCOM received no outside publicity and therefore no support that the bureaucracy could not overcome. The only leverage that General Meyer had to apply was his own position that was increasingly weak and ineffectual as his four-year tour wound to its close. The proposition, while not aborted, simply died in the womb.

The Congress was somewhat more successful. They, recognizing the same issues that General Meyer did, pressed DOD to fix the problems. DOD, rather than compromise, resisted to an inordinate but predictable degree, which ultimately resulted in congressionally mandated binding legislation.

Congress was successful because it operated externally to the DOD. Had Congress been unable to gain outside support, the law may never have been passed. However, once raised in the public eye, support for the congressional initiatives became overwhelming.

A constituency for dramatic SOF reform came from many sources. Retired military, former Secretaries of Defense, and Federal officials as well as former CINCs and serving mid-level military staffers all reinforced the Meyer view that Congress had acquired. Because the concept sprang from outside the DOD womb, it was allowed to fully develop. With the problems exposed to public scrutiny as well as the self-defeating DOD responses, the direction and tenor became uncontrollable and the results predictable.

The issue was very poorly played by the military establishment. In a political town, DOD leadership misread the issues, the depth of conviction and the political sensitivities, and overplayed a poor hand. Congress, which was dealing the cards, called the bluff. Had DOD made even a modicum of a commitment toward SOF reforms, the legislation may never have occurred.

The first SOF reform law, a direct result of the Grenada action, was an amendment to the FY87 Defense Appropriation Act passed in October of 1986. This created the U.S. Special Operations Command (USSOCOM), established the organizational mechanics of the program and provided a framework for growth. Establishment, let alone growth, however, was bitterly fought by DOD.

This resistance, clearly felt and appreciated by Congress throughout 1987, resulted in even more restrictive and definitive legislation in October of 1987—the Nunn–Cohen Amendment to the 1987 DOD Authorization Act passed 16 April 1987. This amendment, introduced by Republican Senator William Cohen and Democratic Senator Sam Nunn, was plainly designed to close the loopholes and obfuscatory actions of DOD in delaying implementation of desperately needed SOF reforms.

The second law made no appreciable difference in the actions of DOD except to make minor compromises while continuing to oppose any substantive changes. The history of this resistance and its results is evolutionary and covers a wide spectrum of issues.

Failed Operations and Missed Opportunities

It seems that the members of Congress who precipitated this legislation have been powerfully struck by two contradictory factors: the repeated mistakes and foul-ups which have occurred in recent years, and the tenacious resistance of the bureaucracy to change. And it seems that they are determined to do their part to see that the United States does not unnecessarily repeat the bitter mistakes of the past.

—Mr. Chris Mellon, Staff Assistant to Senator Cohen
(District of Maine) on the congressional perception
of the Pentagon attitude toward SOF reform

Before, during and after STRATSERCOM's bureaucratic "life," special operations requirements continued. Some, such as the *Achille Lauro* and TWA hijacking, were very visible and emotional events. Others, less well publicized, nonetheless left a lasting impression upon the Congress and caused them to take up General Meyer's fallen banner and become committed to the implications of the Meyer conflict probability model.

No single action or incident caused Congress to decide that the binding legislative creation of USSOCOM was necessary. The congressional impetus toward involvement in operational matters was evolutionary in nature. Many things from many directions slowly generated an overwhelming movement toward solving by law what DOD was unwilling to repair on its own accord.

Serious congressional interest began with the failed Iran Raid in April of 1980 and culminated with the relatively minor dispute over support to Air Force special operations aviation funding in September of 1987. The most obvious and emotional SOF issues exposed to Congress were the public terrorist incidents. These, combined with testimony, studies and intuition, turned Congress down a legislative path that it reluctantly but inevitably followed.

Prior to 1986, Congress was relatively willing to observe the various military problems in the SOF area and to register opinions and comments from the sidelines. This was in keeping with Congress' normal and historical reluctance to delve into specific operational military matters or to issue detailed guidance. Beginning in the spring of 1986, this attitude abruptly changed as Congress became increasingly frustrated with DOD's intransigence toward recognizing and repairing severe SOF problems.

The congressional action that opened the SOF Pandora's Box was the effort by Senators Goldwater and Nunn and Congressmen Nichols, Daniels, and Hutto in the course of the hearings concerning re-organization of the DOD—the popularly titled Goldwater–Nichols Defense Reorganization Act of 1986.

The hearings revealed deep and long-standing flaws in the manner in which America's defense was managed. Ultimately, the feeling of Congress was so strong that the "system was broke and did need fixing" that they broke with tradition and passed by a wide margin a restructuring requirement of Department of Defense that rivaled in scope the original 1947 Defense Re Organization Act. Throughout this process, both the civilian and military DOD leadership testified in both open and closed sessions that the proposed law was unnecessary.

A spillover of the Goldwater–Nichols hearings was a review of DOD SOF. Leading the charge was Senator William Cohen and Congressman Dan Daniels. Their in-depth studies, hearings, and analysis coupled with reinforcing material from Goldwater–Nichols, led them to conclude that the DOD management of SOF was even more derelict than its overall management practices. Worse, the SOF deficiencies were routinely experienced in the practical world of failed execution whereas the DOD management failures were partially undeveloped supposition. Nonetheless, the military establishment reacted even more heatedly toward SOF legislation than it did toward Goldwater–Nichols. As a senator said after a particularly heated hearing:

> Dealing with the (military) leadership is like being in a time warp. We try to discuss an operational shortfall or a glaring obvious structural problem and they ignore the issue and talk about what a great job everyone is doing. One of us is blind. Someone must drive them to work in the morning.

In fall of 1986, after six months of hearings, Congress passed a sweeping restructuring of the DOD SOF elements. This Act, commonly called the Hutto Amendment, was attached to the FY87 Defense Authorization Bill. As

good investment. He initiated a program of capability exercises, CAPEXs, to demonstrate SOF to the bill payers.

The CAPEXs, held on the average of one each quarter, demonstrated a variety of SOF counterterrorist skills. Usually attending were major administration figures such as the Vice President and Secretaries of State and Defense and their immediate staff as well as key senators, congressmen, and their staffs. They were duly impressed by the demonstrations, but disturbed by some of the background noise.

Often on the visits, they heard of significant shortfalls in SOF aviation, particularly Air Force fixed-wing. They were exposed to maintenance problems that went well beyond the ability of the unit to resolve. They discerned quality problems with some members of the JSOC staff. Over time, Congress concluded that JSOC and its people were exceptionally competent, but suffered from institutional problems beyond their ken.

With this as background, Congress noted some SOF/counterterrorism successes. Unfortunately, none were American.

Israel had conducted a highly successful raid into Uganda to rescue its hostages at Entebbe. The German counterterrorism unit, GSG9, had rescued an aircraft of hostages in Mogadishu. The British Special Air Service had successfully stormed the Libyan Embassy at Princess Gate in London. Lastly, the Soviets had successfully won release of three hostages in Beirut after their Spetznaz special forces became involved. If they can, why can't we?

Throughout the period, the shadow of Afghanistan played in the recesses of the congressional minds. The rebels had managed to bring the Russian stabilization attempts to a virtual standstill. Initially, without covert U.S. aid, the rebels had not won but they hadn't lost either.

Large segments of technically superior Soviet troops were incapable of defeating the mujahideen. With increasing amount of congressionally approved covert aid, the rebels were able to defeat Soviet units in direct combat and to regain control of key areas.

The aid program began in small amounts in 1980 and grew each year until the level reached a total of $1 billion by 1987. The nature of aid also grew. Initially, it consisted almost entirely of Soviet small arms, but by 1986, it included sophisticated weapons such as Stinger air defense missiles and artillery pieces as well as state-of-the-art tactical communications.

This appeared to be an excellent paradigm for future operations in the Third World. However, considerable testimony with the Intelligence Oversight Committees displayed the traditional inter-service bickering and vacillation that plagued CIA efforts to develop a smooth supporting system.

Later on, in the spring and summer of 1987, Congress saw a darker side of SOF problems at home. The Iran–Contra affair provided a hint of what might happen if covert operations were not systematically controlled, managed, and organized under some form of oversight. The very organizational dispersion of forces and diffusion of responsibility made improper use of SOF a real possibility. As Lieutenant Colonel Oliver North stated in his 10 July 1987 testimony:

> Mr. Casey had proposed establishment of an "off the shelf, self-sustaining, stand-alone entity," that could perform covert political and military operations without accountability to Congress.

Senator Warren Rudman, the Minority Leader of the Iran–Contra committee, stated: "If you carry this to its logical extreme, you don't have a democracy anymore." Lurking behind the senator's statement was a real concern that the CIA would use the military SOF capability as a tool to circumvent congressional oversight and restrictions. This "conspiracy" theory was a key aspect of the hearings as well as the Army special operations trial revolving around the Army "Yellow Fruit" program. Congress felt it imperative that if there was to be a quality SOF program, it would have to be brought under congressional oversight. Ad hoc closet organizations would not be acceptable.

While reviewing the contemporary history of SOF operations, Congress was also exposed to numerous non-operational stimuli. They all pointed toward major SOF organizational shortfalls. Concurrently, many highlighted the absolute intransigence of DOD to recognizing or resolving obvious shortfalls—a restatement of historical tradition.

While the Meyer conflict probability model went from a left to right slope, the DOD enactment of self-directed change was on a reverse climb.

The Battle Joined

This is another type of war, new in its intensity, ancient in its origins—war by guerrillas, insurgents, assassins; war by ambush instead of combat; by infiltration instead of aggression; seeking victory by eroding and exhausting the enemy rather than engaging him.

—John F. Kennedy at West Point, June 1962

It came through loud and clear that he saw a new kind of threat coming for which conventional armies, navies, and air forces weren't ready to fight.

—General Maxwell Taylor commenting on the JFK speech

As 1986 began, a small but very influential group of congressmen and senators began to seriously think of establishing legislative bandages to the SOF/LIC hemorrhage. Senators Goldwater, Nunn, Cohen, Kennedy and Rudman in the Senate Armed Forces Committee and Congressmen Daniels, Nichols, and Hutto in the House worked on diverging paths. Their collective opinion began to coalesce as the creation of USSOCOM became an inevitable event. Over the year, they reluctantly concluded that they not only had a right but a duty to act.

In addition to the operational issues and events previously discussed, they were besieged with other input ranging from testimony to letters to studies to DOD reaction to personal observations. These served as the intellectual and conceptual base for the USSOCOM creation.

U.S. and Soviet Special Operations Study

Commissioned by the Special Operations Panel of the House Armed Services Committee, written by Mr. John Collins and published in April of 1987, the study, commonly called the Hutto Report for the Chairman of the House Armed Services Committee subcommittee, outlined in great detail the relative objective position of U.S. and Soviet SOF forces, their general condition, history and future potential. It served as the conceptual basis of Congressman Dan Daniels' SOF reorganization proposal for a sixth service.

In the introduction, Chairman Hutto outlined the opening salvo on what would be an increasingly dense barrage against the SOF status quo.

> ... virtually every macro/command control, planning, and SOF force posture problem derives mainly from misunderstandings. Few members of the U.S. Government and military establishment fully appreciate special operations threats, capabilities, limitations, and relationships with the rest of our security apparatus.

The study outlined a detailed survey of internal U.S./DOD problems effecting LIC/SOF issues. It particularly highlighted the following:

> Department of Defense is primarily concerned with counter-terrorism and SOF specific items whereas LIC is clearly the greatest long-term threat and the one that Department of Defense/NCA is least prepared to address.
>
> The recently created USSOCOM (Oct 86) is doomed to failure in its present form because it has no budget, there is no coordination at the NSC or OSD level and the senior leaders of the services neither like nor understand the issues.

The conclusion the author reaches is that the SOF command line must be more unified and include control of all SOF forces, the authority and planning apparatus for SOF must involve the highest levels of the military and civilian decision-making apparatus, and quality people must be provided to the organizations.

Following are some key extracts:

> U.S. leaders normally acknowledge a sharp boundary between peace and war (many believe the latter is an aberration, despite conclusive evidence to the contrary), and severely restrict domestic security activities. Traditionalists in charge of our military establishment dislike elites. Those proclivities, in various combinations, account for the low priority U.S. policymakers historically have assigned most special operations. They also limit allowable targets, as well as techniques ...

> AirLand Battle doctrine pays lip service to SOF intelligence, direct action, deception, and PSYOP missions, but the Department of Defense as a general rule slights special operations during mid- and high-intensity conflicts ...

> Uncertain priorities provide a shaky platform for USSOF planners, who cannot be sure which view will prevail. It is also difficult to select personnel and train units, when the popularity of roles changes rapidly. ... Every USSOF component experiences similar problems ...

Future U.S. counterterror capabilities depend on steps to strengthen the control structure, settle conceptual disputes, lift the most debilitating legal limitations, and tighten links with allies. Prognoses based on dissimilar assumptions about "progress" in such respects variously predict improvement, impairment, or project straight lines. All seem premature.

Joint Low-Intensity Conflict Project Final Report

This was an in-house military study on the state of LIC/SOF within DOD and was prepared by military personnel. It was published in August of 1986 by the Joint Air Force-Army LIC Project at Fort Monroe, Virginia.

Initially, the report escaped serious notice by Congress though it was referred to in the initial hearings for the SOF re-organization conducted by the Senate Armed Forces Committee in 1986. With the publication of the Hutto SOF study, it received wider congressional study as a military validation of the problems Hutto indicated.

Its key points were summarized:

> Four themes prevail throughout the report: As a nation, we do not understand low-intensity conflict; we respond poorly without unity of effort; we execute our activities poorly; and we lack the ability to sustain operations.

The press picked up the report in September of 1986 during the height of the hearings on SOF reorganization and used its contents to validate the congressional reform effort. Most widely quoted was:

> ... Petty quarrels among the military services, lack of coordination between civilian and military officials, and a total lack of planning have created an atmosphere that encourages confusion and inaction at best and mistake and blunder at worst. ... We are not now institutionally postured to conduct low-intensity conflict operations ...

Sam Sarkesian Speech

Presented initially as a lecture at the National Defense University in March of 1983, this speech was later published as part of a book and was "must-read" literature during the SOF hearings in 1986. Professor Sarkesian was a political science professor at Loyola University and testified several times on the subject of SOF organization and problems subsequent to the NDU lecture.

Professor Sarkesian accurately described the organizational outcome and necessity of USSOCOM. Equally interesting is that a member of Professor Sarkesian's presentation panel was Mr. Kenneth Burgquist, who protested the structural recommendations. Mr. Burgquist's opposition would later return to haunt him with Congress as his nomination for the Assistant Secretary of Defense Special Operations/Low Intensity Conflict (SO/LIC) was received by the Senate Armed Services Committee.

Dr. Sarkesian presented the structure and rationality for a drastic SOF re-organization within the Department of Defense. He traced the history of U.S. attitudes toward SOF and the very predictable bureaucratic opposition to SOF programs and personnel. He made several recommendations as being essential if the U.S. was to successfully meet its conflict requirements:

- Create a unified command.
- Assign all SOF forces to the command under service components.
- Establish a position of Assistant Secretary of Defense for SOF/LIC matters that reports directly to the Secretary of Defense.
- Establish an LIC coordinating unit at the National Security Council level.

Concurrently, he warned that "… organizational strategy without a conceptual synthesis cannot overcome bureaucratic tendencies, status quo power plays, and organizational mindsets."

The ultimate USSOCOM legislation exactly replicated Dr. Sarkesian's proposals as did the bureaucratic response.

Mr. Burgquist's rejoinder was most indicative of the latter:

- A National Security Council-level SOF representative might not work.
- A unified command would not work.
- Service SOF assets should not be assigned outside of the service.

Mr. Burgquist was later nominated by DOD to be the Assistant Secretary of Defense (SO/LIC) to implement the binding legislation.

Lack of SOF Competence at the Highest Managerial Levels

Throughout the 1986–87 period, Congress received repetitive testimonials on the inadequacy of the DOD SOF establishment and the inability and lack of desire of DOD to correct its own shortcomings. The testimony did not originate from the usual group of anti-militarists or isolated service iconoclasts but from respected lifelong DOD professionals—both civilian and military. They represented the very heart of the defense establishment. This compendium of testimony, exactly parallel to other non-DOD input, was crucial in swaying

Congress' attitude toward enacting binding and non-traditional legislation. The key was a letter from Mr. Noel Koch.

Mr. Koch had served for five years within DOD as the Principal Deputy Assistant Secretary of Defense for International Security Affairs. He was charged with the responsibility of revitalizing SOF within the DOD and was subordinate to Mr. Richard Armitage. In the summer of 1986, he abruptly resigned from his post over disgust with how DOD was handling the Initiative 17 action (the Army would take over the long-range rotary wing SOF penetration mission from the Air Force), as well as other SOF-related issues.

His letter, quoted in part below, was a dramatic statement concerning the attitude of the senior DOD leadership toward efforts to fix glaring SOF problems. It was credited with being perhaps the most important single document to convince the Senate Armed Services Committee that binding SOF legislation was needed to overcome DOD's stubborn intransigence toward fixing glaring shortfalls. As a DOD "insider," he confirmed in great detail what Congress had suspected. His specific details were even more dramatic than the attitude he revealed on the part of the senior DOD leadership.

The letter or the resignation should not have been a great surprise. Mr. Koch, in an *Armed Forces Journal* interview of March 1985, hinted at the major underlying problems that he was ultimately unable to resolve.

> I have argued that the principal failing of SOF is simply that the services ... have little more than an intuitive sense of what those forces ought to be doing ...
>
> If you go back, Kennedy said we needed these forces. And he said we needed a whole new strategy. Grudgingly, he was provided with the forces over an extended time. But there never evolved a strategy to go with them. ... SOF rarely has been used to do what it was designed to do.
>
> ... the number of Combat Talons [MC-130s] that the CINCs plan to have at their disposal is far in excess of the number of Combat Talons that are in the inventory. ... So we've been after the Air Force to increase its inventory, and ever since the need was recognized back in 1980, it's been slipped every year.
>
> ... our national defense strategy ... is woefully deficient at the low-intensity end of the spectrum ...
>
> ... the biggest problem with STRATSERCOM was that the Army invented it.
>
> ... If you look at the services programs ... you'll see that they don't change very much or very fast in their emphasis. The traditional "core" will get funded first and foremost, then the programs that are peripheral to the individual service's core interests, missions, and traditions "compete" for the resources that are left. For the services, SOF has never been a core program.

William Colby Letter

Received in the fall of 1986, the Colby letter was directed toward the House Armed Services Committee and Congressman Dan Daniels' efforts toward

SOF re-organization. It immediately received wide circulation on the Hill and was an important factor in the overwhelming SOF reorganization committee vote conducted less than two weeks later.

Mr. Colby was a retired Director of the CIA, a veteran of the OSS and a key member of the USLIC program in Vietnam. As an old "Establishment" hand, he lent considerable credibility to the congressional SOF initiatives. Key comments were as follows:

> In the ultimate test, does it work? America's special operations have been found wanting. It is long past time to repair them.
>
> The creation of an Assistant Secretary of Defense (SO/LIC) with direct access to the SECDEF will have the benefit of "… lifting him out of the multi-layered military and civilian bureaucracy which has smothered these forces in their parent services …"
>
> The Pentagon has shown little enthusiasm for the idea, of course, consistent with its traditional disdain for elite forces, but it took similar outside intervention by a President, John F. Kennedy, to force it to develop these forces in the first place. These congressional sponsors are showing the same initiative that he did, and the military will be better for it. So will the nation …

The Latham Memorandum

In August of 1987, the Senate Armed Services Committee received a copy of a Memorandum from the recently resigned Assistant Secretary of Defense (Command, Control, Communications, and Intelligence), Mr. Donald Latham. The memo, written upon his resignation from DOD, was directed toward his boss, William Howard Taft IV, the Deputy Secretary of Defense. Mr. Taft was the principal player in all key SOF issues and the manager of the DOD program toward SOF. Mr. Latham, like Mr. Koch, had decided to resign because of his dissatisfaction with the DOD approach to LIC/SOF issues. The memo was hard evidence to Congress that what they had been told about DOD attitudes and techniques regarding SOF issues/directions was true. As a result of this memo as well as other reinforcing information, Congress felt compelled to pass even more binding SOF legislation in the fall of 1987.

General E. C. Meyer (Ret) Input

It is the opinion of many key congressional players of the time that the role of General Meyer was absolutely fundamental to the ultimate decision to pass the original binding legislation in 1986 and the follow-up legislation in 1987. He provided a degree of credibility, insight, experience, and vision unequaled by any other single source.

General Meyer, as Army Chief of Staff, had attempted to fix the SOF problems with his own STRATSERCOM proposal in the wake of the Iran failure. He was intimately familiar with the ways of the DOD bureaucracy and presented a degree of integrity and vision that was unsurpassed.

General Meyer acted at several different levels during the course of the congressional SOF investigations. He testified regarding the proposed legislation, he testified and corresponded on the matter of the nomination for the Assistant Secretary of Defense for Special Operations/Low Intensity Conflict position and was a member of the Special Operations Advisory Group reporting to the Secretary of Defense. Additionally, he routinely met informally with key congressional leaders throughout the process. Simply put, what he said carried great weight. His message was simple and consistent:

- There is no comprehensive LIC/SOF strategy.
- The bureaucracy/services will not create a valid strategy or capability on their own accord.
- There are many traps and pitfalls that the defense establishment will use to dilute and defer any mandated legislation.
- Effective change must be implemented.

Reinforced by the testimony of other senior retired officers and analysis during the 1986–87 period, Meyer's input largely overwhelmed the DOD attempts to put a bright face on a bad situation. Members of the House Armed Services Committee and Senate Armed Services Committee were universal in mentioning the strength and import of the Meyer testimony in convincing them to support strong binding legislation for SOF. Without the bolstering of the retired community, it is doubtful that Congress would have been so confrontational in consideration of the united front presented by DOD.

Goldwater–Nichols Hearings

Throughout the fall of 1985, the Senate Armed Services Committee and the House Armed Services Committee held extensive hearings regarding the re-organization of the DOD. The ultimate result of the investigation was the most sweeping adjustment in the way of "doing business" since the original Department of Defense Organization Act of 1947. The key players for Goldwater–Nichols were the same players that reviewed the problems in SOF and participated in the SOF re-organization acts of 1986 and 1987.

The Goldwater–Nichols hearings validated the congressional perception that the DOD machinery was definitely broken and did need mandated repair. Concurrently, it became quickly apparent to the various committee members that SOF/LIC was being particularly victimized by the overall DOD shortcomings. However, Goldwater–Nichols alone could not fix the SOF organizational problems. Clearly, the fixes had to be separate. The SOF micro-fixes could not be instituted until the Goldwater–Nichols macro adjustments were made.

Beginning the hearing process was a staff report by Mr. Jim Locher of the Senate Armed Services Committee entitled "Defense Organization: The Need For Change." This study, a two-year undertaking, was a truly monumental omnibus review of the entire DOD. It concluded with 16 major findings and 12 recommendations.

As a precursor for the SOF review, the Jim Locher study outlined in painful detail the organizational inability of DOD to resolve its internal problems. These key issues were raised:

- Lack of authority of the Secretary of Defense, the Chief of the Joint Chiefs of Staff and the CINCs.
- The input vice output orientation of the Department of Defense management and resource system.
- Inability to develop competent integrated strategy and advice to the National Command Authority.
- Imbalance between the services and joint requirements that result in continual degradation of joint interests.
- Conflict between readiness and modernization.
- Inadequate mechanisms for change coupled with stubborn refusals by all services to make serious adjustments that reflect needs.

Key recommended changes included the following:

- Abolition of the Joint Chiefs of Staff and creation of a board of retired or very senior military officers to replace the Joint Chiefs of Staff. This board would provide direct military advice to the National Command Authority.
- The board would have a deputy chairman with functional authority.
- The board would provide all views to the National Command Authority, not just an agreed upon viewpoint.
- Each service would create a joint duty career specialty.

- Assign component commanders and their forces directly to each CINC while eliminating the service command authority.
- Eliminate the service secretariats.

Ultimately, the approved bill incorporated the bulk of the recommendations in some form. The overwhelming congressional impression was that the Department of Defense was critically incapable of handling its affairs in an effective manner due to "the system" and its historic inability to internally adjust to evolving needs.

Congress, however, did not fix its collective mind as a result of the study. The supportive testimony provided that resolve. The hearings held between 16 October and 12 December 1985 spanned the breadth of DOD expertise. Previous Secretaries of Defense, Chiefs of the Joint Chiefs of Staff, and Service Chiefs testified as did all sitting senior DOD officials. The breadth of experience and the degree of dialogue was unprecedented in its dissection of the DOD management system.

The retired DOD leadership was strongly in agreement with the general conclusions of the Locher study. While they disagreed with abolition of the Joint Chiefs of Staff, they strongly supported the necessity of a stronger chairman and a greater role and authority for the CINC. Concurrently, they generally agreed that the existing Planning, Programming, Budgetary System (PPBS) was detrimental to efficiency and contemporary needs.

The present DOD leadership, while disagreeing with the study conclusions and recommendations, was decidedly unconvincing in its defense of the status quo. The collective congressional impression was that the Locher study combined with expert experienced testimony had built an irrefutable case for binding legislation.

Key congressmen and senators, exposed to SOF issues in the course of the Goldwater–Nichols hearings, discerned the same problems they had unearthed during the course of the Goldwater–Nichols hearings. The organizational problems were the same. The bureaucratic response was the same. The necessity for legislation was the same.

Army Special Operations Trials

Beginning in the spring of 1986 and continuing in various forms throughout 1987, the Congress was exposed to a series of Army and Federal trials targeted against military personnel assigned to General Meyer's special operations office on the Army Staff, ODSO. These trials, widely reported in the media and occasionally reaching the point of national notoriety, focused attention on Army management and support of SOF issues.

Many articles took the position that the post-Meyer leadership was conducting "payback" for the SOF personnel who had enjoyed great power and influence over the establishment bureaucrats. The Army presented its case as simply trying to clean up irregularities in money and influence.

Assistant U.S. Attorney for Washington, D.C., Ted Greenburg, brought Federal charges against an ODSO member and operator of a covered program entitled Yellow Fruit, Lieutenant Colonel Dale Duncan. Additionally, given near carte blanche authority by the Army to investigate Army irregularities, he swore charges against the Deputy Chief of Staff for Operations and Plans, Lieutenant General Fred Mahaffey and the Assistant Chief of Staff for Intelligence, Lieutenant General William Odom, for obstruction of justice. He forwarded a classified study to the Department of the Army recommending sweeping charges against many Army staff members and outlined what he felt were gross irregularities in how Army SOF did business.

Much of the Greenburg study was leaked to and reported by the media, particularly during the height of the special operations trials in 1986. Concurrently, the Army also conducted its own parallel investigations of SOF irregularities. These too were the leaked subject of media attention. (Both programs were classified.) The articles, reinforced by the trials/hearings created congressional perceptions that Army SOF was in disarray and that the Army leadership was undermining hard won gains. Rather than "exposing improprieties in SOF" as was the Army/Greenberg intent, the issues just further convinced Congress that the bureaucracy was attempting to dismantle SOF—the good as well as the bad.

Ultimately, one NCO was acquitted. No charges were placed against three investigated officers who subsequently resigned. One officer was tried in both Federal and military court and imprisoned (Dale Duncan). The jury chose not to accept the clearly stated cover requirements that Duncan undertook as part of his cover. One officer was tried, imprisoned, and released in return for cooperation and one officer was tried, convicted, imprisoned, and released by the Court of Military Appeals, which accused the prosecution of gross malfeasance of office. All the trials were closed to the public, which heightened the impression that the Army was conducting a "star chamber" trial of its best SOF staffers.

Selected members of the Senate Armed Services Committee were exposed to a declassified portion of an Army 15-6 investigation regarding SOF funding use/abuse. The 15-6 is an Army form of a preliminary grand jury investigation and was conducted by personnel with no previous experience or knowledge of SOF operations.

The 15-6 was an omnibus review of all financial programs within the ODSO program and involved the same people brought to trial as well as other members of the ODSO staff apparatus. The investigating officer, a Finance Corps colonel, personally selected by the Vice Chief of Staff of the Army, spent over a year conducting the investigation.

The 15-6, contrary to the impression left by Army statements and press releases, was generally supportive of the SOF staff. In fact, the report concluded that much of the later, post-Meyer senior leadership was probably at fault for failure to adequately supervise and to provide timely guidance, especially as to the changes in philosophy between Meyer and his successor, General John A. Wickham. It went on to conclude that the conditions surrounding the initial establishment of many SOF programs was as indicated by the defendants and contrary to the view presented by the prosecution. It also noted the thorough accounting by ODSO of the budget growth and necessary legal underpinnings.

It recommended that charges be dropped against several ODSO personnel.

The 15-6 was reviewed by lawyers for the Commander, Military District, Washington, as the investigating officer's superior. They concluded, to the amazement of the Senate Armed Services Committee, that the generals should be exonerated and the subordinates be charged. This further heightened the congressional perception that the military did not really understand or support the type of SOF programs that were essential for contemporary success. As a minimum, the trials and attendant publicity indicated that serious warts existed in SOF and the oversight programs.

Major General Scholtes' Testimony

Major General Richard Scholtes, Commanding General Joint Special Operations Command and Grenada SOF operations, testified in closed session to the Senate Armed Services Committee on 4 August 1987. This testimony, perhaps more than any other single event, convinced Congress that they would have to take drastic measures if the problems in SOF were to be resolved.

General Scholtes testified regarding his experience as the commander during the Grenada rescue operation, Urgent Fury. The hearing was closed to the public. In it, he was measured, neutral, and generally supportive of the events. "We muddled through" was the description one member gave of Scholtes' testimony.

Speaking in the morning, he returned in the afternoon for a lengthy private session with Senators Nunn, Cohen, Kennedy, and Warner at Brigadier General Wayne Downing's suggestion to Jim Locher. He was significantly more detailed and persuasive regarding SOF organizational and operational problems. The information became the primary impetus solidifying congressional sentiment to impose further necessary SOF reforms.

General Scholtes was reported to have made the following points:

- The Joint Chiefs of Staff planning system and input was seriously flawed. He had insufficient time to plan and was prohibited from dealing with key operational elements until late in the process.
- The intelligence was very bad and resulted in poor plans, poor execution and unnecessary loss of life.
- The command lines were poor, unclear to all the players, and resulted in inadequate, confused battlefield management.
- The tactical penetration lift assets were inadequate and caused the initial strike force to conduct sequential rather than simultaneous operations. When helicopters were damaged, the follow-on targets had to be cancelled.
- The integration of all participants was very poor and resulted in serious communications problems between forces and an essentially uncoordinated plan.
- The lack of competent force planning necessitated a change of H Hour, which endangered the primary strike force.
- There was no transition plan between the SOF and conventional forces, which caused unnecessary confusion on D-day and resulted in misuse of some SOF assets.
- The Atlantic Command staff, responsible for the operation, had no SOF expertise and did not appreciate the unique SOF operational requirements.

This testimony was received after lengthy public statements and formal testimony by the military that Grenada had minimal execution problems and that the "system" worked. Congress was left with the impression that either the Department of Defense did not recognize its own deficiencies or that it simply refused to acknowledge their existence. To quote a participant in the Scholtes' testimony, "This borders on criminal neglect. We've got to do something. What in God's name would have happened if they [the Cubans] had a decent defense?"

Senator Nunn, being more polite, commented that the testimony "was profoundly disturbing to say the least." At this point, the Senate Armed Services Committee determined that it essentially had no choice but to decide upon further binding SOF legislation.

SOF Airlift

Between the Scholtes' testimony and the end of September 1987, the SOF reorganization bill took a back seat in terms of congressional interest as the annual budget battles unfolded. It took a relatively minor Air Force decision regarding SOF airlift funding to push the reorganization back into the spotlight.

Since Desert One, SOF aviation had been a topic of great interest on the Hill. Of particular significance was the necessity to modernize the aging Air Force MC-130 (lift), AC-130 (guns) and EC-130 (communications) SOF penetrators.

The MC-130 and its variants is a highly sophisticated aerial refuellable aircraft designed to carry and support SOF personnel deep into enemy territory. During the Iran rescue, there were only seven such aircraft in the entire Air Force inventory. As this was inadequate, three "vanilla" refuellable EC-130s were "borrowed" from the national command, control, and communications assets at Kessler AFB. One was lost at Desert One.

In the aftermath of the rescue attempt, Air Force promised that it would enhance and upgrade the MC-130 fleet, the last aircraft having been received in 1968. At $30 million apiece, upgrading required serious Air Force tradeoffs with high visibility tactical fighter aircraft. During each budget cycle between 1980 and 1987, Air Force performed the decrement dance.

The Air Force would place one or two MC-130s "above line" (funded) in the initial budget programs. This would be accompanied by several public pronouncements of support for SOF aviation. As the process became more definitive, the "above line" MC-130s would quietly be slipped to the "program" (unfunded) years, without publicity.

Concurrently, the Air Force could not make up its organizational mind regarding the place of SOF airlift. The Air Force SOF airlift unit, the 1st Special Operations Wing at Hurlburt Field, Florida, gravitated between Tactical Air Command and Military Airlift Command. The state of maintenance of the Special Operations Wing was well-below Air Force average due to low maintenance priorities. Not only did the wing have a hard time finding a home in the Air Force, it had a very difficult time getting spare parts in its changing mailboxes.

The Senate Armed Services Committee, observing this program each year, began to harden its attitude toward the Air Force and DOD SOF airlift programs. By the beginning of 1986, patience had run out. Senators Goldwater and Nunn wrote a very direct letter to Secretary of Defense Casper Weinberger. These specific comments are notable:

> We are particularly concerned that six years after the tragedy at Desert One, we appear to have made few significant improvements in this essential capability. … It is discouraging to note that today we have exactly the same number of MC-130 Combat Talon aircraft (14) … as we had at Desert One, and two fewer HH-53 Pave Low helicopters than we had in May of 1980 (seven today, compared with nine in 1980).

> The apparent failure of the Department of Defense to overcome existing shortfalls in a timely fashion raises serious questions regarding the department's ability to establish priorities …

This situation continued through the summer of 1987 and did not go unnoticed. In exasperation, Senator Nunn sent another letter to Secretary Weinberger in August. This letter, even blunter than the 1986 correspondence, was intended to terminate the decrement dance in favor of the SOF operational needs. Its key points were as follows:

- No improvement had been made in SOF airlift requirements since Desert One in spite of Air Force statements of support.
- The Secretary of Defense would be required to certify that the SOF programs would be funded.
- Until the certification was received, certain critical Air Force program funds would be sequestered.

Secretary Weinberger provided the certification to the Senate Armed Services Committee. Six weeks later, Senator Nunn and the Senate Armed Services Committee were informed that Air Force had reprogrammed SOF aviation procurement funds into other programs. At this point, late September, Senator Nunn indicated to Senator Cohen, the bill's sponsor, that the SOF reorganization amendment to the FY87 Defense Appropriation Bill should be pursued. DOD had burned its last bridge behind it.

The very definitive nature of the SOF reorganization ran totally contrary to congressional history and tradition. There was no "pork" involved in the bill. It was a politically innocuous issue for the Congress and it ran against the tradition of congressional avoidance of delving into operational military matters. Yet it was sponsored with emotion and passion by those congressmen and senators exposed to SOF issues over the 1980–1987 period.

The collective congressional wisdom was that they not only had a right to pass the act but a duty—a duty that became ever more clear as the evidence of DOD ineptitude, disregard for the obvious, and avoidance of reforms became apparent. However, DOD did not stand idle while its house was being attacked.

The Pentagon—Action and Reaction

For every action, there is an equal and opposite reaction.

—Newton's Third Law of Motion

We didn't cope with irregular warfare in Asia ... and rather than recognizing that we didn't learn our lessons, we are turning back again in the hope that the next war will be a conventional war.

—Lieutenant General (Ret) William Yarborough

All the white corpuscles are running to the source of infection.

—Anonymous White House Official

By January of 1986, Department of Defense was aware that there was an increasing sentiment on the Hill for binding SOF legislation. Concurrently, DOD recognized that it couldn't completely stonewall the issue as service budgets would be held hostage. The defense of the status quo began to take several forms.

The first was a continuous flow of testimony that problems were being recognized and being worked upon but that time was necessary and Congress shouldn't "tinker" with a delicate system. The second approach was to execute several internal SOF reorganizations in the hope that that would stave off binding legislation.

Supporting testimony for DOD SOF efforts came from several elements of the Executive Branch. Principal defenders were John Poindexter and Richard Armitage.

Poindexter, National Security Advisor to the President, sent a letter to the Senate Armed Services Committee on 1 October 1986, in which he said in part:

> ... you should not conclude that management and oversight of sensitive operations have been neglected in the past. I can assure you that this is not the case, and that personnel and coordinating groups within the NSC have supported the President's participation in such matters on a continuing basis. ... I urge you to reconsider the need for restrictive detailed legislation on this sensitive issue. If the conference agreement contains

> mandatory language, it would present potential constitutional problems because it would impermissibly limit the President's authority as Commander-in-Chief.

A review of Article I and Article II of the Constitution by the Senate counsels disagreed with the admiral's interpretation of constitutional law. Mr. Armitage, the Assistant Secretary of Defense for International Security Affairs, repeatedly testified throughout 1986 that directive legislation was unnecessary and would be counterproductive. He asked for time to fix internal problems and promised substantial adjustments. Unfortunately, the DOD internal reforms, when closely reviewed, convinced Congress that they had received hollow testimony.

It was clear to DOD by the summer of 1986, that it would have to make a substantive organizational change of its SOF structure to avoid legislative direction. Prior to 1986, DOD had attempted two SOF organizational efforts. Neither organization was viewed by Congress as meeting the need.

The first organization, proposed in 1983 to the Secretary of Defense, would create a SOF sub-command under Readiness Command at MacDill AFB. That effort was so patently inadequate that even the Office of the Secretary of Defense rejected it as insufficient. A second JCS proposal in 1984 was more successful. It created the Joint Special Operations Agency (JSOA).

JSOA was created as a two-star directorate within the JCS, subordinate to the J3. It had no assigned forces and a small staff. Its job was to "coordinate" SOF issues and to provide the interface between JSOC and the joint staff. It had no operational or command responsibilities. It was hoped that JSOA would quiet critics who contended that JSOC and its forces had no "voice" in Washington and that there was no planning capability above the tactical level.

Between its creation and 1986, there was a rising crescendo external to DOD that the "fixes" were not working. Real-world operational failures coupled with continued indicators that planning and management was mediocre at best caused widespread press comment and external demands for change. Adding to the fire was the revelation that the SOF SEALS could not deploy to the *Achille Lauro* because three separate aircraft broke down. The assignment of a non-airborne qualified armor officer with no SOF background as the new JSOA commander did not add credibility to DOD's efforts.

Recognizing the inexorable pressure for change and the inevitability of its occurrence, DOD developed an SOF reorganization plan in January of 1987. This plan was viewed by external sources as inadequate and a cosmetic attempt to avoid the binding legislation which had to be enacted by April.

The key points of the Department of Defense restructuring of the Joint Special Operations Agency were as follows:

- The name of Joint Special Operations Agency was changed to the Special Operations Forces Command (SOFC).
- The commander would be upgraded to a three-star position.
- While he would still remain subordinate to the J3, he would have coordination authority with the Assistant Secretary for Special Operations and Low Intensity Conflict.

Critics immediately pointed out the inadequacy of the changes and the obvious attempt to maintain the service turfs and control of SOF elements while avoiding implementing the FY87 directives.

The SOFC Commander still remained subordinate to the J3, a staff officer. He had no direct access to the Secretary of Defense and reported to Richard Armitage who was on record as opposing SOF management reforms. Further,

- The commander was a three-star who could act on a basis of equality with neither the CINCs or the Service Chiefs.
- SOFC had no resource authority.
- SOFC had no assigned forces. Moreover, SOFC exercised no function during a crisis other than passing information between the JCS and JSOC.

Almost immediately, Congress received testimony from retired military and knowledgeable civilians that the changes were inadequate and cosmetic. The Special Operations Advisory Group was virtually unanimous in its opinion that the efforts were short sighted and inadequate. In March of 1987, they formally told the Secretary of Defense the organization was flawed and that continued Department of Defense support for such measures would be a disservice.

Mr. Noel Koch was even harsher in his criticism in a letter to Senator Cohen in September of 1987.

> The Special Operations Force Command offers nothing we do not already have in the neutered JSOA if JSOA had been permitted to do its work, if the excellent work it did do had been taken seriously, and if it had been permitted the necessary level of proponency. … The Director of the Joint Staff insisted that the Director of JSOA didn't have to fear being plowed under by his superiors. He did, and he was …
>
> I do not believe the system which leads to such abuse is capable of correction by the individuals who run it. The proposal put forth by the Pentagon for addressing the current situation is very near to a prima facie case of contempt of Congress, and its own best argument for strong legislation.

By the spring of 1987, DOD had attempted three separate internal SOF reforms. Each was viewed as a cosmetic half-way measure to solve serious problems. Each attempt was increasingly viewed by Congress as an effort to circumvent the will of Congress and the widespread call for serious SOF reforms. These actions served only to harden Congress' resolve that DOD was incapable of self-reform and that they would have to become intimately involved and directive to fix the pressing problems.

On 15 October 1986, Congress passed the first of two pieces of binding SOF legislation. The second, reinforcing legislation, was passed in October of 1987. Both were amendments to the Defense Appropriation Acts of each respective year.

The first amendment was passed as a result of incontrovertible evidence that DOD had serious SOF problems it would not fix. The second was passed in consideration of equally strong evidence that the military establishment had no intention of willingly enacting the first.

The Law

Well, you know, terrorism is an easy thing to ignore.

—Said to me by the Director of the Joint Staff

However grim the circumstances, the system is incapable of self-correction even in its own self-interest.

—Noel Koch

By the fall of 1986, both houses of Congress were pursuing parallel SOF reorganization paths. Congressman Dan Daniels introduced a bill that would create a National Special Operations Agency—a sixth service. On the Senate side, Senators Nunn and Cohen introduced a bill designed to "enhance the capabilities of the U.S. to combat terrorism and other forms of unconventional warfare."

The Senate proposal embodied three key points:

- It created a unified command exclusively for SOF.
- It created the position of the Assistant Secretary of Defense for Special Operations/Low Intensity Conflict.

It recommended that the President create an SOF coordinating board on the National Security Council

Both the House and Senate propositions were a significant departure from history. The House version totally bypassed the JCS and placed a civilian in charge of a military command.

The Senate approach, while maintaining conventional staff and command lines, was the first attempt by Congress to establish a military command in law. Further, it delved directly into Executive Branch prerogatives regarding staff management. Both propositions were an accurate reflection of the concern and despair felt by the Congress in getting meaningful voluntary change from the defense establishment.

The House and Senate met in joint committee session to develop a compromised SOF reorganization. On 2 October 1986, a compromise was reached and what the Department of Defense would not do, Congress mandated. The amendment, attached to the FY87 Defense Authorization Act, contained eight key provisions.

It established the position of an Assistant Secretary for Special Operations and Low Intensity Conflict (SO/LIC). He would report directly to the Secretary of Defense and provide civilian interface and oversight for Department of Defense SO/LIC programs.

It created a Unified Combatant Command for SO/LIC to be commanded by a four-star flag general or flag officer. It directed that all active and reserve SOF elements be assigned to the headquarters.

A Major Force Program category was established for the Command and its elements. Force Program 11 (MFP 11) would create program visibility for SOF forces and permit line item inspection by Congress.

Special operations Commanders would be assigned to both the European and Pacific combatant commands and they would hold flag or general officer rank.

A Sense of the Congress was established recommending that the President designate a Deputy Assistant to the President for National Security Affairs for Low Intensity Conflict. This would provide a capability to centrally manage Executive Branch LIC programs.

The Secretary of Defense was required to submit to Congress not later than 120 days after date of enactment, a plan on how DOD would implement the law. Further, the President was required to report within one year to Congress, not the Armed Services Committees, the state of SOF/LIC programs.

Lastly, the President was required to activate the Unified Command headquarters within 180 days.

The Intent

The logic and language of the law is best understood in the context of the congressional objectives that gave birth to its creation. Senator William Cohen, the Senate sponsor, introduced the proposal as embodying the following points:

1. Provide close civilian oversight for LIC activities;
2. Ensure that genuine expertise and a diversity of views are available to the National Command Authorities regarding possible responses to LIC threats;
3. Improve interagency planning and coordination for LIC, and;
4. Bolster U.S. special operations capabilities in a number of areas, including joint doctrine and training, intelligence support, command and control, budgetary authority, personnel management, and planning.

Senator Cohen's introductory comments paid homage to several hard facts of bureaucratic life on both sides of the Potomac. Low-intensity conflict and SOF/counterterrorism operations absolutely required interagency coordination to be successful. Failure to do so had been repetitively demonstrated. Further, LIC was viewed as requiring a long-term strategy and resourcing through "country teams" that could only be coordinated at the national level. This necessitated a National Security Council-level mechanism for White House policy coordination.

The administration proposal for a three-star command was inadequate in that a three-star officer would not have direct access to the National Security Council. Further, with lesser rank and without equal status in the Unified Command Plan, the three-star commander would have minimal influence and authority on what was obviously becoming a high probability conflict problem.

A military command without direct civilian leadership would have neither the political foundations nor oversight requirements necessary to successfully manage the resources and requirements deemed appropriate.

Lastly, the agreed upon bill reinforced the concurrent Goldwater–Nichols Defense Reorganization Act. It established a clear chain of command and provided for a strong war fighting CINC with a distinct mission. It made the Joint Chiefs a servant of USSOCOM rather than superior to it.

Necessity Breeds Invention

As unusual as the direction of the law was, the specificity was even more so. The Joint Explanatory Statement, issued by both House and Senate conferees on 2 October 1986, provides insight into Congress' view of Department of Defense's attitude toward internal changes in the face of mounting necessity.

> The conferees determined that there are serious deficiencies in the capabilities of the U.S. to conduct special operations and to engage in low intensity conflicts ... the conferees determined that legislation is necessary to overcome the unending resistance in the Department of Defense to necessary organizational and other reforms of special operations forces.
>
> The conferees carefully considered the degree of specificity to include in this provision. Although several elements of this provision are more specific than may normally be expected in legislation, the conferees determined that the seriousness of the problems and inability or unwillingness of the Department of Defense to solve them left no alternative ... The conferees determined that the failure to act forcefully in this area and at this time would be inconsistent with the responsibilities of the Congress to the American people ...
>
> ... the conferees agreed to require that authorized revisions of the programs and budgets approved by the Congress for SOF be made only by the SECDEF after consulting with the commander. This mechanism is designed to protect SOF funding from reallocation

> by the Military Departments. ... this mechanism was necessary to counter the low priority that the Military Departments have traditionally assigned to SOF funding and the tendency of the Departments to shift such funding to meet their higher priorities.

Clearly, Congress saw a need to fix a badly broken mechanism of national power projection. Concurrently, they saw over time, that the defense establishment was simply unwilling to make the bold necessary internal changes. Further, it was clear to them that DOD would go to great lengths to prevent changes from occurring above its bureaucratic pain threshold. Congress was to learn that there is a long leap between passage of a law and its implementation, particularly implementation within the spirit of congressional intent. This situation would breed deeper resentments, more hardened resolve on both sides and culminate in an even more binding piece of legislation in 1987.

Let the Games Begin

You guys think you can tell people what to do, but if they don't want to do it, they're not going to do it.

—Said to me by the Director, Joint Chiefs of Staff

We recognized the danger to our security associated with this erratic fiscal support and fragmented management of SOF, and, in partnership with the Congress, moved to institutionalize SOF within Department of Defense. ... we look forward to continuing our partnership with the Congress in sustaining our SOF capability in the 1990's.

—Secretary Carlucci, SOF Posture Statement

Hold until relieved.

—Major Howard's orders for Pegasus Bridge, 6 June 1944

As history would predict, regulations and reality do not always follow parallel courses at the higher echelons of government. Every SOF wound that Congress attempted to bandage continued to bleed and fester between the enactment of the original amendment in 1986 and its follow-on strengthening legislation in 1987.

While the military establishment might have invoked Emperor Hirohito's guidance to "endure the unendurable," it did not do so. Unlike the Japanese, the bureaucracy did not accept the situation but continued to fight its interpretation of bureaucratic seppuku.

From the moment of the SOF enactment, DOD unleashed a panoply of defenses to inhibit directed change. The primary focus of these efforts centered on the Assistant Secretary of Defense position, the headquarters location, SOF airlift, and the bedrock issue of the budget. Virtually every ploy in the bureaucrats' inventory was exercised.

This was quickly detected by Congress who maintained the pressure on the Joint Special Operations Agency but remained largely unsuccessful in seeing its intent come to fruition. Finally, in disgust, Senator Cohen, acting for the Congress, added another more strengthening amendment to the original SOCOM organization as part of the FY88/89 Defense Authorization Act.

The key items were that the budgetary authority of the CINC was even more clearly spelled out as well as the role and functional duties of the Assistant Secretary of Defense. Additionally, the Secretary of the Army was directed to fill the position of the Assistant Secretary of Defense until a nomination had been confirmed. The reason for this additional legislation was clearly laid in the lap of DOD and its inability to conduct meaningful compliance or change.

> The conferees agreed that insufficient progress has been made by the Department of Defense in implementing the reorganization of SOF mandated ... The conferees decided that congressional action was necessary to remove a number of bureaucratic obstacles to meaningful progress. The action of the conference committee reaffirms the commitment of the Congress to correct serious deficiencies in the capabilities of the U.S. to conduct special operations and to engage in low intensity conflict.

> As was the case last year, the conference committee was forced by bureaucratic resistance within Department of Defense to take very detailed legislative action in mandating the urgently needed reorganization and reform of special operations and low intensity conflict capabilities, policies, and programs. The conferees recognized that their recommendations represent a degree of specificity that, under normal circumstances, should be avoided in legislation. In this instance, however, Congress could not acquiesce to efforts in Department of Defense to delay or block implementation of the law—the conferees expressed their willingness to continue to play an extremely active legislative role until such time as the congressionally mandated reorganization and reform are fully and effectively implemented.

Despite the reinforcing legislation, the same battles were fought by DOD on the same issues over the 1987–88 period. The issues are still not resolved.

National Security Council Policy Board

The NSC Policy board was established. However, no principal assistant was named. The board remained moribund and produced no direction or management that could be discerned.

Headquarters Location

The location of USSOCOM became either an emotional or a substantive issue depending upon the view. The SOF law did not direct a headquarters location. However, this quickly rose to a leading issue.

External retired military and the majority of interested Congressmen and Senators had hoped that USSOCOM would be established in the Washington,

D.C., area. The Special Operations Advisory Group formally stated its views in a letter to the Secretary of Defense in March of 1987:

> ... we feel that had we been consulted we would have recommended against the placement of USSOC at MacDill AFB, Florida. It is our view that, given the sensitivity, political/military character, and importance of the challenges to which USSOC will have to respond, the command should be located in the Washington D.C. area.

The feeling of the non-DOD personnel was that the unique requirements for LIC and counterterrorism operations demanded ready access to the Washington, D.C., agencies and decision-making apparatuses. Experienced retired military felt that if the CINC were not present within the D.C. area, he would fall victim to the classic bureaucratic ploy entitled the "Key West Solution," given a flag and a phone book and never asked to speak and hopefully forgotten.

The counter argument placing the headquarters in the old Readiness Command facilities at MacDill AFB, Florida, centered around fiscal realities and operational needs. General James Lindsay, the first USSOCOM commander stated:

> Many in Congress would have preferred to see the headquarters placed here in the capital region, but by locating in Tampa, we were able to use the facilities and a selected pool of experienced and qualified joint staff officers of the disestablished readiness command to form the nucleus of the new command. ... By staying in Florida, we have left those things which need to be taken care of in Washington to our Washington office and the Pentagon staffs while keeping our own headquarters staff free to deal with operational and resource issues.

Cynics took a different tack. Experienced Washington watchers felt that a USSOCOM at MacDill was the bureaucratic equivalent of Siberia. Should the CINC be in Washington, he would have the opportunity to routinely meet with the Secretary of Defense, very senior officials and possibly the President during the course of the business day and during the all-important social life of the capitol. This would provide great potential to overturn or circumvent the bureaucratic management of SOF issues and isolate the senior military leadership from the ultimate decision-making process.

A one-star liaison in the Pentagon could be viewed with a jaundiced eye. The brigadier general would not have open access to senior leaders. He certainly would not be considered as having the same weight of testimony as the CINC himself. And, he would be interested in future promotion—a point his own service might not overlook.

Assignment of Forces

What should have been straightforward and without rancor became a very divisive issue regarding the SEAL inclusion under USSOCOM. The problem went to the core of the traditional Navy approach to control of forces.

The original intent of all players, including Congress, was that the Navy SOF elements, the SEALs, less SEAL Team 6, the counterterrorism force, would remain under Navy control. Accordingly, SEAL teams were assigned to Commander-in-Chief, U.S. Pacific Fleet and Commander-in-Chief, U.S. Atlantic Fleet.

Upon review, it became evident that USSOCOM could not fulfill its charter unless all SOF elements were assigned to the headquarters. This issue was raised in the JCS by General James Lindsay and was strongly objected to by the Navy and Navy Secretary John Lehman. General Lindsay did not back down and Congress became aware of the issue by the spring of 1987.

DOD supported the position of the Navy and rather than support a debate, simply stated the desired situation as fact without comment. The Assistant Secretary of Defense (ISA), Richard Armitage, indicated the strategy in a statement before Senator Kennedy's Force Projection Sub-Committee of the Senate Armed Services Committee on 1 April 1987.

> With the exception of the Naval Special Warfare Groups, all SOF stationed in the U.S. will be assigned to USSOCOM, including the JSOC ...

> Naval Special Warfare Groups currently assigned to the U.S. Atlantic Command and U.S. Pacific Command will remain assigned to their respective CINCs.

The committee felt that this was an unacceptable arrangement in light of the operational requirements and mission taskings of USSOCOM. Accordingly, Senators Kennedy and Warner specifically requested, in a 19 May 1987 letter to Secretary Weinberger, that the SEALs be assigned to USSOCOM. No specific reply was received on the subject.

By the fall of 1987, the SEAL issue had become a major bureaucratic battle. The Secretary of Defense and his principal on the issue, Richard Armitage, had been besieged from external sources with demands that the SEALs be passed from CINCPAC and CINCLANT to USSOCOM. Equal pressure was applied by the Secretary of the Navy and the Chief of Naval Operations that this must not happen.

Congress was also marshaled by the navy lobby in an attempt to forestall compliance. Several people contacted friendly Senators and Congressmen and asked them to bring pressure to bear on the Secretary of Defense to prevent SEAL reassignment. Leading the charge was Senator John McCain from Arizona, an ex-naval aviator and POW in Vietnam.

He both called the Secretary of Defense and wrote a letter explaining the problems with SEAL assignment to USSOCOM. Additionally, the Secretary of Defense received numerous letters and calls from people supportive of the navy position throughout the August–September 1987 period.

They cited the needs of the war fighting CINCs for the SEALs and indicated that compliance would violate the spirit of Goldwater–Nichols by reducing CINC influence and capability.

Finally, just prior to his resignation, Secretary Weinberger penned a personal note at the bottom of an implementing directive assigning the SEALs to USSOCOM. His margin comment was reportedly, "I want this to happen."

Informed of the decision, the Chief of Naval Operations and the Secretary of the Navy confronted the Secretary of Defense, who confirmed the reassignment. Shortly after Mr. Carlucci's elevation to Secretary of Defense, Navy Secretary Jim Webb requested that Mr. Carlucci overturn the Weinberger decision. He did not grant the request.

Preventing assignment of naval forces to any element that was not a naval headquarters had reached the level of a sacred duty with the Navy. Historically, the Navy has jealously guarded having its forces used for anything other than "in support of" non-naval elements. This is contrary to Army and Air Force practice where they routinely subordinate elements to the local theater commander.

At the height of World War Two, President Roosevelt found it necessary to divide the Pacific Theater in half, giving half to General Douglas MacArthur and half to Admiral Chester Nimitz to prevent a catastrophic breakdown in strategy execution. Contemporaneously, the byzantine command relationships being exercised in the Persian Gulf are an accurate depiction of the bedrock naval refusal to permit forces to be subordinate to anyone not wearing a Navy uniform.

The Position of the Assistant Secretary of Defense (SO/LIC)

The issue of the SEALs, however, was minor compared to the severe combat waged over the issue of a civilian Assistant Secretary of Defense.

Whereas the SEAL issue affected only one service, capitulation on the Assistant Secretary of Defense could have a mortal effect on the entire JCS and service efforts to retain control of SOF issues.

The FY87 SOF Amendment directed that Department of Defense create a position of an Assistant Secretary of Defense (SO/LIC) and specified that he have direct access to the Secretary of Defense. Further, it stated that he would be directly in the reporting chain for CINC SOCOM. If enacted, this would create several problems for the bureaucracy.

Firstly, it gave SO/LIC visibility and influence beyond the range of the Joint Chiefs of Staff. Secondly, it provided a superior civilian voice that could interact with the mandated SO/LIC Advisory Council on the National Security Council, which could provide executive direction of SOF policies beyond the control of DOD. Thirdly, it gave the CINC and his programs the capability to circumvent the JCS/services normal control mechanisms. Opposition by the defense establishment took two forms, organizational and nominative.

On 20 February 1987, the Office of the Secretary of Defense formally complied with the mandated requirement to report on progress regarding the implementation of the SOF reorganization. In it, the Office of the Secretary of Defense stated that it could not create a separate Assistant Secretary of Defense as Title 10, USC, limited Department of Defense to 11 Assistant Secretary positions. Instead, it recommended that the position be subordinated to the Assistant Secretary of Defense (ISA), Richard Armitage. Further, it indicated that the position was being filled on an interim basis by Mr. Larry Ropka and a 54-man staff working from offices in Rosslyn.

The Special Operations Advisory Group, asked by the Secretary of Defense to comment after the fact, did so in March of 1987. Signed by General (Ret) E. C. Meyer, it stated in part:

> We would suggest that its overall tenor is embarrassingly and disappointingly tentative. This is true for what is contained in the report and even more so for what is omitted. ... We believe that the apparent cause of this delay [in implementing the law] could be fairly attributed to the attitude regarding SOF prevalent within Department of Defense that precipitated this legislation in the first place.

> We feel strongly about the failure ... to nominate the ASD. The reasons stated ... is an argument that, if valid, should have been made last October when the law was enacted and brought up at this time. This appears to be a way of delaying the establishment of a viable OASD (SO/LIC) for several months. ... The proposal to staff half of the 54 billets assigned to the ASD again puts the cart before the horse. In our opinion, the ASD nomination should be made as expeditiously as possible independent of the Title 10 issue. Also, we note that a staff of 54 is approximately half the size of other offices of like rank and its projected placement in Rosslyn can call into question Department of Defense's resolve in meeting even the minimal requirements of legislative intent.

The Meyer letter was an accurate summary of the congressional and retired DOD leadership reaction toward the initial Office of the Secretary of Defense ploy. No specific action was undertaken by Congress in reply, though the Kennedy Sub-Committee held hearings in April on the overall SOF reorganization subject.

On 1 April, Assistant Secretary of Defense (ISA) Richard Armitage, indicated to the committee that

> We are establishing the ASD (SO/LIC). … The recommendation for the ASD(SO/LIC) will be forwarded to the President by mid-April …

In an apparent bow to mounting pressure regarding the location of the ASD offices, he went on to say,

> Once established, the ASD and his Principal Deputy will be located on the E ring of the Pentagon with the other ASDs … The remainder of the organization will be located in Rosslyn due to space limitations within the Pentagon.

Despite the testimony, no nomination was forthcoming and the Acting Assistant Secretary of Defense, Mr. Larry Ropka, a subordinate to Mr. Armitage, continued to work with his partial staff from Rosslyn. By May, Congress was thoroughly disgusted with the DOD opposition to implementing the Assistant Secretary of Defense provisions, and Senators Kennedy and Cohen sent a blistering letter to Secretary Weinberger on the subject.

The Secretary informally replied that a nomination would be forthcoming soon and the hold on statutory nominations was lifted as a good faith gesture in early July.

Two candidates were under serious consideration during this period. One, Kenneth Burgquist, was working within OSD and another, Bill Cowan, was on the staff of Senator Rudman, Republican from New Hampshire. A third candidate, Mr. Larry Ropka, never received serious consideration due to his close association with Armitage and his unfailing support of the "no change, nothing is broken" bureaucratic argument to SOF fixes.

Cowan was a retired Marine Corps Lieutenant Colonel with extensive SOF background. He had worked in the secret Army intelligence organization, ISA, and as part of Mr. Noel Koch's office of Principal Deputy to the Assistant Secretary of Defense (SO/LIC) responsible for SOF affairs under Mr. Armitage. He had a solid SOF reputation and was known as an independent thinker with strong principles.

Mr. Burgquist was the Deputy Assistant Secretary of Defense (Manpower and Reserve Affairs) and had been employed by the CIA. He was a close friend of Mr. Armitage and often spoke on SOF issues.

By early June 1987, it was common knowledge that Burgquist had the inside track on the nomination though no formal announcement was made. This began a sub-rosa war on the Hill.

A number of senior retired military objected that Burgquist was unqualified for the position and would be a clone of Mr. Armitage, who was on record as the spearhead of the DOD opposition to the binding legislation. Further, Burgquist himself was on public record as opposing the entire SOF reorganization and the Assistant Secretary of Defense position in particular. The Sarkesian lecture comments at the National Defense University in 1983 were liberally quoted as well as more recent statements.

The Special Operations Advisory Group, and others, believed that retired Lieutenant General Sam Wilson would have been the best choice. Several very strong letters were transmitted to key congressional leaders opposing Burgquist and recommending Wilson. Strongest among these were letters from General (Ret) Bob Kingston, ex-CINC U.S. Central Command, a very experienced SOF commander, and Lieutenant General (Ret) William Yarborough, the first Special Forces commander.

By July 1987, no nomination was formally made and Congress was increasingly impatient with DOD stonewalling on the nomination as well as implementation of the rest of the law.

Mr. Donald Latham, Assistant Secretary of Defense (Command, Control, Communication And Intelligence), resigned on 17 July and accurately summarized the congressional feeling in a memo to the Deputy Secretary of Defense, William Howard Taft IV.

Unfortunately for himself, Mr. Burgquist did not step aside from the fray. As information came to him regarding the nomination, he took the offensive. He phoned several members of Congress and wrote letters to others. He attempted to counter the arguments and to impugn the critics and the opposition candidates, Mr. Cowan in particular. By September, Congress was thoroughly sick of the Burgquist affair and reached the same conclusion as Shakespeare's Queen Gertrude who says "The lady doth protest too much, methinks."

Particularly noxious was an attack on Cowan by Burgquist in a letter to Senator Warren Rudman and an unspecified attack on Senator Kerrey. In October 1987, Senator Kerrey exercised his parliamentary rights and placed a hold on the nomination on the floor of the Senate. This effectively delayed any formal hearing and served to cast Burgquist's judgment in doubt.

The hold meant that a formal hearing on Burgquist would be moot. Accordingly, the Senate Armed Services Committee did not act on the nomination and it adjourned for Christmas. By law, this meant that the White House would have to re-submit the nomination in the new calendar year for approval. This provided an opportunity for a more amenable nomination to the Assistant Secretary of Defense position. However, early on in this period, Congress, in an attempt to break the deadlock, took corrective action.

On 15 October, Congress passed the second supplemental bill to strengthen USSOCOM and to overcome some of the blatant OSD intransigence to implementing the provisions of the original law. A key provision was that until an Assistant Secretary of Defense nomination was approved by the Senate, the Secretary of the Army would be the Acting Assistant Secretary of Defense. This was done to circumvent the continued subordination of Mr. Ropka to Armitage and to provide the CINC with a strong supportive voice during the critical budget and organizational issue battles.

Though this action provided some relief for the problem, it was a temporary measure. Throughout the fall period, several key senators attempted to gain Secretary Weinberger's support to withdraw the nomination and to substitute a more suitable candidate. They were unsuccessful.

When Frank Carlucci replaced Caspar Weinberger as Secretary of Defense in December, this was viewed as an opportunity to break the logjam. Carlucci paid an informal courtesy call to key members of the Senate Armed Services Committee in January. During this meeting, the Burgquist nomination was broached with Carlucci in the hope of convincing him to alter the selection. Mr. Carlucci made no commitment though he expressed some concern regarding the senators' negative attitude toward SOF implementation steps by the Office of the Secretary of Defense.

In January 1988, several senior people approached White House Chief of Staff Howard Baker to change the nomination. Recognizing that the White House would have to re-submit a nomination for Assistant Secretary of Defense as the original had not been acted upon within the calendar year, it was hoped that a new name could be speedily confirmed. This was not to be.

In mid-February, the White House informally notified the Senate Armed Services Committee that a nomination would be forthcoming. The nomination was to be Mr. Charles Whitehouse, previously ambassador to Thailand and a career diplomat. As of mid-March, the nomination had not been formally offered.

Ultimately, the Assistant Secretary issue became a test of wills. The Office of the Secretary of Defense did not want an Assistant Secretary with separate access to the Secretary of Defense or who would be a civilian lever for the CINC that could circumvent JCS and service control steps. Congress, well-schooled in the ways of bureaucratic manipulation, wanted exactly those capabilities in the position.

The Office of the Secretary of Defense attempted to fight the issue with alternative propositions, then offered a person who would most likely comply with the institutional desires rather than the intent of Congress. Finally, the White House removed the initiative from its subordinate and nominated an individual (retired Ambassador Charles Whitehouse) who appeared to be an independent actor acceptable to the Hill. Unfortunately, even if approved, he would have less than six months of effective service before a new administration took over. Perhaps by the strange rules and values of the Washington bureaucracy, DOD had "won."

The Budget

Perhaps no single item of the SOF reorganization has been such an object of rancor as the USSOCOM budget authority. This is the bedrock issue for the success or failure of the SOCOM reorganization.

The heart of DOD and the ultimate primal function of each service is to gain resources. Under the Planning, Programming, and Budgeting System, the battle is fought with three services competing through the Secretary of Defense for congressional approval. Under the Department of Defense reorganization Act of 1947, only defense "agencies," defined as the service entities of the Army, Navy, and Air Force, could develop and execute a formal budget.

The war-fighting CINCs, with assigned service component combatant forces, were totally dependent upon each service chief to provide the resource wherewithal. Control of the budget was the most jealously guarded and protected of all service prerogatives.

Under the Planning, Programming, and Budgeting System, there was no requirement for a concerted DOD budget strategy with tradeoffs between services or mutually supported programs. Each service made its own decisions and its own tradeoffs independent of the greater strategy.

Goldwater–Nichols attempted to adjust this lack of strategic vision. By requiring the CINCs to be involved in the Defense Review Board process as well as during the budget "building" process and by requiring separate budget testimony from the CINCs, Congress hoped that CINC needs would receive greater influence in the system.

Reinforcing that approach, the SOF Reorganization Act of FY87 attempted to create a CINC "with a checkbook." Further, it provided a blank check to re-program funds into SOF programs. The intent was battled with the greatest passion by Office of the Secretary of Defense.

Giving a CINC the same budgetary status as a service would totally undermine the control mechanisms of the services. They would have to provide resources at a directed level for forces assigned to SOF. This would be a particularly bitter pill in that SOF had historically "not been a core program." Traditionally, when service cuts were made, SOF led the way; with checkbook clout, CINC USSOCOM could terminate that philosophy.

From the Secretary of Defense level, the prospect of another member at the Defense Resources Board table was decidedly unsettling. Gathering a budget consensus between three services was difficult enough; adding a fourth player could be unmanageable. Worse, if the system worked, every CINC would have grounds to become part of the budget decision-makers; then all semblance of control by OSD and the services would terminate.

In sum, if CINC USSOCOM had his own budget, he would be successful in executing the intent of Congress. Without it, he would be bureaucratically neutered. Little wonder that this issue became the most vicious and terminal.

The initial DOD approach to the CINC budget issue was to ignore it, with polite references to developmental inclusion. However, the CINC headquarters were clearly not invited to the basic service budget processes.

Congress created Program 11 for SOF, which set up a joint U.S. Special Operations Command to leverage the capabilities of the services, and provided for Major Force Program 11 (MFP 11), a dedicated funding mechanism for special operations that is independent of the services

As the budget system went through its process from January to September, USSOCOM was not invited to participate in the service developments. Forced to do detective work on the nature of the SOF budget, USSOCOM estimated that it could only identify approximately 85 percent of funding by August, the final period before the Defense Resources Board review. In this manner, the services could feel free to reprogram or cut true SOF funding without raising visibility. Even when identified, SOF funding was cut with impunity, violating the requirement for prior consultation with CINC SOCOM.

During the 1987 budget decrement scrub, the Defense Resources Board was directed to make a 10 percent cut of the DOD budget. SOF, with 2 percent of the total budget, took a 10 percent cut. Particularly hard hit was SOF aviation, the heart of the long-standing battle between Congress and DOD.

In 1984, the Army and Air Force had agreed in Program Decision Memorandum 17 (Initiative 17) that the Army would take over the long-range rotary wing SOF penetration mission from the Air Force. This meant that Army would have to purchase the MH-47E helicopter as the penetrator of the future and Air Force RH-53 Pave Low helicopters would convert to solely sea-air rescue birds. As 1986 evolved into 1987 and the resource implications of the switch became known, both sides became less and less enthusiastic.

Finally, before the decrement Defense Resources Board session, the Army unilaterally cut out the MH-47E program as well as the CV-22 tilt rotor Osprey, the alternative aircraft. After several phone calls from Congress and external sources, the Secretary of the Army, John Marsh, directed that Army restore the MH-47Es. This created great consternation within the Army and the Office of the Secretary of Defense PA&E (a Pentagon budgetary agency), the budget gurus: now the Army would have to make internal tradeoffs from non-SOF aviation programs such as the Apache attack helicopter and LHX programs in particular.

Finally, in the January Defense Resources Board, it was agreed upon after spirited exchanges between CINC USSOCOM and the Army, that Army would purchase 17 MH-47Es in FY88 and the remaining 34 over the next four years. This would meet the validated need for 51 MH-47Es. The Army Posture Statement submitted to Congress in March 1988, reflected five MH-47Es in FY88 and a total of only 17 through five years. This did not go down well.

Throughout the 1987 period it was apparent to most observers that DOD had no intention of providing CINC USSOCOM a budget. Repeated queries regarding when the headquarters would have a budget were met with comments that the CINC wasn't ready for a budget yet, implementing guidance, was being developed and that the system was very "delicate."

With backs to the wall after very pointed congressional queries, DOD money managers reluctantly exposed their strategy. Particularly revealing was an exposition by a senior member of the Office of the Secretary of Defense budgetary agency in January 1988.

> It's a question of legal interpretation. We have a position from the General Counsel that says we have fulfilled the legal requirement of the Act by providing for CINC participation in the Defense Resources Board process, by having his input during the formulation, and by identifying the SOF lines within each Service. We do not interpret the Bill to require that CINC SOCOM have the same budget authority or participation in the same sense as a Defense Agency. If Congress meant that to happen, then they should have said so. We have no plans now to expand the USSOCOM budget role beyond what it already has. Even if we gave them a separate budget, he doesn't have the people to run it ... We would

be very hesitant to include the CINCs at the same degree of participation as the Services. The system simply could not handle it. It is difficult enough to manage three voices let alone a roomful of equal voices ... SOF has a highly vocal but small lobby on the Hill that doesn't really appreciate what we have done. It is my impression that they are primarily focused on counterterrorism and don't really understand all the issues.

We have heavily involved the CINCs in the budgetary process but there is only so far we can go and still preserve the system.

The Office of the Secretary of Defense position was not unique. The senior Army money manager, Major General Richard Woods, echoed the budgetary agency concept.

We have received no implementing guidance for a USSOCOM budget and do not plan any deviations from our present approach until directed to do so ... SOF issues are highly visible and sensitive with a vocal lobby on the Hill. While they are important, we don't think they are more important than basic Army issues—particularly in a time of declining resources.

If SOF issues are important, Congress will fund them. I can't see decrementing the Army base programs for what is essentially a deviation from the direction the main army is going.

This attitude remained totally unchanged throughout the period between the original FY87 amendment and the further strengthening established by the FY87 amendment. DOD was simply not going to permit CINC USSOCOM to have a budget authority separate and distinct from the services.

A review of the FY88 amendment makes the intent of Congress crystal clear on the budget issue. The Secretary of Defense was to ensure that "the commander of SOCOM receives sufficient forces to discharge his responsibilities ... particularly his responsibilities involving development and acquisition ... and management of resources for special operations as a separate budget activity."

Further, the Secretary of Defense was to "specify that the SOCOM commander have authority to exercise the functions of the head of an agency under Chapter 137 of Title 10" and that he may "conduct internal audits and inspections of purchasing and contracting actions through the SOCOM inspector general."

Despite the blinding clarity of congressional intent, DOD was simply not going to provide USSOCOM a direct budget authority. As of the budget hearings in March of 1988, USSOCOM was still dependent on each service to resource its assigned forces. Both sides realized that once the CINC received direct budget authority, the ability of DOD to resist would be dramatically reduced—hence the depth and duration of the resistance.

Epilogue—The Irony of it All

The irony of the USSOCOM legislation is that Congress had no original intention of enacting it. It was only through the perceived rigid intransigence of DOD that Congress was forced to pass a law that went contrary to all historical tradition against involvement in operational matters. Congress had hoped that the threat of binding legislation would be enough to cause DOD to make the needed SOF reforms.

The compromise efforts were never made to a degree that felt adequate. Congress felt it had no choice but to legislate needed improvements in consideration of DOD's stubborn refusal to repair obvious problems.

From the failed Iran Raid in 1980 until the spring of 1987, Congress was content to send informal messages and comments to DOD that it was unhappy with SOF programs and to suggest adjustments. A convergence of impatience and bureaucratic requirements arose in May 1987 that forced Congress' hand.

The Senate Armed Services Committee and the Readiness Sub-Committee of the House Armed Services Committee drafted proposed SOF reorganizations for DOD. The Senate Armed Services Committee developed a dual track strategy, one based on bureaucratic necessity and one on subjective but fervent desires.

The House Armed Services Committee bill would create a sixth service for SOF. This ran contrary to the direction the Senate was taking on its Goldwater–Nichols Defense Re-Organization Act and would undermine its efforts to strengthen the role of the CINCs and the Chairman. But, without an alternative SOF proposal, the Senate would have little leverage when Congressman Dan Daniels' sixth service proposal went into Joint Committee. The Senate Armed Services Committee proposal would provide a suitable parliamentary device.

By writing draft binding legislation, the Senate Armed Services Committee hoped that it would send a sufficiently strong message across the Potomac to force meaningful change within DOD. Should the Pentagon provide some positive effort toward problem resolution, the intent of the Senate Armed

Services Committee was to drop its legislation, drop the Daniels legislation and satisfy the subject with a Sense of the Senate resolution on SOF of a non-binding nature. Following a traditional path, the Senate was hoping to use the USSOCOM proposal as a tool of compromise rather than a club.

In what was perceived by the Hill as a Neanderthal-like series of responses, DOD refused to pick up the gauntlet. Still, it did not seal the proposal's fate; it took a precipitate, deliberate act on the part of the DOD to accomplish that.

Throughout the summer of 1987, the Congress and DOD kept at loggerheads. DOD, attempting to stave off legislation and satisfy congressional interests, offered several organizational changes as proof of positive intent. The proposals for the restructuring of the Joint Special Operations Agency were viewed as bureaucratically protective, inadequate to the need and an affront to obvious requirements.

The proffered Joint Special Operations Agency, headed by a three-star and subordinate to the J3, Joint Chiefs of Staff, was viewed as an organization with no effect on the overall problem. Senior retired military consistently testified publicly and in private informal meetings that the DOD changes were inadequate to the need. The Commander, Joint Special Operations Agency, had no assigned forces. He was subordinate to the J3. He had no access to the Secretary of Defense. He was vulnerable and beholden to promotion whims.

The DOD changes were viewed as a smokescreen to protect bureaucratic turf, service fiefdoms, and avoidance of necessary changes. However, the USSOCOM Bill was not placed in the hopper over Joint Special Operations Agency, but over the relatively inconsequential issue of SOF aviation.

A major limiting factor in the Iran raid was the availability of refuelable SOF MC-130s in combination with the mechanically unreliable RH-53 Sikorsky helicopters. In the aftermath, the services and the Joint Chiefs promised quick corrective action to ensure more and better airlift. Concurrently, the theater CINCs consistently emphasized the need to upgrade the aged and limited SOF aviation fleet.

Consistently, the services would not fund the upgrades and the Secretary of Defense would not force them to do so. The traditional ploy utilized by the Air Force in particular and by the Army in part was to play the Planning, Programming, Budgetary System violin.

During the budget developmental process, SOF aviation would be indicated as an "above line" funded issue accompanied by appropriate public statements of support. Once the final budget battles were joined but while discretionary choices still remained within the services, SOF aviation would be slipped to "below line" issues. In the event that DOD was required to make tradeoffs, the services consistently offered SOF aviation as an item to be cut to make budget levels.

Between the Iran rescue and the final passage of USSOCOM, not a single new MC-130 was produced, in spite of vehement statements by Air Force of its support to SOF aviation. Despite the contrary noise level, SOF airlift was consistently funded in the "out years," apparently never to be programmatically realized.

In early 1986, Senators Nunn and Goldwater requested that Department of Defense submit a Five-Year Plan to upgrade SOF aviation. The upgrade would reflect the DOD validated SOF requirement. As eloquently testified by Mr. Noel Koch, the request was studiously ignored or sidestepped.

Impatient with the tactics of ignoring and delay, Senator Nunn sent a formal letter to Secretary Weinberger in September of 1987 requiring the Secretary to certify compliance with the Five-Year Plan. The Congress would sequester funds from certain critical Air Force programs until the certification was made.

Several attempts were made by the Secretary's office to work with the Senate Armed Services Committee to eliminate the requirement and to plumb the depths of congressional intent. These met with a solid rebuff. Accordingly, in September of 1987, the Secretary certified that the Five-Year Plan would be accomplished. The sequestered funds were released.

Six weeks later, Congress was informed that much of the SOF aviation funds were undergoing reprogramming actions out of SOF aviation.

A key senator, when informed of this by a staffer, picked up a notebook, slammed it against the wall of his office and said in a loud voice, "Son of a bitch! That's it!" USSOCOM was shortly passed as binding legislation within the FY87/88 Defense Appropriations Act.

The Department of Defense, instead of shoving the glass aside, took a deep draught of its own hemlock.

The above account is a compilation of first person congressional interviews. The information is a consistent representation of their statements. They have requested to remain unnamed.

From the Phoenix to the Product

On May 1, 2011, Osama Bin Laden was killed by a special operations force, probably the only force that could have achieved such an outcome.

This was not the end of the rise of SOF as a valued part of the defense establishment, but it was, as Churchill stated, surely the end of the beginning.

The disaster of Desert One worked as the catalyst that made the outcome of 1 May possible. All the aspects and elements that grew out of Project Honey Badger were physical contributors to the assault force success.

SOF Intelligence elements pinpointed with exceptional accuracy, the location of the target personality.

The assault force trained with diverse inter-agency support and participation that had been honed over many years subsequent to Goldwater–Nichols and Nunn–Cohen Amendments to SOF structure and support.

SOF aviation elements carried and supported the force to and from the objective over diverse terrain and stealth to and from the objective.

Joint SOF and interdepartmental headquarters synthesized all intelligence leading up to the operation, assigned joint SOF elements to the task and finally oversaw the operational aspects of the strike operation itself.

The forces and capabilities that have been created, while represented by the Osama Bin Laden strike, were underwritten by the Americans who perished at Desert One. The operational successes, post Osama Bin Laden, are partially but not completely known. And that is a good thing. Exposure is not a benefit for such people or programs.

That which has been exposed illustrates that the Iran rescue attempt was truly a good thing.

SOF Chronology

To fully appreciate the history of this period, it is necessary to re-acquaint oneself with pertinent facts bearing on the issues.

1980

- SOF Department of Defense budget $441 million.
- Department of Defense and Air Force validate requirement for 12 new MC-130s.
- Initial aid buildup in El Salvador.
- Between 1980 and 1987, over $1 billion provided as significant aid to Afghanistan. $1.2 billion through FY86.

March

- Ambassador Puzzoli refuses security improvements to embassy in Managua, Nicaragua.

April

- Failure at Desert One.

May

- Holloway Board makes presentation.

June

- Secretary of Defense institutionalizes SOF/counterterrorism forces in Department of Defense structure.

October

- HQ Joint Special Operations Command activated; General E.C. Meyer develops STRATSERCOM proposal.

1981

- Congress authorizes Department of Defense to assist in drug interdiction; Task Force 160, Army SOF aviation unit formed.
- Initial CSA-directed SOF Mission Area Analysis (MAA).

March

- Second SOF MAA.
  – CSA directs "wedge" funding of Army SOF assets/restructuring.
- SeaSpray SOF aviation unit organized.

April

- U.S. ambassador in Lebanon ambushed/escaped.
- President signs *National Security Defense Directive #17* that outlines aid program for Contras at a level of $19.5 million.

December

- General Meyer presents STRATSERCOM proposal to Service Chiefs in the "Tank."
- General Dozier kidnapped.
- Air Force funds for 12 MC-130s in FY83/84, later slips funding to "out" years.

1982

January

- Initial free elections in El Salvador.
- First Contra strikes in Nicaragua.

March

- General Dozier rescued.

April

- Falklands Campaign begins.

May

- Department of the Army Special Operations provides initial support to El Salvador/Honduras.

August
- Bashir Gemayel returned to Beirut by covert U.S. Army forces dispatched to Beirut.

October
- General Vessey becomes Chairman, JCS.

1983

January
- Noel Koch tasked by Secretary of Defense to brief counterterrorism issues to Joint Chiefs of Staff and to develop a command plan.
- CIA hires PR firm in Miami for the Contras.

March
- John Marsh sends letter to Caspar Weinberger expressing concern regarding influx of SOF requirements from CIA to Department of the Army without clear legal guidelines.
- National Defense Special Operations Symposium. Dr. Sam Sarkesian presentation.

April
- OSD directs that Joint Chiefs correct SOF deficiencies by 1991
- President Reagan publicly christens the Contras as "Freedom Fighters."
- Neil Koch briefs Joint Chiefs Ops Deputies on counterterrorism deficiencies.
- U.S. Embassy in Beirut bombed July.
- Kissinger Central American Commission formed.
- Department of the Army operation "Yellow Fruit" initiated.

August
- Filipino politician Benino Acquino assassinated.
- U.S. famine relief workers in Ethiopia kidnapped.
- U.S. joint exercise Big Pine begins in Honduras.
- Contra/CIA strike against Nicaraguan POL facilities.

October
- Joint Chiefs initiate internal study on terrorism.
- Marine barracks at Beirut bombed.

- Grenada student rescue initiated.
- Joint Chiefs propose SOFC Command as a sub-command at Readiness Command.
- Yellow Fruit program halted by DA.

1984

- Air Force and Army sign Initiative 17 on transferring SOF aviation to Army.
- CIA initiates major operational endeavors in El Salvador. CIA mines Nicaraguan harbors.
- Joint Special Operations Agency created within Joint Chiefs of Staff.

January

- SOCPAC/SOCEUR positions created.
- Kissinger Commission report released February.
- USS *New Jersey* shells Lebanon.

March

- CIA Station Chief in Beirut, William Buckley, kidnapped.

April

- President signs National Security Decision Directive (NSDD) #138, which outlines terrorism as a threat to national security and outlines plans and needed improvements.
- President signs NSDD #124, which outlines actions to be taken against the Sandinistas.
- President determines that drugs are a threat to national security and authorizes Department of Defense to increase support to drug interdiction.

May

- Duarte elected in El Salvador.

July

- Venezuelan airline hijacking.

August

- Libyan Embassy shootout in London continues until September.
- Army begins 15-6 investigation of Department of the Army special ops funding.

- Boland Amendment passed that halts CIA aid to Contras.
- North–Secord "Enterprise" initiated.
- Congress authorizes "sophisticated" weapons aid to Afghan rebels.
- NSDD signed outlining U.S. policy toward low-intensity conflict in Philippines.

November
- Kuwaiti airliner hijacked in Iran.

December
- Air Force SOF aviation priority is placed #59 in Air Force budget.

1985

- Air Force recognizes requirement for 21-MC 130s, does not fund in "near term."
- House Armed Services Committee requires Air Force to submit SOF aviation master plan.
- 900 deaths attributed to terrorism.

March
- Noel Koch article in Armed Forces Journal on SOF issues.
- El Salvador elects a legislature.

April
- NSDD directs major increase in Afghan aid.

June
- Hijacking of TWA airliner to Beirut.
- General P. X. Kelley directs Marine Corps upgrade of SOF.
- Congress approves $27 million in aid to Contras.

August
- Rome airport bombing.

October
- *Achille Lauro* terrorist hijacking.
- Locher Study on Department of Defense organization to Senate Armed Services Committee.

- Sense of the Congress on the necessity for Department of Defense to better manage SOF issues attached to FY86 budget.

November
- Goldwater–Nichols Defense Reorganization hearings held by the House Armed Services Committee and Senate Armed Services Committee through Christmas.

1986
- Command and General Staff College publishes FC 100-20, Low Intensity Conflict.
- SOF budget for Department of Defense is $1.2 billion.
- Army SOF trials begin.

January
- Caspar Weinberger opens Low Intensity Conflict (LIC) conference at Fort McNair.
- Joint Air Force/USA Center for Low Intensity Conflict (CLIC) established.
- Secretary of Defense speech on LIC.
- Secretary of State speech on LIC.
- Goldwater–Nunn letter to Secretary of Defense expressing concern over lack of support to SOF aviation.

February
- Filipino President Marcos flees to Hawaii.

March
- Air Force announces $3 billion Five-Year SOF aviation upgrade.
- Stinger ground-to-air missiles are sent to Afghan rebels.
- Russell article in *Military Logistics Forum* published attacking Air Force failure to support SOF aviation needs.
- Department of Defense announces $4.3 billion SOF aviation upgrade and validates 34 MC-130s needed by 1991.
- Disco bombed in Berlin.
- Libya bombed by U.S.

May

- Senator Cohen introduces original USSOCOM organization bill in Senate.
- Congress approves $100 million for Contra aid.

July

- President approves concept to mount a rescue of hostages in Beirut.
- CJCS, in Senate Armed Services Committee testimony, proposes a three-star JSOA as a "trial balloon."

August

- Joint Low Intensity Conflict Report published.
- Boland Amendment lifted.
- General (Ret) Meyer letter to Senator Cohen on SOF reorganization.

September

- Press coverage begins on Joint LIC Report.
- Pakistan airliner hijacking.
- Noel Koch letter to Senator Cohen.
- Bill Colby letter to House Armed Services Committee.
- Senator Nunn statement on Senate floor condemning Air Force SOF aviation support.

October

- Plan for a hostage rescue in Beirut cancelled.
- Poindexter SOF testimony to Senate Armed Services Committee.
- Joint House–Senate Explanatory Statement on FY87 SOF Reorganization Amendment.
- FY87 SOF Reorganization enacted in law.
- Defense Resources Board directs reduction of SOF aviation programs to $1.5 billion. SOF upgrade will be based on modifications of existing aircraft rather than new buys.

November

- *Armed Forces Journal* article on SOF reorganization.
- *Al-Shira Magazine* reveals arms for hostages deal.
- Oliver North fired by President.

1987

- Department of Defense SOF budget is $1.7 billion.

February

- Department of Defense submits mandated report to Congress on its progress in implementing the SOF reorganization law.
- Department of Defense proposes a three-star Special Operations Forces Command (SOFC) as an alternative to USSOCOM.

March

- Special Operations Advisory Group letter to Secretary of Defense criticizing Department of Defense actions in failing to implement SOF reorganization.
- P-11 funding program designator established to track SOF resources.

April

- John Collins publishes SOF Study for House Armed Services Committee.
- House Armed Services Committee opens SOF hearings.
- USSOCOM activated.

May

- Kennedy–Cohen letter to Weinberger placing a hold on confirmation actions until an Assistant Secretary of Defense (SO/LIC) is nominated.
- Army 15-6 results changed by Commanding General, Military District of Washington.

June

- President establishes LIC Board on NSC.
- President signs tasking the Executive Branch to develop a unified national strategy for LIC.

July

- Iran–Contra hearings begin.
- Latham Memorandum to Deputy Secretary of Defense Taft outlining reasons for congressional distrust of Department of Defense on SOF issues.

August

- Major General (Ret) Scholtes, retired JSOC commander, testifies in closed session on Grenada SOF problems.

September

- Senator Nunn sends a letter to Secretary of Defense on failure of Department of Defense to support SOF aviation.

October

- General (Ret) Kingston letter to Senator Cohen on Assistant Secretary of Defense (SO/LIC) necessary qualifications.
- Lieutenant General (Ret) Yarborough letter to Senator Cohen recommending Lieutenant General (Ret) Sam Wilson as Assistant Secretary of Defense.

November

- Task Force 160 attacks Iranian minelayer in Persian Gulf.
- USSOCOM strengthened with additional legislation in FY 87 Defense Authorization Act.

1988

- SOF budget is $2.5 billion or 1 percent of total Department of Defense budget FY88-92 (budget proposal is $10.5 billion).

January

- Defense Resources Board supports providing USSOCOM 17 MH-47E helicopters in FY88 and a total of 54 by FY92.
- Department of Defense publishes SOF posture statement.

February

- Army budget reflects support of 5 MH-47Es in FY88 and a total of 17 by FY91.
- General Lindsay testimony to House Armed Services Committee.

Joint Task Force Organization

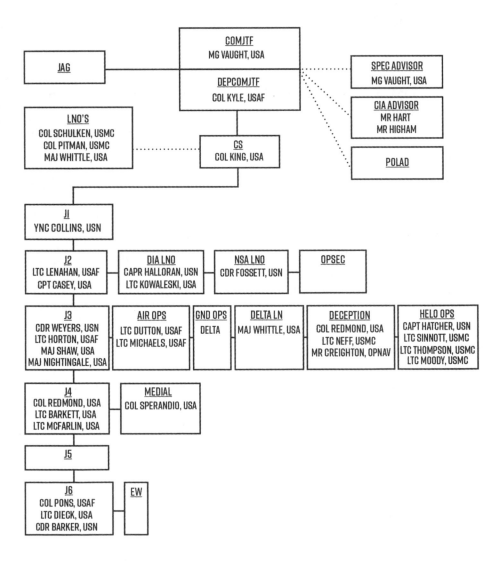

COMJTF
MG VAUGHT, USA

DEPCOMJTF
COL KYLE, USAF

JAG

SPEC ADVISOR
MG VAUGHT, USA

CIA ADVISOR
MR HART
MR HIGHAM

POLAD

LNO'S
COL SCHULKEN, USMC
COL PITMAN, USMC
MAJ WHITTLE, USA

CS
COL KING, USA

JI
YNC COLLINS, USN

J2
LTC LENAHAN, USAF
CPT CASEY, USA

DIA LNO
CAPR HALLORAN, USN
LTC KOWALESKI, USA

NSA LNO
CDR FOSSETT, USN

OPSEC

J3
CDR WEYERS, USN
LTC HORTON, USAF
MAJ SHAW, USA
MAJ NIGHTINGALE, USA

AIR OPS
LTC DUTTON, USAF
LTC MICHAELS, USAF

GND OPS
DELTA

DELTA LN
MAJ WHITTLE, USA

DECEPTION
COL REDMOND, USA
LTC NEFF, USMC
MR CREIGHTON, OPNAV

HELO OPS
CAPT HATCHER, USN
LTC SINNOTT, USMC
LTC THOMPSON, USMC
LTC MOODY, USMC

J4
COL REDMOND, USA
LTC BARKETT, USA
LTC MCFARLIN, USA

MEDIAL
COL SPERANDIO, USA

J5

J6
COL PONS, USAF
LTC DIECK, USA
CDR BARKER, USN

EW

Eagle Claw: What Happened

WHAT HAPPENED

The Plan

- First night: USS *Coral Sea* decoys Soviet "trawlers" away from USS *Nimitz* (carrying eight RH-53D Navy minesweeping helicopters to be used for the mission).
- Three Air Force MC-130E Combat Talons take off from Masirah Island (Oman) carrying the Delta Force, accompanied by three EC-130E aircraft that carry fuel bladders to refuel the helicopters at a rendezvous called Desert One.
- One MC-130E lands at Desert One and sets up navigation aids for the remaining force. Radio silence is maintained.
- Remaining fixed-wing aircraft arrive and drop off Delta Force. EC-130Es remain to refuel helicopters.
- Fixed-wing aircraft depart Desert One for Masirah, where MC-130E crews board other aircraft for transport to Wadi Kena, Egypt. There they ready themselves for the second night when they are to transport an Army Ranger force to secure Manzariyeh airfield, Iran, where hostages will be extracted by C-141s.
- Helicopters depart Desert One and drop off Delta Force at Desert Two, a hide site 50 miles southeast of Tehran and then proceed to their own hide site elsewhere.
- Delta Force meets with in-country agents at Desert Two led by Dick Meadows, providing trucks for overland movement to a warehouse in Tehran where they will laager.
- Delta Force moves to the embassy compound (while a Special Forces team goes to the foreign ministry) and has 45 minutes to extract the hostages. Incomplete intelligence makes the extraction process difficult, requiring the clearance of 27 acres and three facility complexes.
- Hostages and escorts move across the street to a soccer stadium to meet with the helicopters for lift to Manzariyeh airfield, while being covered by

an Air Force AC-130 gunship. The possibility of Iranians gaining a position to hinder the helicopter extraction is an ever-present concern.

- MC-130Es deliver Rangers to Manzariyeh airfield to hold it and prepare for arrival of C-141s (from Saudi Arabia), and hostages in helicopters from Tehran. Other AC-130s provide covering fire.
- Hostages arrive at Manzariyeh airfield by helicopter and depart in C-141s with Delta Force. Helicopters are destroyed in place.
- Carrier-based fighters provide suppression of any Iranian Air Force activity during the extraction process.
- Air-to-air refueling provided as needed on return trip.

The Mission

After five months of planning and preparation, the *Eagle Claw* participants were deployed for mission execution. Just after 1900 on the 24 April 1980, the eight helicopters (called "Bluebeard") departed from the *Nimitz*, nearly 60 miles off the coast of Iran. They had been preceded by the EC-130 refuelers ("Republic") and the MC-130s ("Dragon"), carrying Delta Force, from Masirah.

Less than two hours into the mission, Bluebeard 6 had an indicator light warn of a main rotor blade spar crack. The crew landed (followed by Bluebeard 8 with Colonel Pitman) and decided to abandon the helicopter after inspecting the rotor blades. The two crews flew back to the carrier.

Penetrating deep into Iran, the fixed-wing contingent ran into a phenomenon called a "haboob," fine dust particles that obscured vision. A short time later they ran into another haboob that was much more intense than the first one. Colonel Kyle attempted to warn the RH-53s, but had no luck with his communications gear. While these presented minor obstacles to the airplanes, they upset the cohesion of the helicopter flight, which had to disperse in order to avoid collision.

The MC-130s and EC-130s arrived at Desert One after midnight without mishap and waited for the helicopters, over an hour past their scheduled arrival time. A Ranger team and Delta troopers set up security around the site and immediately had problems. A bus full of Iranian civilians had to be stopped and detained as it was passing through, and a fuel truck (probably run by smugglers) was shot with a LAW rocket when it refused to stop. In the light of the burning fuel, the raiders could see the driver escape in a pickup truck that was following the tanker.

Six helicopters out of the original eight made it into Desert One. However, Bluebeard 2's secondary hydraulic system indicated failure, and Lieutenant

Colonel Seifert made the call that it was "no go" for that helicopter. With only five helicopters left, Colonels Beckwith and Kyle were forced to conclude that the mission could not go on, as six had been the agreed minimum needed for the operation. A disappointed Kyle radioed General Vaught (who was headquartered at Wadi Kena) and Washington recommending mission abort, return to base and go the following night. Vaught recommended approval of the plan to President Carter and Carter agreed. Vaught instructed Kyle, per previous plan, to return all forces to the respective bases and be prepared to launch the next night. Due to distance, this required the helicopters to take on more fuel than they had, taking only enough to run the Night Two mission, which was relatively short legged.

As the force prepared to depart, Bluebeard 3 helicopter hovered into Republic 4 EDC-130 and started a conflagration that spread to other aircraft and killed eight Air Force crew. In the confusion, Kyle made sure that all the live personnel were accounted for, released the Iranian civilians, and loaded up the surviving C-130s to evacuate the area. Unfortunately some of the helicopters could not be reached for "sanitizing" and their classified material (including names of Iranians working for the Americans) fell into the hands of the revolutionary government.

After takeoffs, the remaining C-130s returned to Masirah.

Aftermath

After the failure of *Eagle Claw*, another even larger and more ambitious rescue planning effort was started with the cover name *Honey Badger*. This was the precursor capability that grew into the SOF capabilities we enjoy today. The standup/continuation was ordered by Carter in the event of the necessity for in extremis rescue. The Iranian hostages and Desert One would continue to haunt Carter and help to elect his successor, Ronald Reagan.

Congress took an immediate interest in the failed operation and both houses opened hearings. These faded rather quickly in favor of the Department of Defense's Holloway Commission. This body examined some 23 issues and provided ten conclusions. This commission, in hindsight, was convened with a pre-ordained agenda to provide the appearance of resolution but not the degree either needed or requested by the Vaught task force. It is noteworthy that the commission never called General Vaught to testify and provided a summary of conclusions without any input or review by him or key members of the task force.

The systemic problems which led to the outcome of *Eagle Claw* would not be comprehensively addressed until the advent of the Cohen–Nunn amendment to the Fiscal Year 1987 National Defense Authorization Act. This set up a Joint U.S. Special Operations Command to leverage the capabilities of the services, and provided for Major Force Program 11 (MFP 11), a dedicated funding mechanism for special operations that is independent of the services. All actions against the specific objections of the services as "not necessary." The enduring legacy of *Eagle Claw*, is the vast array of highly competent Special Operations elements we enjoy today as the Phoenix that rose from the ashes of Desert One.

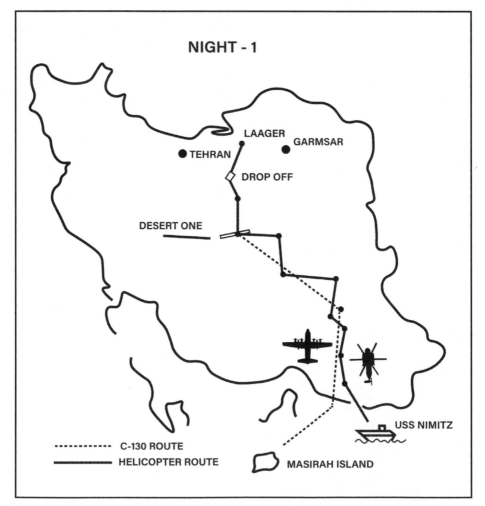

Map of the planned operations for the first night in Desert One.

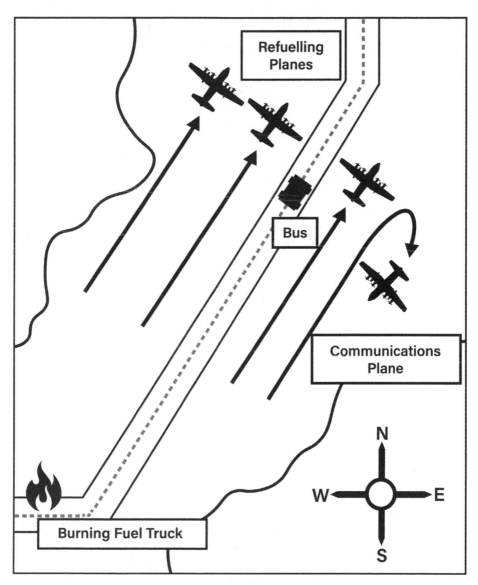

A bus is stopped and a fuel track burns after being attacked during Desert One.

FOG

FOG—The Field Operating Group

In the aftermath of Desert One, and as part of the Honey Badger program, Generals Vaught and Meyer determined that an internal Army Intelligence and Support element was essential. This was due to the proven inability and unstated but profound lack of interest on the part of the CIA in providing quality HUMINT to possible Army intervention. General Meyer was adamant that no U.S. Army personnel would be risked without reliable quality intelligence, preferably by U.S. Army personnel.

The concept was reinforced by the success of the three Berlin-based Detachment A NCOs who successfully "cased" the Foreign Minister's building where chargé d'affaires Bruce Laingen plus two other hostages were being held.

The organization was conceived to do several things:

- Provide covert/clandestine in country intelligence.
- Develop specific targets.
- Provide in country hosting/support to any forces introduced.
- Potentially host/manage appropriate proprietary firms in country.

Jerry King, our original JTF Chief of Staff, was selected by General Vaught to head it. Vaught would be King's boss but FOG would work through Operations Directorate, Special Operations (ODSO) (Longhofer) for all support, resources and taskings. King and Longhofer as well as Friedel developed a list of likely members. Composition would include men and women spanning wide demographics and likely technical skill sets, such as baggage handlers, bank clerks, pilots, agri-business, etc.

Longhofer and King worked closely with CIA Clan Operator Rudy Enders in finding people as well as establishing a training and vetting program—primarily in Florida.

Several things became apparent. King did not want to work through Longhofer, but he had to as ODSO held all the funds and authorities.

Lieutenant General Odom, the ACSI, (Army) immediately tried to wrest control. Vaught went to Meyer who stuffed Odom.

This was turf issue for Odom who did not want an operations entity overseeing an intelligence element. Throughout the evolution of FOG (later Intelligence Support Activity, later the ISA) Odom routinely intervened and demanded a controlling vote despite Meyer's refusal. Ultimately, under General Wickham, FOG/ISA was transferred to Odom's Directorate where he promptly put the brakes on its activities. Only world events and the emergence of JSOC requirements placed it, again, in the operational mainstream.

Funding a Deeply Classified Program

Money and how to hide it as well as cover the members became the major sticking issues in the creation. At this point, Department of Defense had no way to cover funds that could not be traced back to Department of Defense, which would be deadly for any FOG folks in-country.

It was necessary to have covered commercial entities out of the U.S. as well as military personnel under cover to those entities be seen as private civilian employees of non Department of Defense-related firms. By this time, the internet had exceeded the capability of Department of Defense to manage it from a policy viewpoint and covered personnel were at great risk of being discovered by the enemy, who were much more proficient than the Pentagon in its protocols.

Accordingly, if Joe X went to Country Y and posed as a commercial vendor and established a business, the adversaries could quickly research the source of funds and chase the rabbit down the hole. We did not want their search to end up within the Beltway. This was a particularly sensitive issue for FOG/ISA, which had to "prep" the operational area and develop local intelligence prior to the operators engagement.

I was the money man and worked closely with CIA and an element at Fort Meade. We finally determined how to transfer funds from Department of Defense to CIA and thence to several foreign banks. Longhofer and I went to the Hill and briefed the key members of the House Armed Services Committee/Senate Armed Services Committee to gain their statutory approval, which was obtained in the form of a private classified bill. This action was diligently ignored by the later Yellow Fruit prosecution, which consistently fought its exposure in the Yellow Fruit defense.

People cover was a lot harder as most of the FOG personnel came from within the Department of Defense. In order to provide a full cover program for FOG and several other assets, Longhofer, working with Enders at CIA Clan Ops, mutually developed the Yellow Fruit program. This placed FOG and others plus the traceable resources outside of the Department of Defense structure, but with a classified funding line I managed within Department of Defense entitled "ELT."

The only personnel aware of this other than ODSO were the Chairman of the JCS, the Secretary of Defense, Generals Meyer and Vessey, Controller of the Army (Larry Keenan), DCSOPS (Otis then Richardson), and Vaught/Moore. I summarized the entire arrangement in a Memo for Meyer, which he initialed.

I prepared similar memos for Meyer for each major spending tranche or re-programming. (These became major headaches for the prosecutor in the later Yellow Fruit courts martial as well as my testimony as to the system.)

King established several civilian firms doing real business, which was used to pay people, especially those not originally part of the Department of Defense. Lieutenant Colonel Dale Duncan, under cover, was installed as a CEO with considerable business in Europe, requiring travel and lifestyle.

When Meyer left, he did not backbrief his replacement as Chief of Staff of the Army, John Wickham, on the program. When Longhofer updated Wickham, he, Wickham, came unglued and ordered it all shut down. He appointed Lieutenant General Thurman with a DCSOPS Directorate titled Technical Management Office (TMO) to dissect the program and kill it.

Meanwhile, the Army began chasing various FOGers-specifically Duncan, trying to find purloined funds. He had bought a first class air ticket for his wife to Switzerland as part of his cover as an International CEO based in Switzerland, which Army subsequently deemed "inappropriate." It all went downhill from there. Mr. Greenberg, Assistant U.S. Attorney for the District of Columbia, got wind of it and started his own investigation and wrote Wickham a letter saying he would hold the Army responsible for all this (which he would expose) unless the Army teamed with him for a joint investigations/trials. Wickham rolled and allowed Greenberg to take charge.

The rest is history except that Wickham tried to short circuit the problem and just disband FOG. Longhofer briefed Marsh on what was going on, how FOG was actually doing meaningful work abroad (returning Bashear Jamael to Beirut with the ODSO), and supporting both Delta and CIA, etc. Wickham and Thurman formally approached Marsh as the Acting Assistant Secretary of Defense for SO/LIC.

Marsh, alarmed at Longhofer's discussion, began his own investigation and determined that FOG, Task Force 160, Delta, and JSOC were totally engaged in real world issues and that their activities were hugely important for national security, albeit covert. When General Wickham and Lieutenant General Thurman asked him to disband FOG and greatly reduce Task Force 160, he unequivocally told them "No!" The Army would robustly resource and support these organizations as major assets within the Army structure.

I testified in all eight trials regarding the money system and rationale for its management. Duncan was jailed for stupidly lying and Longhofer as well for just being uncooperative and "sustaining illegal activities in a position of authority." Longhofer spent eight months in the gentleman's Fort Leavenworth and was fully exonerated by Chief Justice Sullivan of the Military Court of Appeals who excoriated the prosecution for malfeasance.

I was written into the "Invisible Book" (as General Downing told me later) and the rest is history ...

The Invisible Book is a slang term used at the higher levels to indicate specific points regarding personalities that are noted, but not overtly stated. Often, these are more compelling than print when making senior personnel decisions.

Memo to General Meyer Ref Joint SOF Airlift Procurement

MEMORANDUM FOR GEN MEYER

SUBJECT: SOF READINESS/SERVICE POM ISSUES

1. SOF aviation took significant hits in the 90-94 process. With the projected program, it will not be possible to achieve the position outlined in the Sec Def June 87 SOF Airlift response to Congress. Key items are as indicated:

ITEM	REQUIRED	SHORTFALL BY FY 94
C130 SOLL II	11	4
C141 SOLL II	13	3
CV 22A	55	55
MH 47E	51	34
MH 60 K	23	22
AC 130U	12	5

2. The IOC for the CV 22 was slipped two years to FY 96.

3. Tenor of Tank session that reviewed SOF readiness was decidedly negative on resource issues. Gen Lindsay/BG Downing briefed Chiefs/CJCS on Readiness of SOF and outlined major funding shortfalls. USAF desired to cut MC and AC programs drastically. USN desired to zero out the small and medium boat infiltration assets. Army did not want to enhance aviation beyond the shortned level. NOTE: this effectively kills the Initiative 17 program with only 17 MH 47E's.

4. Primary CINC Concerns were;

> Lack of penetration assets from all Services
> Old, insufficient and breaking USAF assets
> Insufficient manning of Theatre SOC's
> Weak/non-existent SOF log structure
> Dual SOF force tasking
> Shortage of Company grade/sr NCO's in CMF 18

5. Primary CINC Recommendations:

> Resource mobility assets at required level
> Develop RC missions for the 200K call-up
> Make 160th SOAG a Tier One unit
> Man the SOC's at the rqd level
> Develop a Theatre SOC LOG plan
> Man 60 SEAL Plts by FY 92
> Fund a SOF Intel architecture
> Validate and resource the SOF language rqmt
> Activate the 3d SF Group
> Establish SOC Korea

6. Senator Cohen received the For the Record Q and A's he submitted to the Sec Def. OSD is now on record as categorically refusing to give US SOCOM a separate budget in the same sense as another Federal Agency. This will not happen without mandated specific legislation.

Declassified

This appendix provides a number of key illustrative documents recently unclassified. They cover the gamut from initial thoughts on a potential operation to the planning charts to the final Concept of Operation to the Flash message from Desert One.

F.1: Initial Planning Paper

This memo was written very early into the program by the J2 for Colonel King, the JTF Chief of Staff and Major General Vaught and was provided to the Chairman. It outlines our initial concept of what would be required to conduct a rescue. This was before the final concept was developed to include the means of transport. At this writing, we were still looking into a truck infiltration. As indicated in the memo, the need for quality in-country intelligence and support was clearly understood.

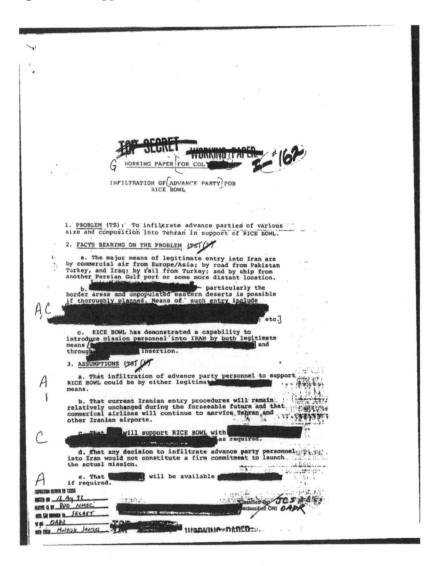

F.2: Diamonds and Rectangles

This is an example of the planning process and charts required by the Chairman. Each of the operational units had one for its activities. The charts for other participating units (e.g., Rangers and the 1st SOW) were integrated at the unit level.

They were overlaid with the other participants to create a summary Operational Chart. This chart, prepared by myself and Marine Captain Jim Magee, was the core of the Chairman's twice daily briefing book. The chart(s) were updated daily as training and/or intelligence indicated adjustments.

The summary chart had a large red line drawn through its entire length that we titled OTW (Over The Wall): the time Delta entered the embassy.

Initially, we were unhappy with forcing creation of this approach by the Chairman as an unnecessary bureaucratic burden. In time, we all learned to recognize its value in planning, and more importantly, how each piece fit into the total operation and where issues could emerge. The system was used throughout the later Honey Badger program and became a standard practice in the new SOF units.

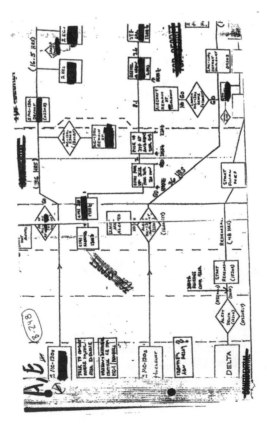

F.3: Help Wanted

The final leg of infiltration to the embassy was a truck movement. It was essential that the trucks be driven by native Iranians with a good knowledge of the streets in the area. The transit from the warehouse to the embassy would be almost a mile and require several turns. Accordingly, a program was developed by the J2 to identify and vet appropriate personnel. Most of them were expatriates who fled Iran when the Shah was deposed. The final pool included several high ranking officers from the Shah's military.

~~TOP SECRET~~

H-7

Item Number: 1

Intelligence Historical Report
J2, JTF 1-79

SUBJECT: Identification/Acquisition of Farsi Linguists to Support SFOD-D

TIMEFRAME: November 1979 - March 1980

SUMMARY:

1. COMJTF directed that US military personnel who speak Farsi be obtained to support SFOD-D ▓▓▓▓ phase for RICEBOWL night no. 2. Minimum of 12 required.

2. Linguists would ▓▓▓▓▓ Iranian ▓▓▓▓▓ to insure that they did not disclose true nature of ▓▓▓▓ if stopped at Iranian ▓▓▓▓

3. Due to paucity of Iranian ▓▓▓ some monitors subsequently became ▓▓▓

4. Initial lists of 3-listening/3-reading qualified personnel (maximum levels possible through language schools) obtained through JTF Service and DIA POC's. Additional names provided by JTF personnel who were acquainted with Farsi linguists.

5. Likely individuals brought TDY to Washington, D.C. for interview by JTF/J2 personnel (posing as DIA representative searching for linguists to support DIA Iranian Task Force). ▓▓▓ provided Farsi linguist used at beginning of interview to test subject's conversational Farsi.

6. Subjects not considered qualified during the interview, or those who failed to volunteer for an unnamed hazardous ▓▓▓▓▓▓▓

CLASSIFIED By COMJTF
DECLASSIFY ON OADR

~~TOP SECRET~~

F.4: Gas

This was written at the specific request of Colonel Beckwith, supported by Major General Vaught. Beckwith wished to arm his force with CS gas as a crowd dispersant if the civilians attempted to interfere—a distinct possibility considering the time required to clear the compound. Initially, both the Chairman and Secretary of Defense were reluctant to authorize any form of gas but Beckwith insisted it as a necessary requirement. The Chairman discussed the issue with Secretary Brown and a reluctant "Yes" was given to Beckwith. Beckwith, an expert at bureaucratic politics, requested the approval in writing.

F.5: Operational SitRep

This is an example of a weekly operational SitRep (Operational Report) prepared by the JTF Staff for the Chairman and Secretary of Defense. It was written on 1 Dec 1980.

~~CONFIDENTIAL~~ *i - 26*

~~TOP SECRET~~

STATUS REPORT

1. (TS) Preparation for the actual operation continues. Six RH-53 helicopters are aboard the KITTY HAWK which is en route to a MODLOC position in the Indian Ocean. Four ███████ are prepared for further deployment ████████ through ████████ to ████████ on order. MC-130s at Hurlburt Field and ████████ are prepared to deploy to ████████ via intermediate base on order. Delta is continuing ████████ and rehearsing in accordance with available information ████████ staff is planning for mission to ████████

2. (TS) Additional training required includes a full rehearsal with ████████ helicopters, MC-130s, ████████ and Rangers. The decision has been made to conduct this additional training and rehearsal at the Yuma Proving Grounds. Movement to the exercise area was completed on 3 December 1979.

   a. JTF Forward, Delta and the helicopter crews are based at the Yuma Proving Grounds.

   b. Two MC-130's and one ████████ are located at Davis Monthan AFB.

   c. ████████ are conducting an ████████ land ████████ exercise at Fort Benning.

3. (U)(TS) The training/rehearsal schedule is as follows:

   a. Monday - Unit functional training (3 Dec 79).

   b. Tuesday - Full rehearsal (4 Dec 79).

   c. Wednesday - Full rehearsal (5 Dec 79).

   d. Thursday - Full rehearsal (if required) (6 Dec 79).

4. (U)(TS) Logistics preparation is continuing on schedule.

CLASSIFICATION REVIEW ED 1256
CONDUCTED ON 12 Aug 92
DERIVATIVE CL BY DDO NMCC
☐ DECL ES DOWNER TO CONFIDENTIAL
REVW ON OADR
DERIVED FROM JS

Classified By: JCS
Declassified ON ████

~~CONFIDENTIAL~~   ~~TOP SECRET~~

F.6: The Final Solution

This document was written by the JTF Staff for General Vaught to pass to General Jones and the Secretary of Defense. It formalized on paper the concept of operations that had been briefed in the JTF spaces.

(S) CURRENT SITUATION

~~SECRET~~

HOSTAGES

50 at Emb

3 at FM

- Reasonably sure we know where they are.
- Kept by 125-150 persons at least a third armed with rifles and pis
- Embassy is 27 acres - with fence 10 - 12 ft high.

LIKELY REINFORCEMENTS

- Up to 140 ~~persons~~ from nearby stations could arrive within 10-15 minutes after the rescue has begun.
- 200 + more in the next 15 minutes.
- Several hundred could be expected within 45 minutes.
- Organized elements of the regular armed forces are not expected during the first hour.
- There is a low probability that the regular armed forces will discover or interfere.

2

F.7: The Plan

This memo memorializes for the Chairman and Secretary of Defense the final outline of the rescue attempt. It was written in late February 1981.

~~SECRET~~   ʯ ⎯I0ᒪ

~~TOP SECRET~~

CONCEPT OF OPERATIONS

(⁷) The operation will be accomplished during a nine day period (7 days for warning and positioning the force and 2 days for execution and recovery). Heavy lift helicopters (RH-53s), AC and MC-130 aircraft, refuelable C-130Es, C-141 airlifters and KC-135 tankers will be used. The helicopters will launch from the Nimitz. Other air operations will be

E conducted from ███████ and ███████

(U) The operation in Iran takes two nights and one day. It is divided into three phases - Insertion, Hostage Release and Extraction.

(⁷) Upon last light of the insertion day, SFOD-Delta (92 Delta

A, E personnel plus ███████████ will be airlifted by 2 MC-130s from ███████ to an isolated desert LZ in Iran.

(U) The first MC-130 will land on the desert LZ and Delta forces will immediately set up blocking positions on the road in order to control any vehicular traffic transiting the area.

(U) The second MC-130 lands desert LZ where number one has secured the area.

-- The first two aircraft will be followed by three C-130Es from

E ███████ Each of these aircraft will have two fuel bladders for a total of 18,000 gallons of fuel available for refueling purposes. Once the C-130Es have landed and are in position, the 2 MC-130s will depart for ███

(U) Concurrently, 7 RH-53s will depart the USS Nimitz to marry up with the forces at the LZ. While at the LZ, the helos will refuel from the C-130Es and load the Delta personnel (the refuel and load evolution should take approximately 40 minutes).

(U) Once refueled and loaded, the helos will fly to a hideout area which is located approximately 100 KM from Tehran.

E (⁷) The C-130Es at the desert LZ will depart for ███████

-- Once the helos reach the hideout area, they will be camouflaged and defensive positions set up. This evolution will be completed prior to sunrise.

~~TOP SECRET~~

~~SECRET~~

Classified By: JCS
Declassified ON: OADR

F.8: We Go

This is a message from Lieutenant General Gast at his forward location to Colonel Pitman on board the *Nimitz*. It outlines that basic plan for execution and advises the helicopter crews as to specific times and requirements. In essence, it is an execution order.

F.9: The Mishap

This is the initial Flash message relayed from Colonel Kyle on the ground at Desert One to Major General Vaught in Egypt and formatted for the JCS. I took this to the Chairman who was in our JTF spaces with the Secretary of Defense and the other Service Chiefs of Staff.

The helicopters had not yet arrived.

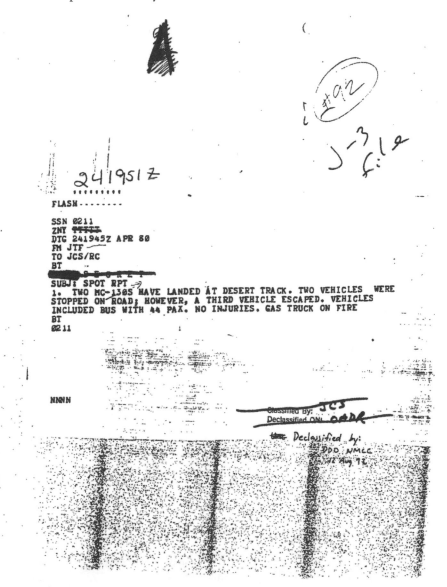

```
2419512

FLASH········

SSN 0211
ZNY
DTG 241945Z APR 80
FM JTF
TO JCS/RC
BT
        S E C R E T
SUBJ: SPOT RPT
1.  TWO MC-130S HAVE LANDED AT DESERT TRACK. TWO VEHICLES  WERE
STOPPED ON ROAD; HOWEVER, A THIRD VEHICLE ESCAPED. VEHICLES
INCLUDED BUS WITH 44 PAX. NO INJURIES. GAS TRUCK ON FIRE
BT
0211



NNNN
                                    Classified By: JCS
                                    Declassified ON: OADR

                                    Declassified by:
                                        DDO, NMCC
```

F.10: Going Forward

This document, not including the contents, was provided by Major General Vaught to the Joint Chiefs of Staff and Secretary of Defense. Its purpose was to outline by service the several organizational steps and force augmentations after the rescue failure. The President had directed that an in extremis rescue attempt could occur and that all applicable DOD elements be either provided or created for that option. The Chairman's "Blank piece of paper" exercise was the core that later became much of today's Special Operations Forces.

This paper specifically recognized the Rangers, the Field Operations Group, the Little Bird helicopters and a significantly upgraded 1st SOW. It also requested the use of the Air Force C-5 heavy airlifter as an expeditionary airfield capable asset, which created a firestorm within the Air Force.

THE JOINT CHIEFS OF STAFF
WASHINGTON, D.C. 20301

11 May 1981

THE JOINT STAFF

MEMORANDUM FOR THE DIRECTOR, JOINT STAFF

SUBJECT: JTF Capability Review

1. Pursuant to standing oral instructions, the enclosed JTF Capability Review is forwarded for review and disposition by the Service OPSDEPs.

2. I wish to express my thanks to members of the Joint Staff who worked tirelessly to complete this important task.

JAMES B. VAUGHT
Major General, USA

Regraded Unclassified when separated from Classified enclosure

Glossary

Key Personalities

General David Jones, Air Force. Chairman, Joint Chiefs of Staff (CJCS)

General Shy Meyer, Chief of Staff, U.S. Army Chief of Staff

Major General James Vaught, Director, Operations Directorate, Army Staff. Commander, JTF *Eagle Claw*/Commander Joint Task Force

Major General William Moore, Major General Vaught's successor as DAMO-OD and overseer of Operations Directorate, Special Operations (ODSO)

Dr. Harold Brown, the Secretary of Defense. Nicknamed Weird Harold by the JTF

Colonel Charlie Beckwith, Commander, Delta. "Chargin' Charlie"

Colonel Charles Pitman, U.S. Marine Corps, helicopter aviation liaison officer

Lieutenant Colonel Rod Lenahan, Air Force. JTF J2

Colonel Jerry King., U.S. Army. Initial Chief of Staff of the JTF

Colonel James Paschall, Army. JTF Chief of Staff on departure of Colonel Jerry King

Stansfield Turner, Director, CIA

Budgetary Terms

"Above the Line" means those items above are funded.

"Below the Line" means those items are not funded. Within the budgetary process, the services retain some flexibility to placing items above or below the line once the budget is Appropriated and Authorized by Congress. This point became very important regarding Air Force funding for new AC and MC 130 procurement.

Other

AGI. Soviet intelligence ship. Tattle Tale. Routinely tracking our carrier task forces and reporting on our operations. There was great concern that if the Soviets discovered or assumed a rescue attempt was underway, they would notify the Iranians and hazard both the hostages and the mission.

Air Mission Commander. AMC. The senior officer responsible for a specific aviation mission. During Desert One, this was Colonel Jim Kyle, U.S. Air Force. The helicopter AMC was Lieutenant Colonel Ed Siefert, U.S. Marine Corps.

Assistant Secretary of Defense/Special Operations/Low Intensity Conflict (ASD-SO/LIC). Controversial office established by Congress to provide civilian oversight to Special Operations programs. Not initially supported by the military services.

The Book. The twice-daily updated binder on the operation provided to the Chairman and other senior personnel. Every JTF staff section contributed. I collated and provided part of the twice-daily briefs.

Chart. This was a schematic prepared for the Chairman that displayed every operational element and its actions throughout the rescue execution. Date/Time was displayed on the top and the respective units at the left vertical. This was always depicted in the diamonds and rectangle format requested by General Jones.

Cover. The name or program used to hide the true identity of either an individual or a business/initiative.

Crazies in the Basement. Term used to describe the Operations Directorate, Special Operations personnel by Army staff.

DIA. Director of Intelligence, Army.

DCSOPS, DAMO-OD. Deputy Chief of Staff-Operations, Department of the Army, Military Operations-Operations Directorate. The G3 of the Army (then Lieutenant General Glen Otis) and his Operational Directorate (then Major General Vaught).

Defense Mapping Agency. DMA. Manufactures special purpose maps for all operational requirements.

Farm. The field and craft training facility of the CIA.

Field Operations Group (FOG). Joint intelligence and support element created by General Meyer to supplement CIA support to potential Army or joint SOF operations. Later, the Intelligence Support Agency (ISA). Often called by insiders the "Secret Army of Northern Virginia."

Human Intelligence. HUMINT. The sine qua non of intelligence, if good. A report from a person regarding an object or issue of interest.

JOGG. Joint Operations Ground Graphic. A type of map primarily used by aviators at a large scale.

Joint Special Operations Command. JSOC. The joint headquarters created after Desert One and at the recommendation of the Holloway Commission to operationally manage future SOF operations. The task was held jointly by both the JTF and the new JSOC during the initial Honey Badger period.

JTF. Joint Task Force; refers to the Iran rescue force. JTF *Eagle Claw.*

Light data: BMNT. Before Morning Nautical Twilight. When it starts to get light. EENT. End of Evening Nautical Twilight. When it gets dark. Both are standard naval navigational terms adopted by all services.

LNO. Liaison Officer.

Midnight Massacre. Saturday Night Massacre. Slang used by internal CIA personnel to describe the severe elimination of HUMINT collectors and assets undertaken when Stansfield Turner became the director.

Mother MAC. Headquarters, Military Airlift Command. Air Force.

NRC. National Reconnaissance Center. Responsible for satellite target selection.

NVG. Night Vision Goggles. In this case, the newly developed PVS 5 NVGs. Used by both ground elements and aviators. Depth perception is a problem with this early version.

National Command Authority. NCA. The most senior civilian and military leadership. Occasionally a term to designate the President without saying directly so.

NSA. National Security Administration. Responsible for tactical Signals Intelligence to the JTF.

Operations Directorate, Special Operations. ODSO. Army staff. The staff and operational element created after Desert One to build and manage U.S. Army SOF elements as well as to be the Joint interface on SOF issues.

Over The Wall. OTW. The time Delta force would actually cross into the embassy compound from Roosevelt Avenue. This point marked the crucial moment of the operation.

OPSEC. Operational Security. The necessity to hide what an organization or entity is doing. In this case, from friendly elements as well as potential enemies. Concerns regarding Russian satellite/overhead images were always a major concern and drove our program exposure.

POLAD. Political Adviser to Chairman or CINCs. Usually seconded from Department of State.

RH-53. The Navy Sikorsky helicopters used for the rescue attempt. The Marine version is the CH-53. The Air Force version is the HH-53. The Helos.

Room 2C840. In the joint staff area of the Pentagon. Previously occupied by JCS-SOD, who became the base element of the Iran rescue JTF.

SeaSpray. A joint CIA-Army helicopter organization created after the failure to perform a variety of essential counterterrorist missions. Later assumed by the CIA when General Wickham desired to excise Army participation. The key assets were the new Hughes MH-500MD helicopters.

SFOD-D. Special Forces Operational Detachment–Delta. The Delta Force. The Unit. The Ranch.

Shooter. Term given to a Delta operative.

SOD. Special Operations Directorate. 2C840.

Special Operations Forces. SOF.

Strategic Services Command. STRATSERCOM. The title of the four-star-level special operations CINC that General Meyer proposed as a resolution for the problems extant with the new SOF forces. This became the present USSOCOM after Nunn–Cohen was passed into law.

Tank. The small meeting room where the Chairman meets with the Service Chiefs and their deputies to receive briefings and make joint decisions. The JTF often briefed issues in the Tank.

Technical Management Office. TMO. Established by General Meyer's successor, General Wickham and headed by then Lieutenant General Max Thurman. Its purpose was to investigate all the Army SOF elements established post-Iran and determine their purpose and viability. Heavily influenced by the Yellow Fruit, Greenberg investigations.

Tiered Forces. SOF and non-SOF elements that are part of the USSOCOM force availability list. Tier One forces were the direct action operators such as Delta Force. Tier Two elements were those usually participating in a support mission. Tier Three were all other existing forces that could be drawn upon.

United States Special Operations Command. USSOCOM/SOCOM. The four-star CINC HQ created in the aftermath of the Grenada operation to manage the newly emerged SOF forces.

Vice Chief of Staff, Army. VCSA. During this period it was General Jack Vessey, later Chief of Staff of the JCS.

Yellow Fruit. Army cover program for emerging SOF capabilities. This was primarily designed, with the assistance of the CIA, to provide an untraceable financial system for foreign operations so as to prevent target foes from tracing operator funds back to DOD. The system allowed covered operations to remain covered.

Yuma Proving Ground. YPG. Army desert test site near Yuma, Arizona. Used for primary training of the JTF elements. Associated with MCAS, Yuma, Marine aviation facility.